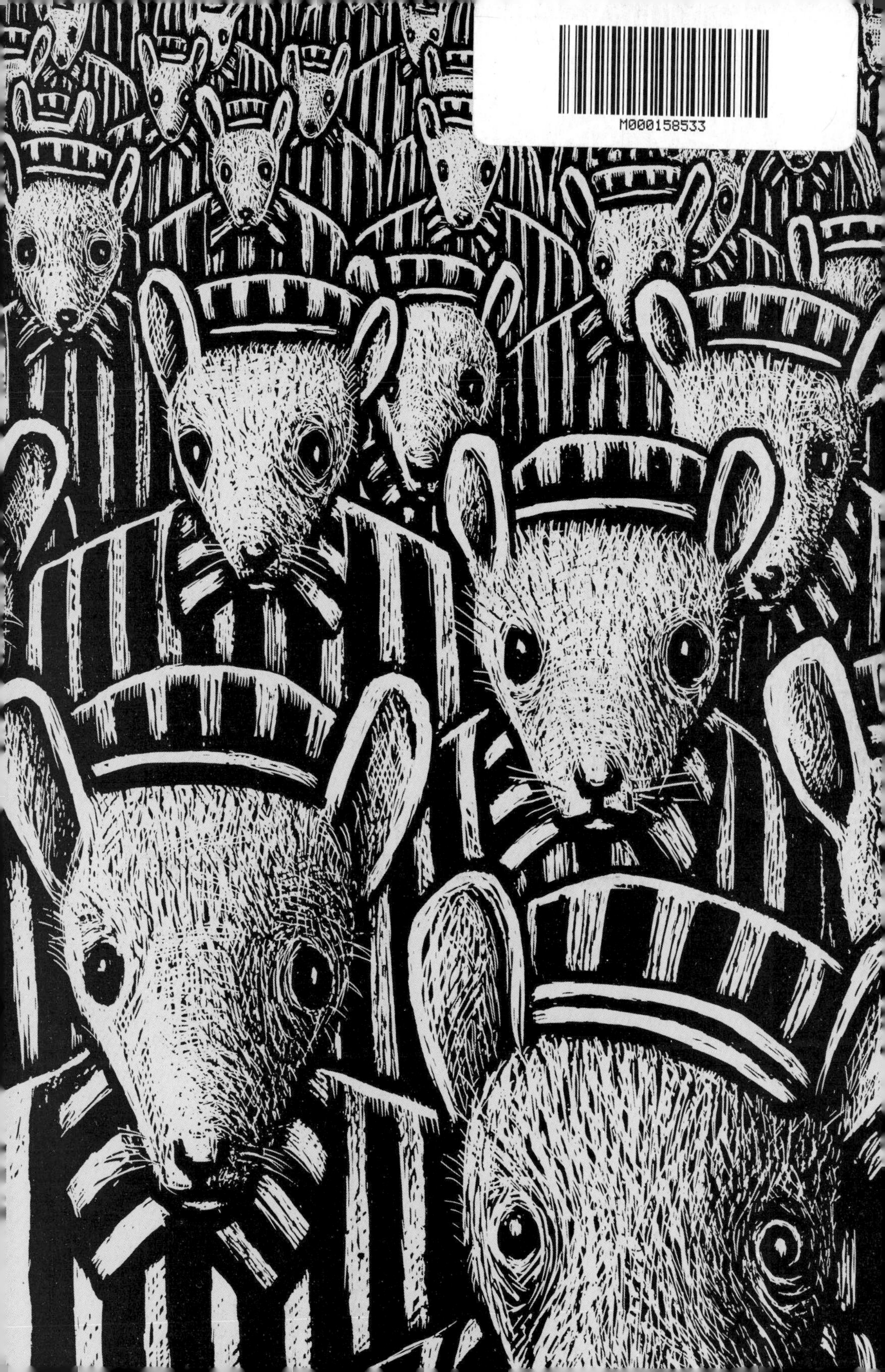

MAUS II

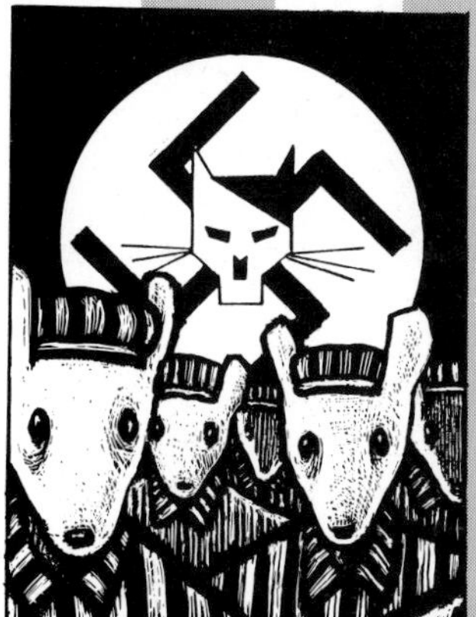

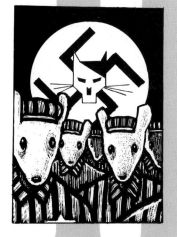

PANTHEON BO

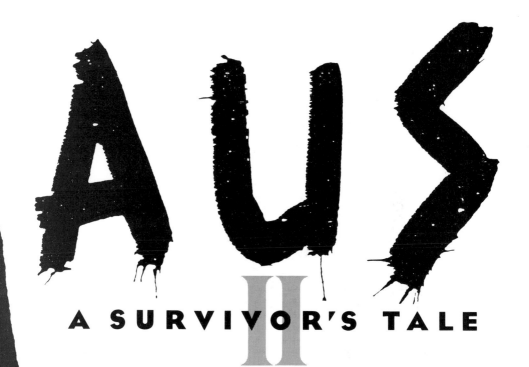

AUS

II

A SURVIVOR'S TALE

AND HERE MY TROUBLES BEGAN

art spiegelman

KS NEW YORK

Thanks to Paul Pavel, Deborah Karl, and Mala Spiegelman for helping this volume into the world.

Thanks to the John Simon Guggenheim Memorial Foundation for a fellowship that allowed me to focus on completing Maus.

And my thanks, with love and admiration, to Francoise Mouly for her intelligence, integrity, editorial skills, and for her love.

All rights reserved under International and Pan-American Copyright Conventions. Published in the United States by Pantheon Books, a division of Random House, Inc., New York, and simultaneously in Canada by Random House of Canada Limited, Toronto.

Chapters one through four were originally published in somewhat different form in Raw magazine between 1986 and 1991.

Library of Congress Cataloging-in-Publication Data
Spiegelman, Art.
Maus: a survivor's tale, II: and here my troubles began/Art Spiegelman.
p.   cm.
ISBN 0-679-72977-1
1. Spiegelman, Vladek — Comic books, strips, etc.
2. Holocaust, Jewish (1939-1945) — Poland — Biography — Comic books, strips, etc.
3. Holocaust survivors — United States — Biography — Comic books, strips, etc.
4. Spiegelman, Art — Comic books, strips, etc.
5. Children of Holocaust survivors — United States — Biography — Comic books, strips, etc. I. Title.
D804.3.S66   1991
940.53'18'0207 — dc20   91-52739

Book design: art spiegelman and Louise Fili

Manufactured in the United States of America

47 46 45 44 43 42 41

"Mickey Mouse is the most miserable ideal ever revealed....Healthy emotions tell every independent young man and every honorable youth that the dirty and filth-covered vermin, the greatest bacteria carrier in the animal kingdom, cannot be the ideal type of animal....Away with Jewish brutalization of the people! Down with Mickey Mouse! Wear the Swastika Cross!"

—newspaper article, Pomerania, Germany, mid-1930s

FOR RICHIEU

AND FOR NADJA

ART SPIEGELMAN, a cartoonist born after WW II, is working on a book about what happened to his parents as Jews in wartime Poland. He has made a series of visits to his childhood home in Rego Park, N.Y., to record his father's memories. Art's mother,

Anja, committed suicide in 1968. Art becomes furious when he learns that his father, **VLADEK**, has burned Anja's wartime memoirs. Vladek is remarried to Mala, another survivor. She complains often of his stinginess and lack of concern for her. Vladek, a diabetic who has suffered two heart attacks, is in poor health.

In Poland, Vladek had been a small-time textile salesman. In 1937 he married Anja Zylberberg, the young-est daughter of a wealthy Sosnowiec hosiery family. They had a son, Richieu, who died during the war.

Forced first into ghettos, then into hiding, Vladek and Anja tried to escape to Hungary with their prewar acquaint-ances, the Mandelbaums, whose nephew, Abraham, had attested in a letter that the escape route was safe. They were caught and, in March, 1944, they were brought to the gates of Auschwitz.

AND HERE MY TROUBLES BEGAN

(FROM MAUSCHWITZ TO THE CATSKILLS AND BEYOND)

CONTENTS

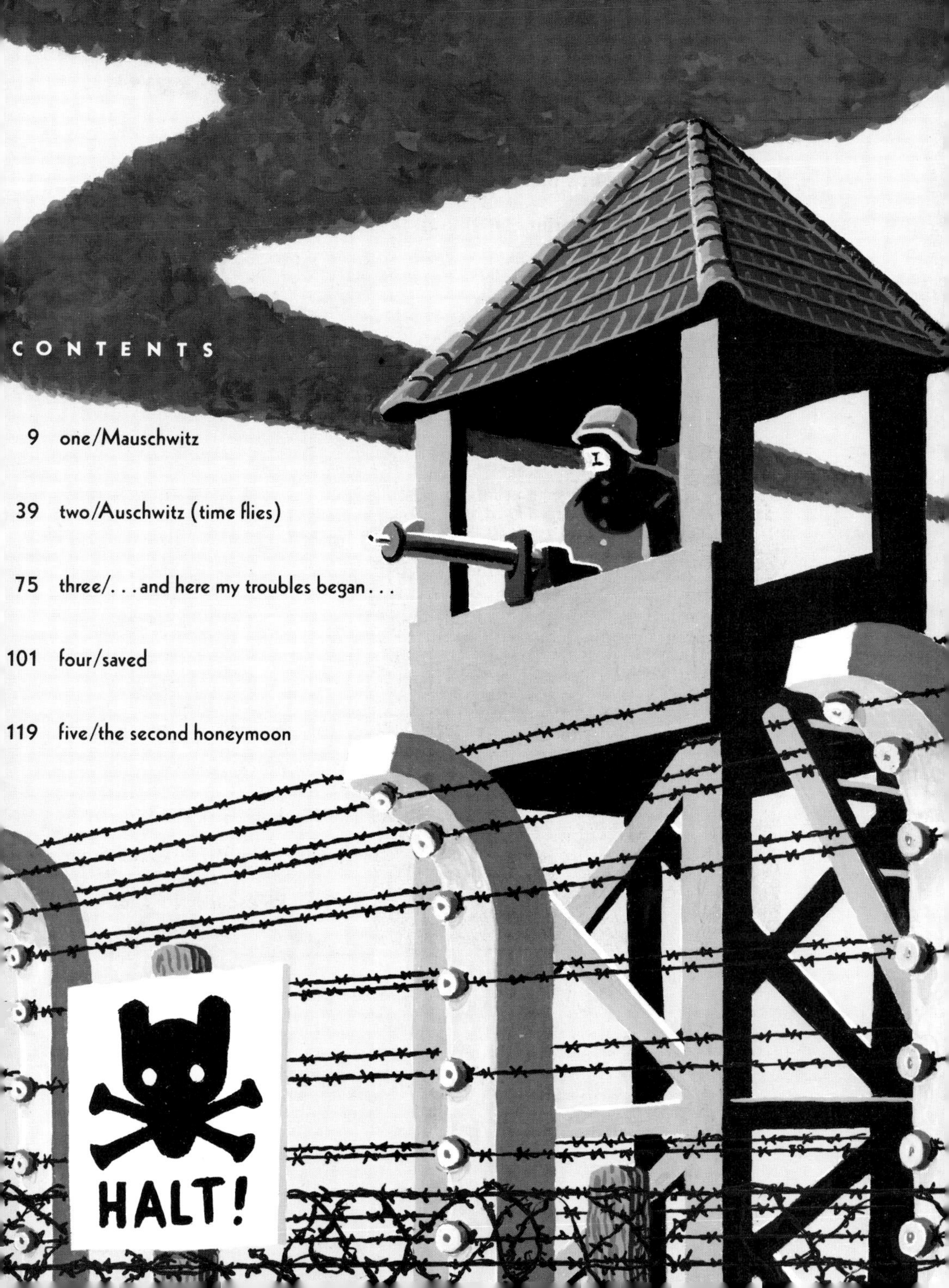

HALT!

CHAPTER ONE

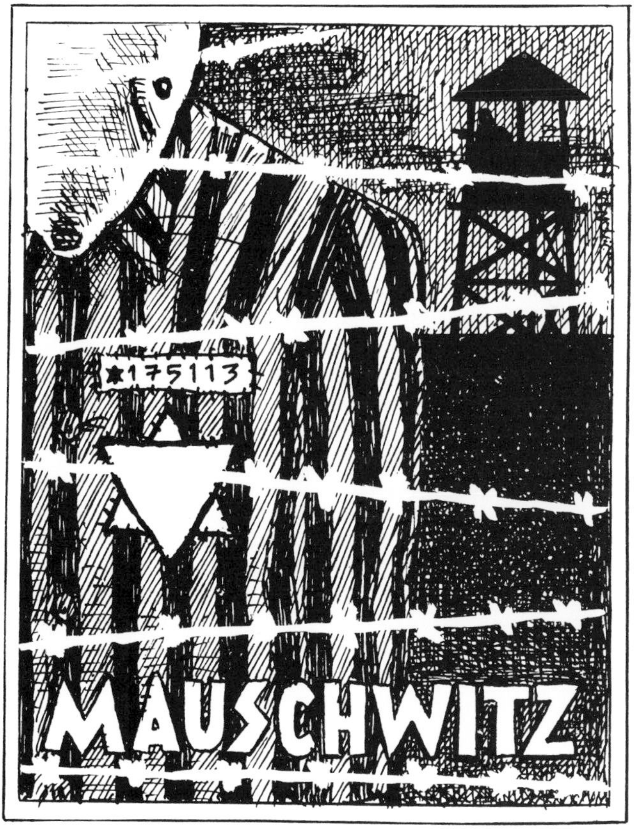

175113
MAUSCHWITZ

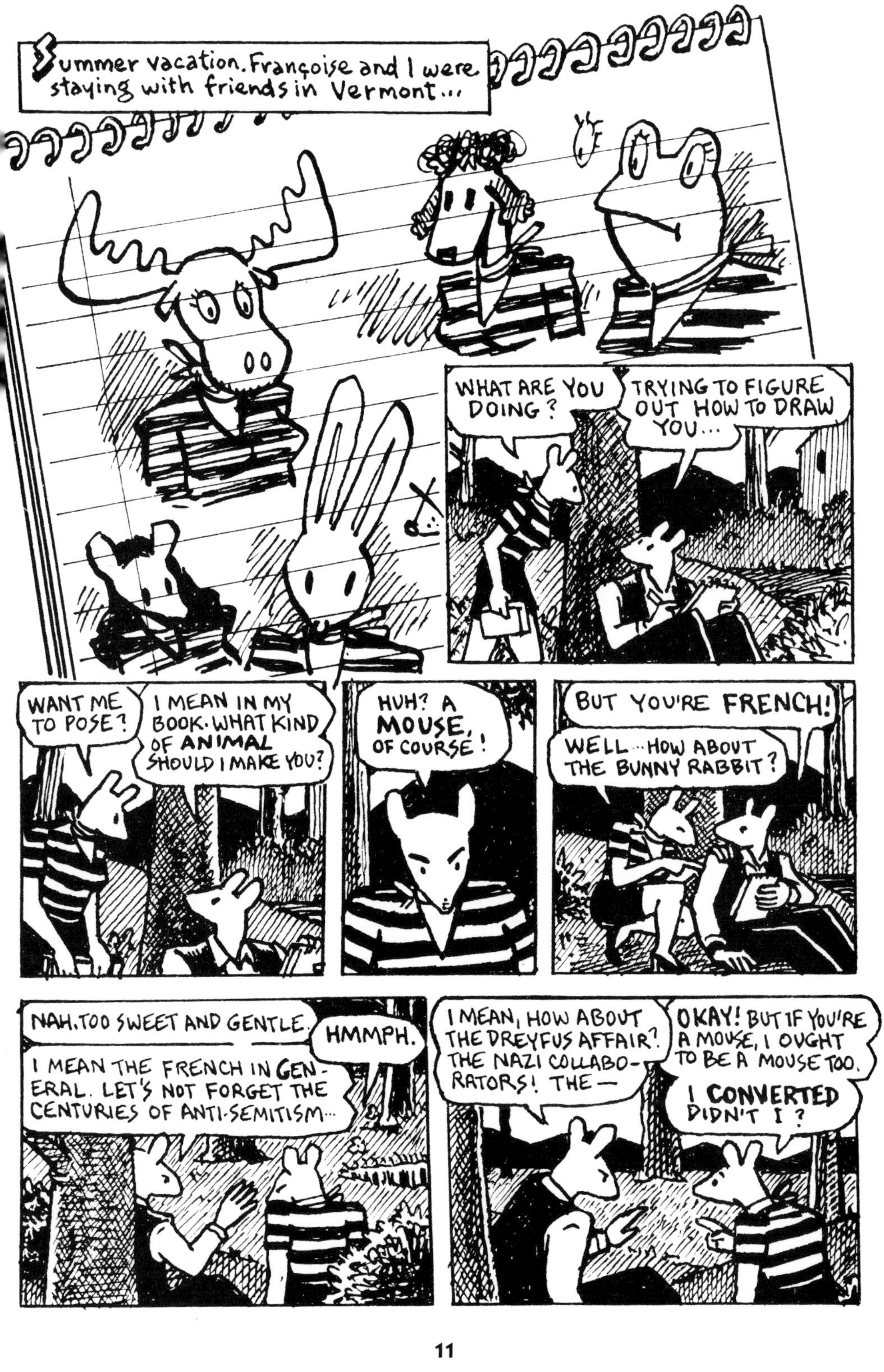
Summer vacation. Françoise and I were staying with friends in Vermont...
WHAT ARE YOU DOING?
TRYING TO FIGURE OUT HOW TO DRAW YOU...
WANT ME TO POSE?
I MEAN IN MY BOOK. WHAT KIND OF ANIMAL SHOULD I MAKE YOU?
HUH? A MOUSE, OF COURSE!
BUT YOU'RE FRENCH!
WELL...HOW ABOUT THE BUNNY RABBIT?
NAH. TOO SWEET AND GENTLE.
HMMPH.
I MEAN THE FRENCH IN GENERAL. LET'S NOT FORGET THE CENTURIES OF ANTI-SEMITISM...
I MEAN, HOW ABOUT THE DREYFUS AFFAIR? THE NAZI COLLABORATORS! THE—
OKAY! BUT IF YOU'RE A MOUSE, I OUGHT TO BE A MOUSE TOO.
I CONVERTED DIDN'T I?

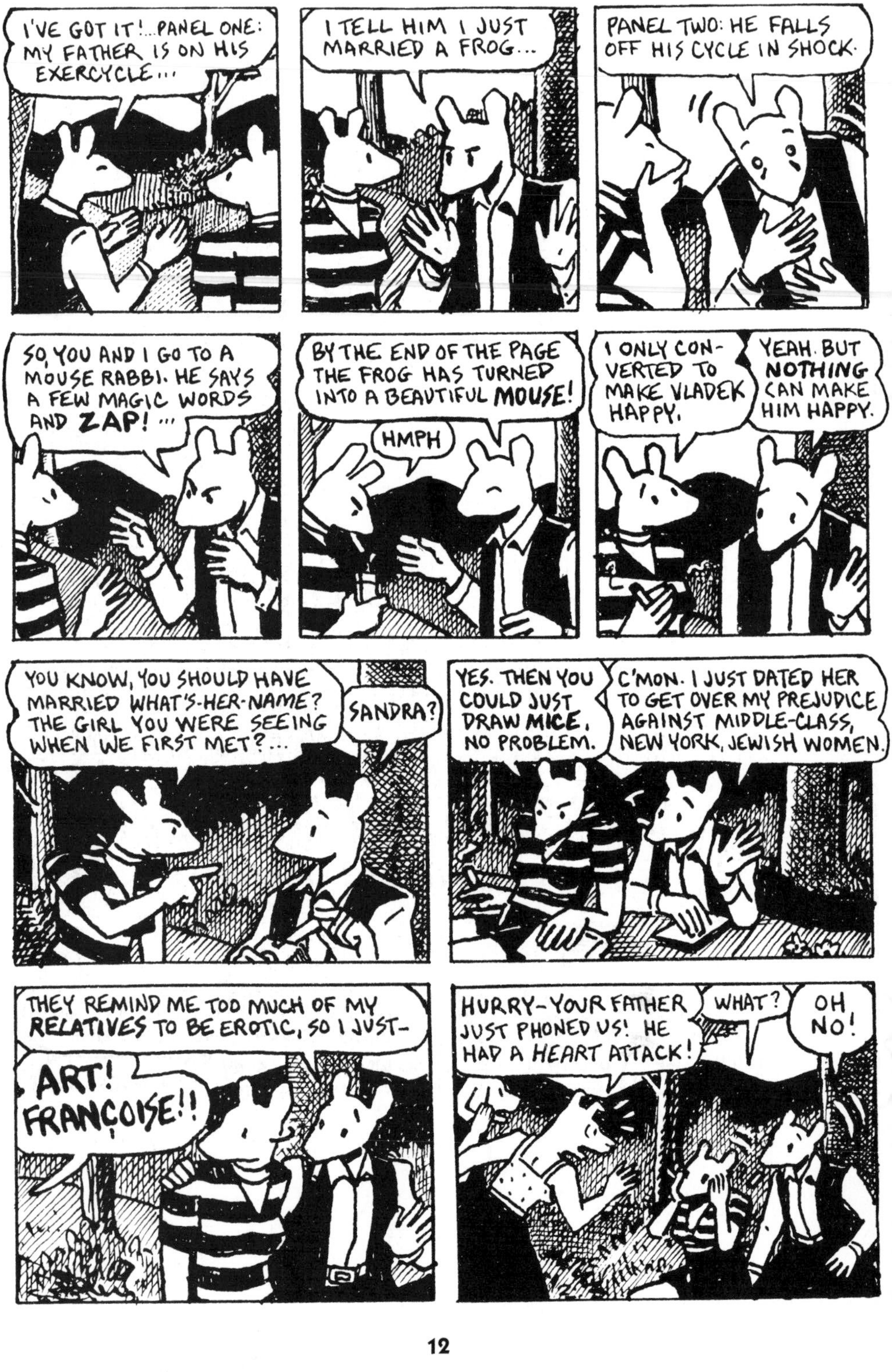

I'VE GOT IT!...PANEL ONE: MY FATHER IS ON HIS EXERCYCLE...
I TELL HIM I JUST MARRIED A FROG...
PANEL TWO: HE FALLS OFF HIS CYCLE IN SHOCK.
SO, YOU AND I GO TO A MOUSE RABBI. HE SAYS A FEW MAGIC WORDS AND ZAP! ...
BY THE END OF THE PAGE THE FROG HAS TURNED INTO A BEAUTIFUL MOUSE!
HMPH
I ONLY CONVERTED TO MAKE VLADEK HAPPY.
YEAH. BUT NOTHING CAN MAKE HIM HAPPY.
YOU KNOW, YOU SHOULD HAVE MARRIED WHAT'S-HER-NAME? THE GIRL YOU WERE SEEING WHEN WE FIRST MET?...
SANDRA?
YES. THEN YOU COULD JUST DRAW MICE, NO PROBLEM.
C'MON. I JUST DATED HER TO GET OVER MY PREJUDICE AGAINST MIDDLE-CLASS, NEW YORK, JEWISH WOMEN.
THEY REMIND ME TOO MUCH OF MY RELATIVES TO BE EROTIC, SO I JUST-
ART! FRANÇOISE!!
HURRY- YOUR FATHER JUST PHONED US! HE HAD A HEART ATTACK!
WHAT?
OH NO!

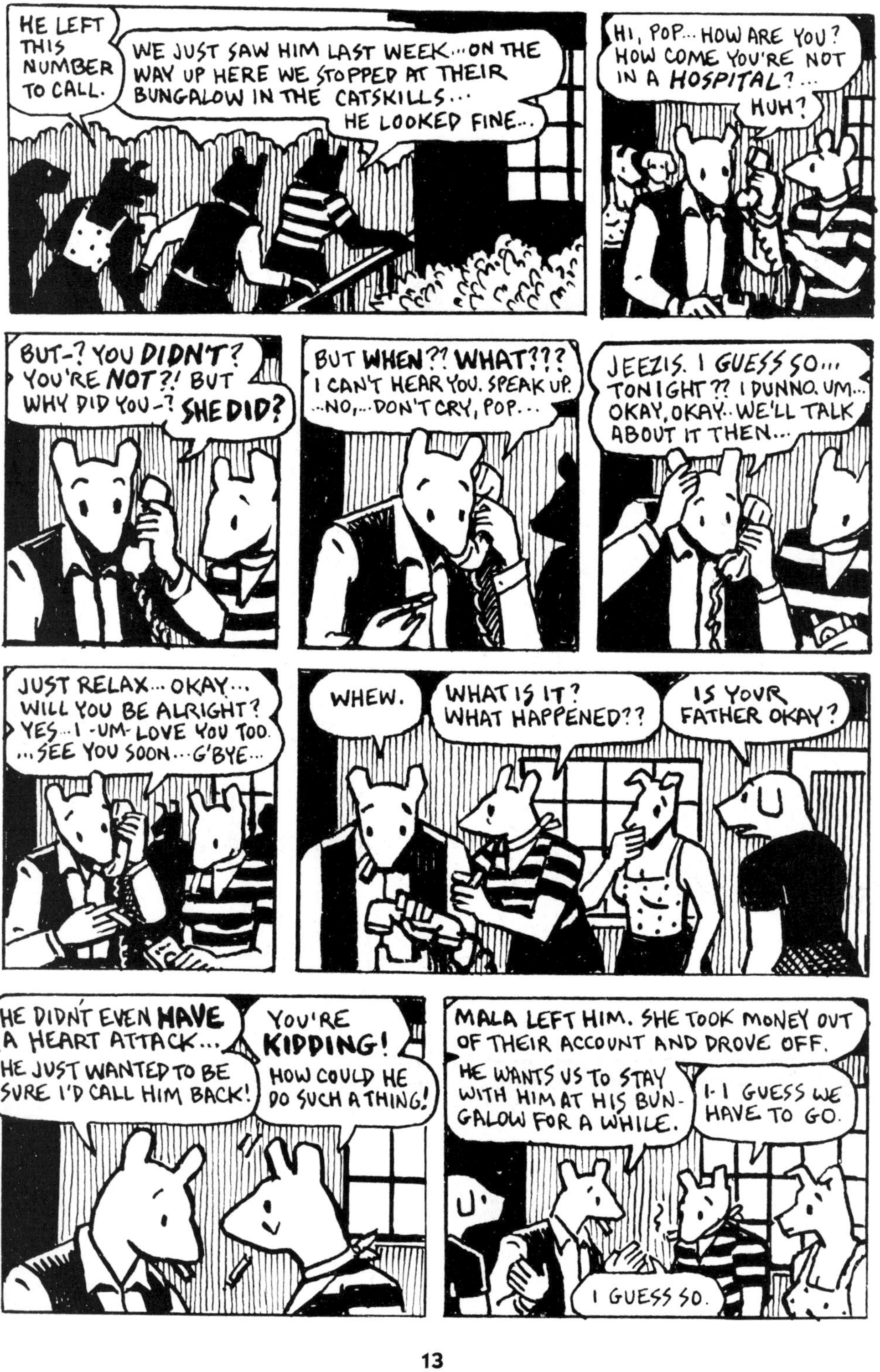
HE LEFT THIS NUMBER TO CALL.
WE JUST SAW HIM LAST WEEK... ON THE WAY UP HERE WE STOPPED AT THEIR BUNGALOW IN THE CATSKILLS...
HE LOOKED FINE...
HI, POP... HOW ARE YOU? HOW COME YOU'RE NOT IN A HOSPITAL?...
HUH?
BUT-? YOU DIDN'T? YOU'RE NOT?! BUT WHY DID YOU-? SHE DID?
BUT WHEN?? WHAT??? I CAN'T HEAR YOU. SPEAK UP. ...NO,... DON'T CRY, POP...
JEEZIS. I GUESS SO... TONIGHT?? I DUNNO. UM... OKAY, OKAY.. WE'LL TALK ABOUT IT THEN...
JUST RELAX... OKAY... WILL YOU BE ALRIGHT? YES... I -UM- LOVE YOU TOO. ...SEE YOU SOON... G'BYE...
WHEW.
WHAT IS IT? WHAT HAPPENED??
IS YOUR FATHER OKAY?
HE DIDN'T EVEN HAVE A HEART ATTACK...
HE JUST WANTED TO BE SURE I'D CALL HIM BACK!
YOU'RE KIDDING!
HOW COULD HE DO SUCH A THING!
MALA LEFT HIM. SHE TOOK MONEY OUT OF THEIR ACCOUNT AND DROVE OFF.
HE WANTS US TO STAY WITH HIM AT HIS BUNGALOW FOR A WHILE.
I-I GUESS WE HAVE TO GO.
I GUESS SO.

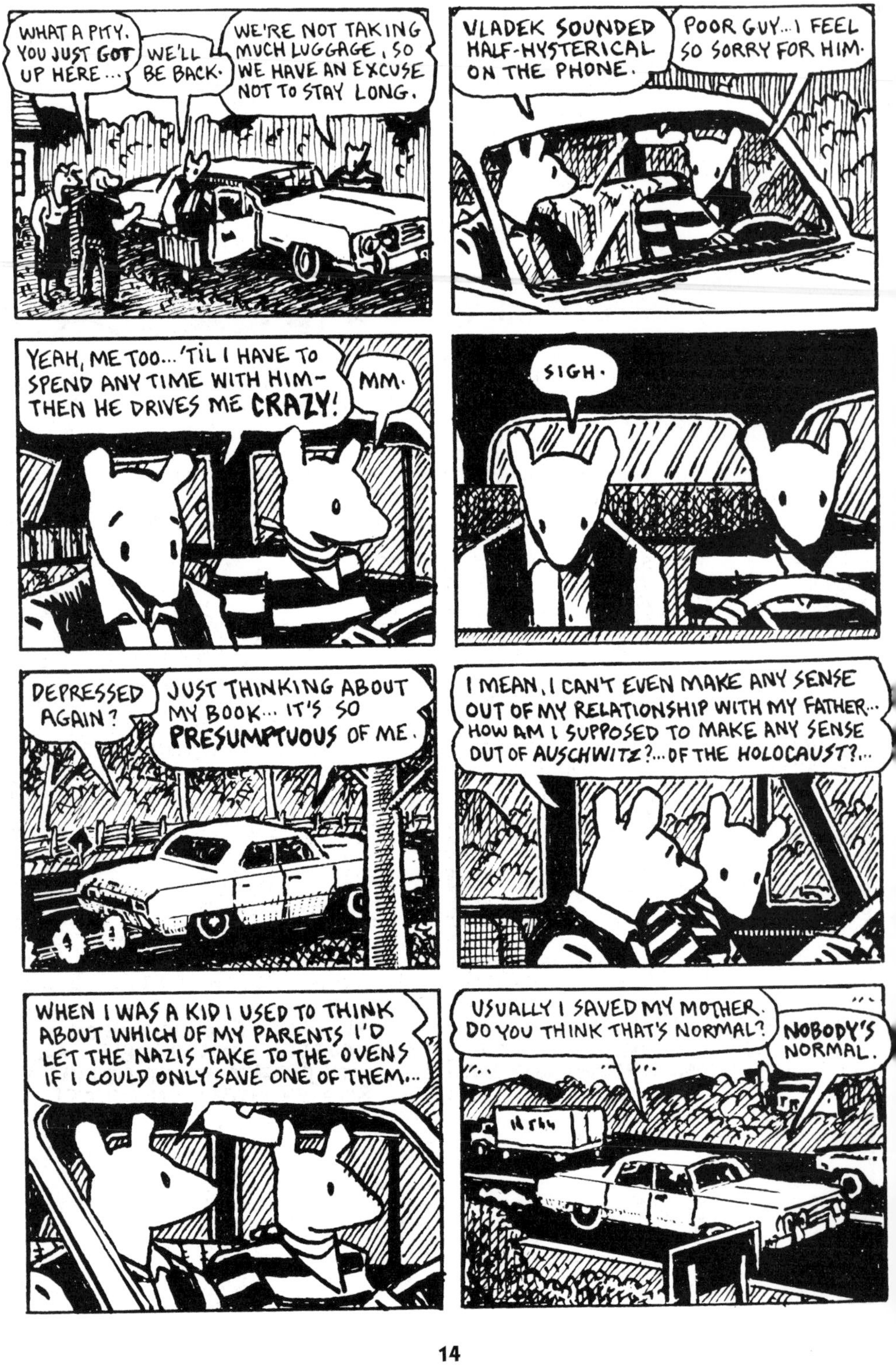
WHAT A PITY. YOU JUST GOT UP HERE...
WE'LL BE BACK.
WE'RE NOT TAKING MUCH LUGGAGE, SO WE HAVE AN EXCUSE NOT TO STAY LONG.
VLADEK SOUNDED HALF-HYSTERICAL ON THE PHONE.
POOR GUY... I FEEL SO SORRY FOR HIM.
YEAH, ME TOO... 'TIL I HAVE TO SPEND ANY TIME WITH HIM- THEN HE DRIVES ME CRAZY!
MM.
SIGH.
DEPRESSED AGAIN?
JUST THINKING ABOUT MY BOOK... IT'S SO PRESUMPTUOUS OF ME.
I MEAN, I CAN'T EVEN MAKE ANY SENSE OUT OF MY RELATIONSHIP WITH MY FATHER... HOW AM I SUPPOSED TO MAKE ANY SENSE OUT OF AUSCHWITZ?... OF THE HOLOCAUST?...
WHEN I WAS A KID I USED TO THINK ABOUT WHICH OF MY PARENTS I'D LET THE NAZIS TAKE TO THE OVENS IF I COULD ONLY SAVE ONE OF THEM...
USUALLY I SAVED MY MOTHER. DO YOU THINK THAT'S NORMAL?
NOBODY'S NORMAL.

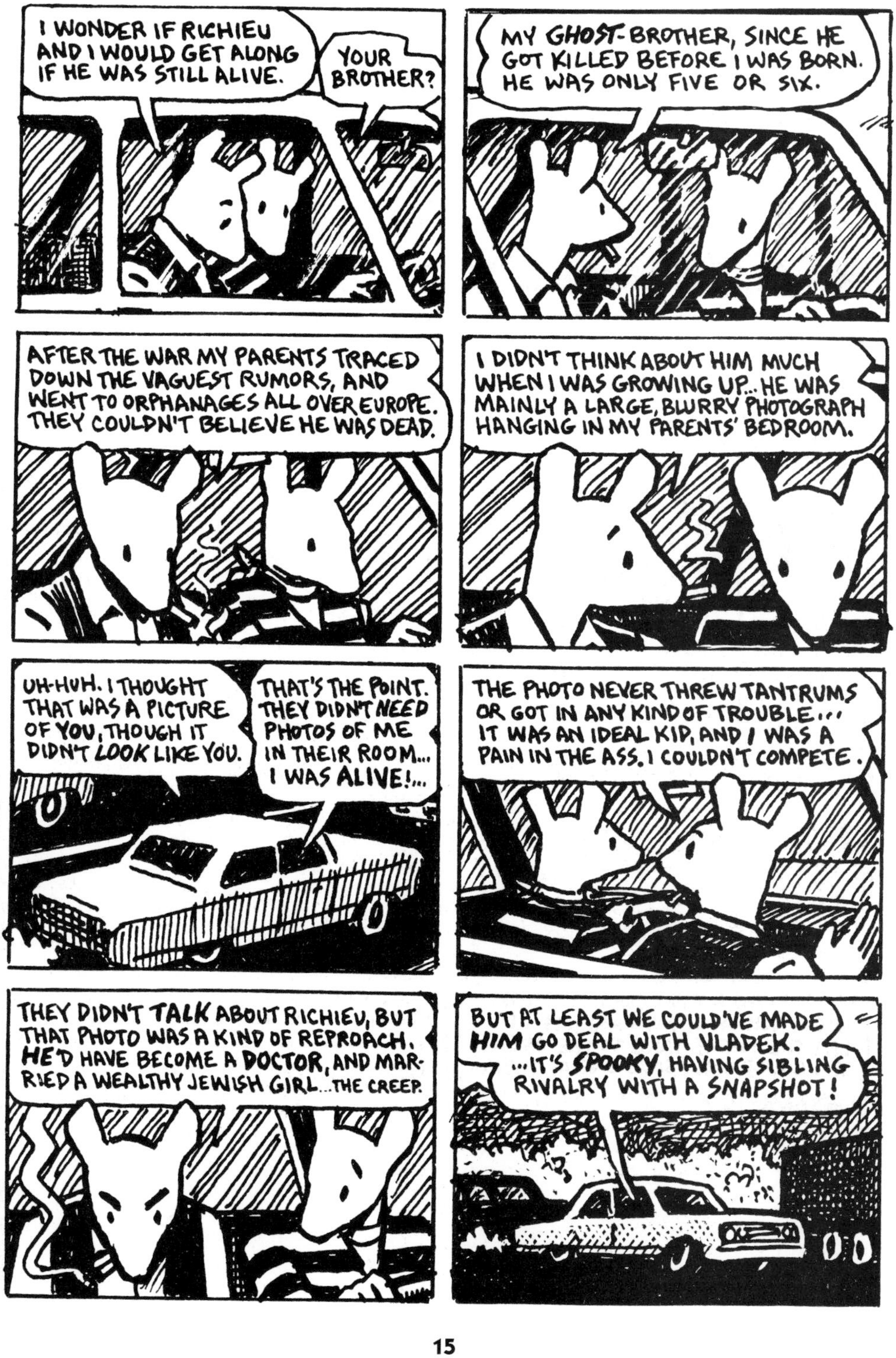
I WONDER IF RICHIEU AND I WOULD GET ALONG IF HE WAS STILL ALIVE.
YOUR BROTHER?
MY GHOST-BROTHER, SINCE HE GOT KILLED BEFORE I WAS BORN. HE WAS ONLY FIVE OR SIX.
AFTER THE WAR MY PARENTS TRACED DOWN THE VAGUEST RUMORS, AND WENT TO ORPHANAGES ALL OVER EUROPE. THEY COULDN'T BELIEVE HE WAS DEAD.
I DIDN'T THINK ABOUT HIM MUCH WHEN I WAS GROWING UP... HE WAS MAINLY A LARGE, BLURRY PHOTOGRAPH HANGING IN MY PARENTS' BEDROOM.
UH-HUH. I THOUGHT THAT WAS A PICTURE OF YOU, THOUGH IT DIDN'T LOOK LIKE YOU.
THAT'S THE POINT. THEY DIDN'T NEED PHOTOS OF ME IN THEIR ROOM... I WAS ALIVE!...
THE PHOTO NEVER THREW TANTRUMS OR GOT IN ANY KIND OF TROUBLE... IT WAS AN IDEAL KID, AND I WAS A PAIN IN THE ASS. I COULDN'T COMPETE.
THEY DIDN'T TALK ABOUT RICHIEU, BUT THAT PHOTO WAS A KIND OF REPROACH. HE'D HAVE BECOME A DOCTOR, AND MARRIED A WEALTHY JEWISH GIRL... THE CREEP.
BUT AT LEAST WE COULD'VE MADE HIM GO DEAL WITH VLADEK. ...IT'S SPOOKY, HAVING SIBLING RIVALRY WITH A SNAPSHOT!

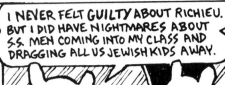

I NEVER FELT **GUILTY** ABOUT RICHIEU. BUT I DID HAVE NIGHTMARES ABOUT S.S. MEN COMING INTO MY CLASS AND DRAGGING ALL US JEWISH KIDS AWAY.

DON'T GET ME WRONG. I WASN'T **OBSESSED** WITH THIS STUFF ... IT'S JUST THAT SOMETIMES I'D FANTASIZE ZYKLON B COMING OUT OF OUR SHOWER INSTEAD OF WATER.

I KNOW THIS IS INSANE, BUT I SOMEHOW WISH I HAD BEEN IN AUSCHWITZ **WITH** MY PARENTS SO I COULD REALLY KNOW WHAT THEY LIVED THROUGH!

...I GUESS IT'S **SOME** KIND OF GUILT ABOUT HAVING HAD AN EASIER LIFE THAN THEY DID.

SIGH. I FEEL SO INADEQUATE TRYING TO RECONSTRUCT A REALITY THAT WAS WORSE THAN MY DARKEST DREAMS.

AND TRYING TO DO IT AS A **COMIC STRIP!** I GUESS I BIT OFF MORE THAN I CAN CHEW. MAYBE I OUGHT TO FORGET THE WHOLE THING.

THERE'S SO MUCH I'LL NEVER BE ABLE TO UNDERSTAND OR VISUALIZE. I MEAN, REALITY IS TOO **COMPLEX** FOR COMICS... SO MUCH HAS TO BE LEFT OUT OR DISTORTED.

JUST KEEP IT HONEST, HONEY.

SEE WHAT I MEAN... IN REAL LIFE YOU'D **NEVER** HAVE LET ME TALK THIS LONG WITHOUT INTERRUPTING.

HMMPH. LIGHT ME A CIGARETTE.

And so, the Catskills...

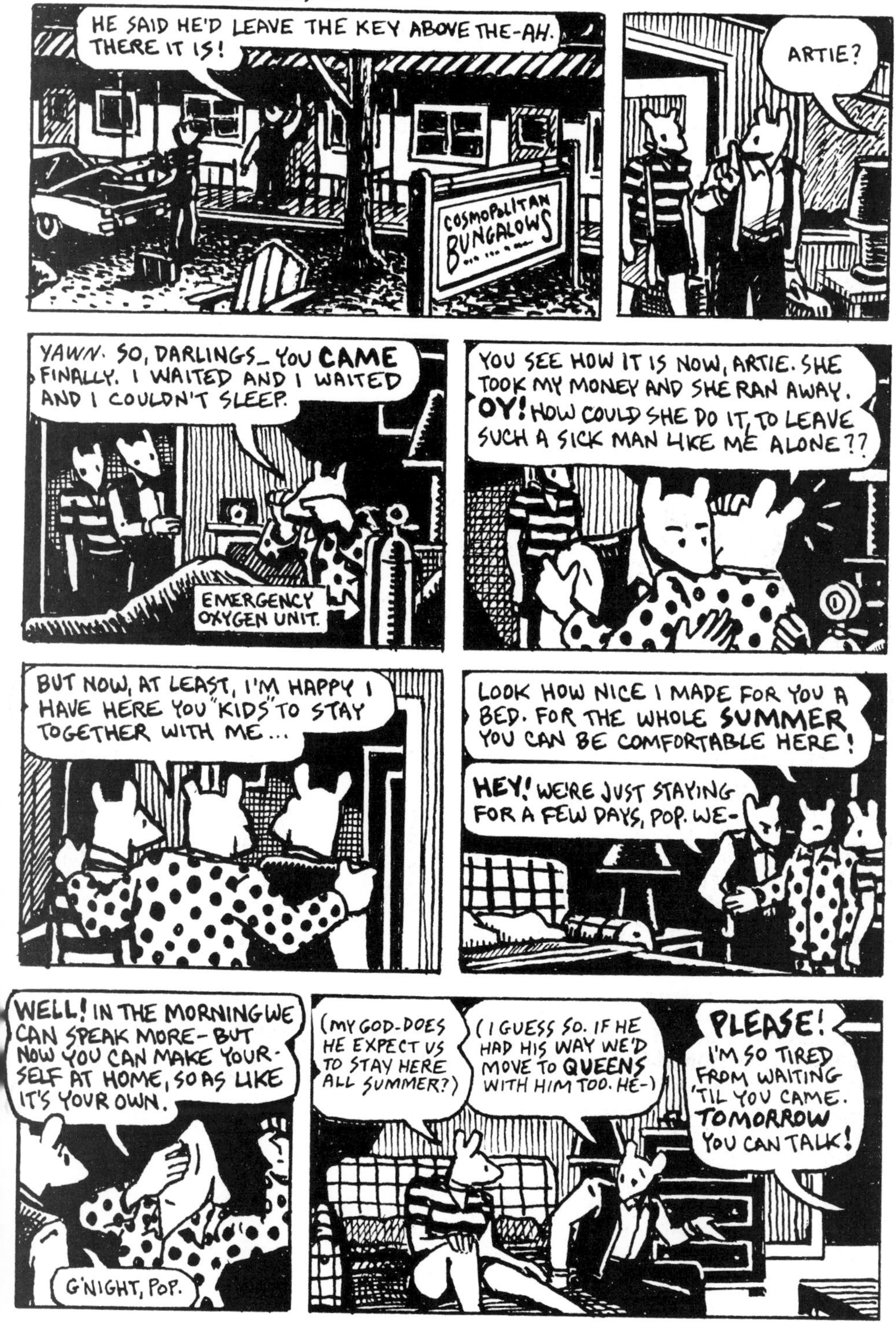
HE SAID HE'D LEAVE THE KEY ABOVE THE-AH. THERE IT IS!
COSMOPOLITAN BUNGALOWS
ARTIE?
YAWN. SO, DARLINGS_ YOU CAME FINALLY. I WAITED AND I WAITED AND I COULDN'T SLEEP.
EMERGENCY OXYGEN UNIT.
YOU SEE HOW IT IS NOW, ARTIE. SHE TOOK MY MONEY AND SHE RAN AWAY. OY! HOW COULD SHE DO IT, TO LEAVE SUCH A SICK MAN LIKE ME ALONE??
BUT NOW, AT LEAST, I'M HAPPY I HAVE HERE YOU "KIDS" TO STAY TOGETHER WITH ME...
LOOK HOW NICE I MADE FOR YOU A BED. FOR THE WHOLE SUMMER YOU CAN BE COMFORTABLE HERE!
HEY! WE'RE JUST STAYING FOR A FEW DAYS, POP. WE-
WELL! IN THE MORNING WE CAN SPEAK MORE- BUT NOW YOU CAN MAKE YOURSELF AT HOME, SO AS LIKE IT'S YOUR OWN.
G'NIGHT, POP.
(MY GOD-DOES HE EXPECT US TO STAY HERE ALL SUMMER?)
(I GUESS SO. IF HE HAD HIS WAY WE'D MOVE TO QUEENS WITH HIM TOO. HE-)
PLEASE! I'M SO TIRED FROM WAITING 'TIL YOU CAME. TOMORROW YOU CAN TALK!

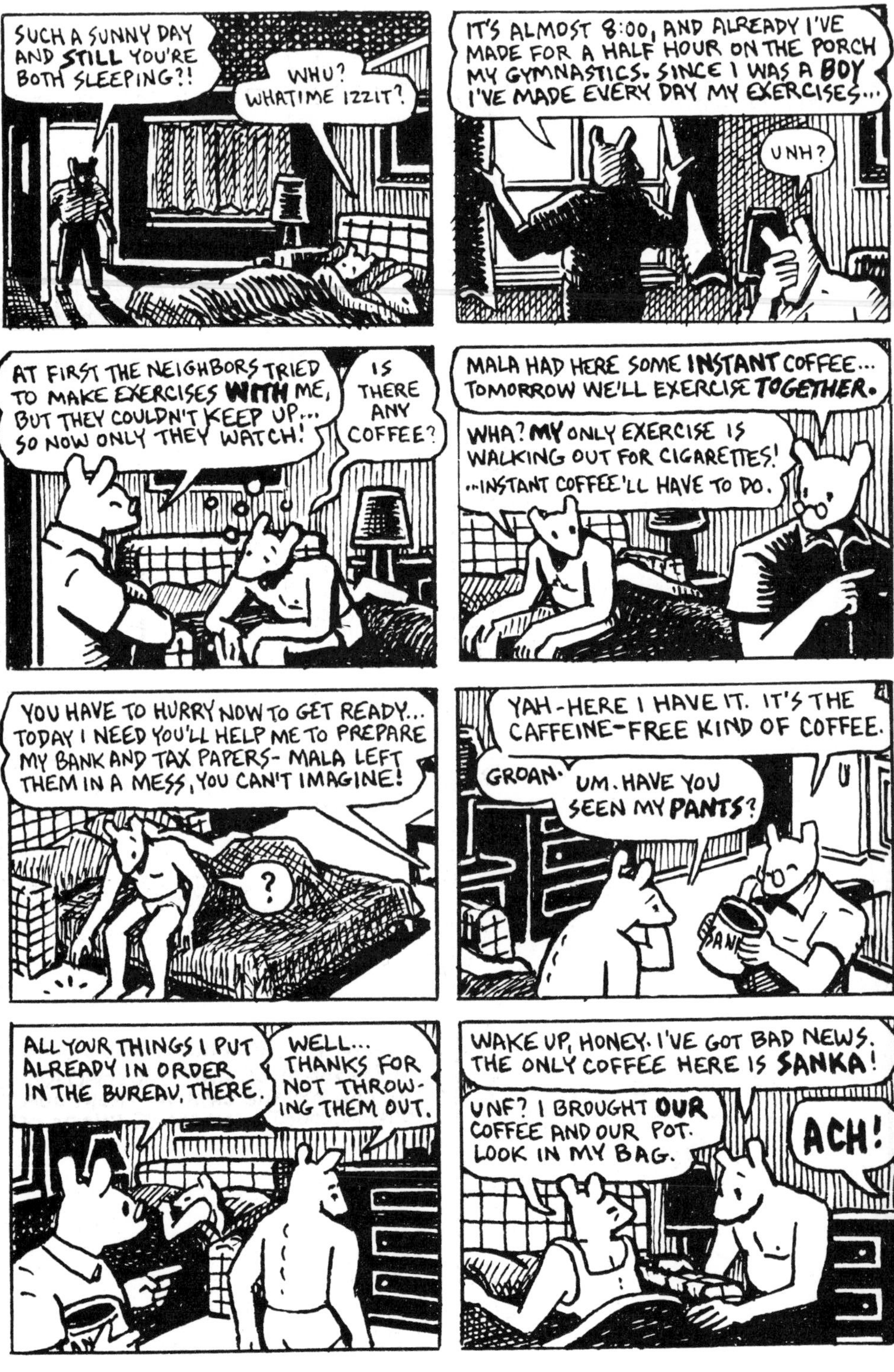
SUCH A SUNNY DAY AND STILL YOU'RE BOTH SLEEPING?!
WHU? WHATIME IZZIT?
IT'S ALMOST 8:00, AND ALREADY I'VE MADE FOR A HALF HOUR ON THE PORCH MY GYMNASTICS. SINCE I WAS A BOY I'VE MADE EVERY DAY MY EXERCISES...
UNH?
AT FIRST THE NEIGHBORS TRIED TO MAKE EXERCISES WITH ME, BUT THEY COULDN'T KEEP UP... SO NOW ONLY THEY WATCH!
IS THERE ANY COFFEE?
MALA HAD HERE SOME INSTANT COFFEE... TOMORROW WE'LL EXERCISE TOGETHER.
WHA? MY ONLY EXERCISE IS WALKING OUT FOR CIGARETTES! ..INSTANT COFFEE'LL HAVE TO DO.
YOU HAVE TO HURRY NOW TO GET READY... TODAY I NEED YOU'LL HELP ME TO PREPARE MY BANK AND TAX PAPERS- MALA LEFT THEM IN A MESS, YOU CAN'T IMAGINE!
?
YAH-HERE I HAVE IT. IT'S THE CAFFEINE-FREE KIND OF COFFEE.
GROAN.
UM. HAVE YOU SEEN MY PANTS?
ALL YOUR THINGS I PUT ALREADY IN ORDER IN THE BUREAU, THERE.
WELL... THANKS FOR NOT THROWING THEM OUT.
WAKE UP, HONEY. I'VE GOT BAD NEWS. THE ONLY COFFEE HERE IS SANKA!
UNF? I BROUGHT OUR COFFEE AND OUR POT. LOOK IN MY BAG.
ACH!

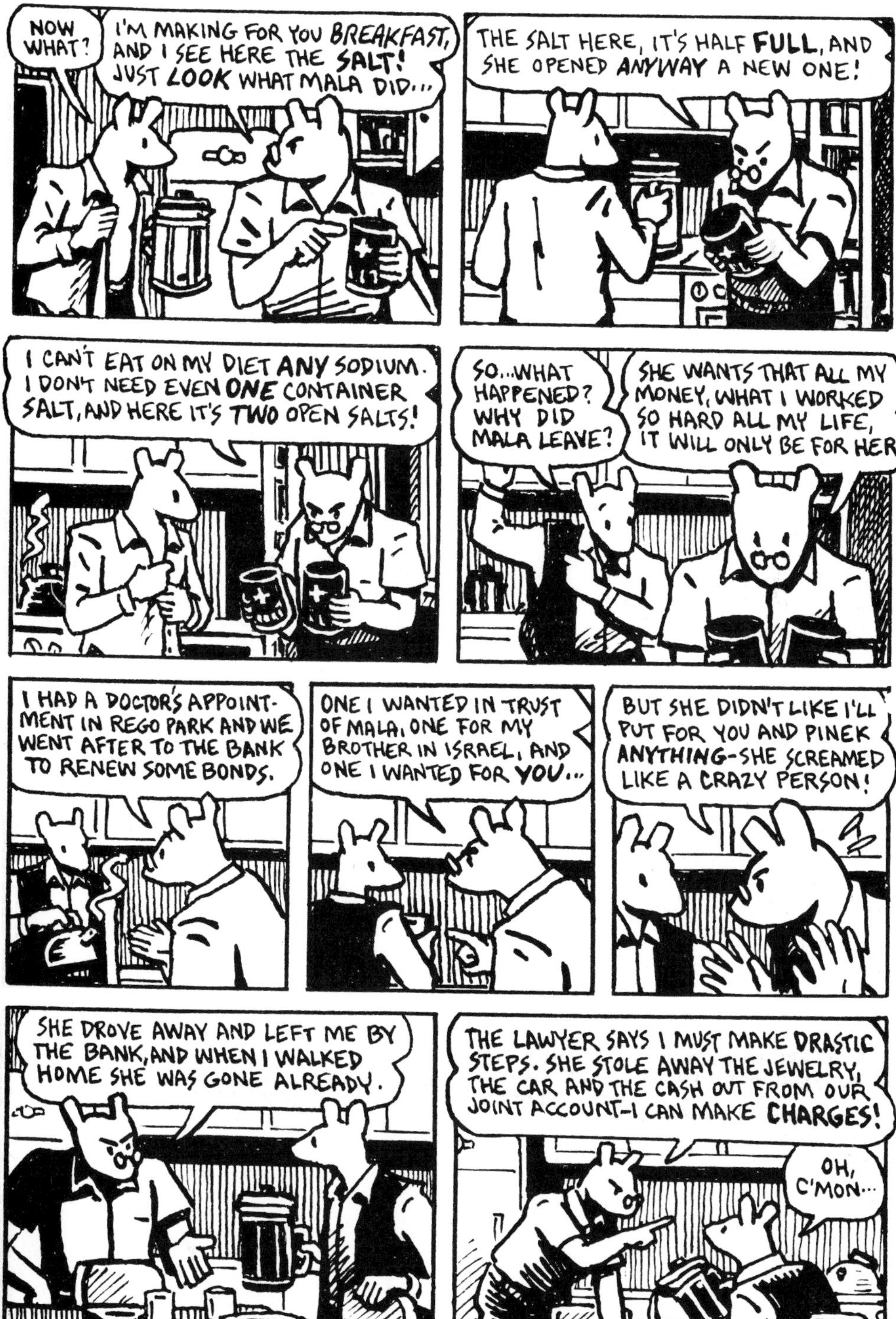
NOW WHAT?
I'M MAKING FOR YOU BREAKFAST, AND I SEE HERE THE SALT! JUST LOOK WHAT MALA DID...
THE SALT HERE, IT'S HALF FULL, AND SHE OPENED ANYWAY A NEW ONE!
I CAN'T EAT ON MY DIET ANY SODIUM. I DON'T NEED EVEN ONE CONTAINER SALT, AND HERE IT'S TWO OPEN SALTS!
SO...WHAT HAPPENED? WHY DID MALA LEAVE?
SHE WANTS THAT ALL MY MONEY, WHAT I WORKED SO HARD ALL MY LIFE, IT WILL ONLY BE FOR HER.
I HAD A DOCTOR'S APPOINTMENT IN REGO PARK AND WE WENT AFTER TO THE BANK TO RENEW SOME BONDS.
ONE I WANTED IN TRUST OF MALA, ONE FOR MY BROTHER IN ISRAEL, AND ONE I WANTED FOR YOU...
BUT SHE DIDN'T LIKE I'LL PUT FOR YOU AND PINEK ANYTHING-SHE SCREAMED LIKE A CRAZY PERSON!
SHE DROVE AWAY AND LEFT ME BY THE BANK, AND WHEN I WALKED HOME SHE WAS GONE ALREADY.
THE LAWYER SAYS I MUST MAKE DRASTIC STEPS. SHE STOLE AWAY THE JEWELRY, THE CAR AND THE CASH OUT FROM OUR JOINT ACCOUNT-I CAN MAKE CHARGES!
OH, C'MON...

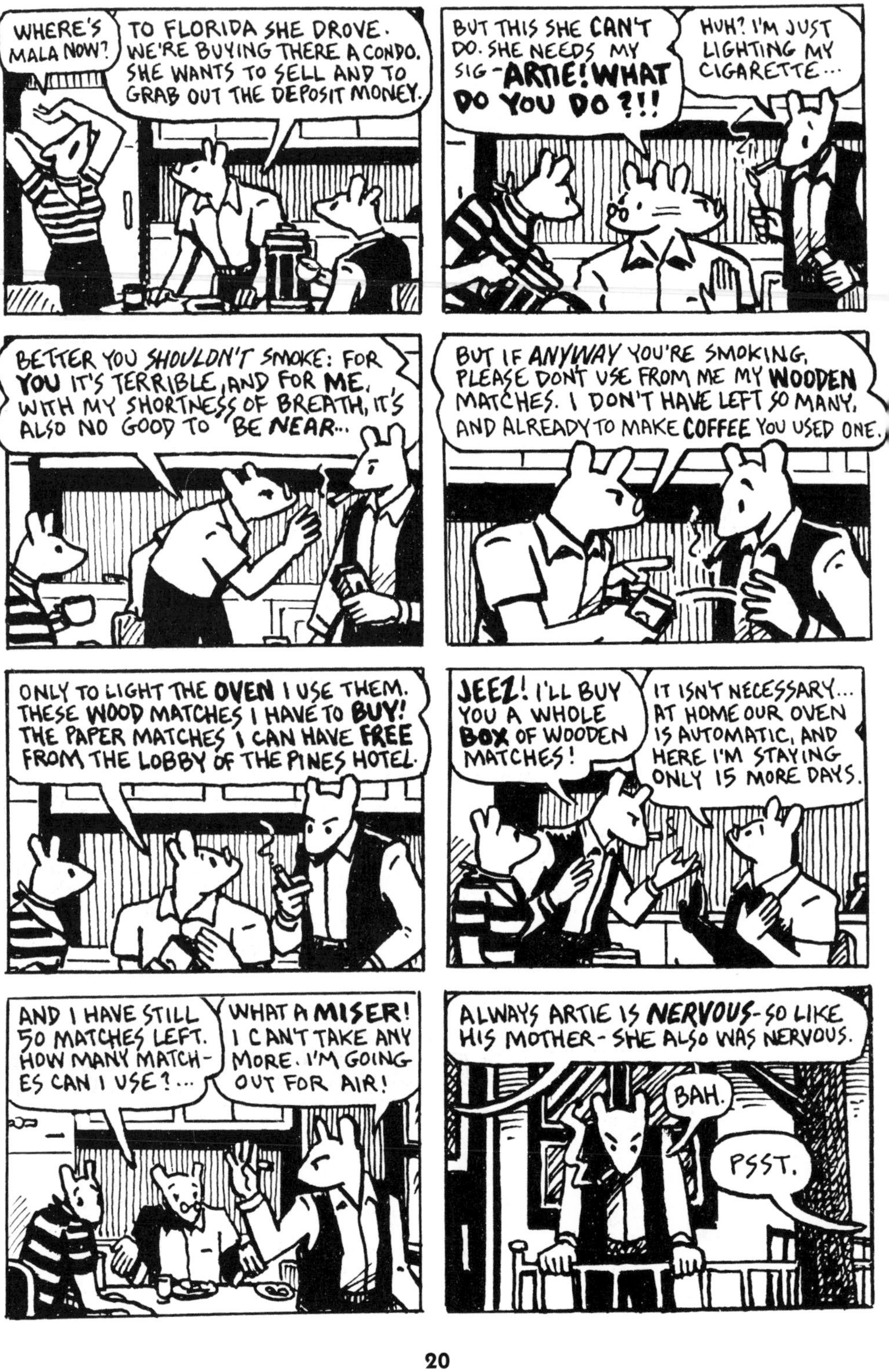

WHERE'S MALA NOW?
TO FLORIDA SHE DROVE. WE'RE BUYING THERE A CONDO. SHE WANTS TO SELL AND TO GRAB OUT THE DEPOSIT MONEY.
BUT THIS SHE CAN'T DO. SHE NEEDS MY SIG- ARTIE! WHAT DO YOU DO?!!
HUH? I'M JUST LIGHTING MY CIGARETTE...
BETTER YOU SHOULDN'T SMOKE: FOR YOU IT'S TERRIBLE, AND FOR ME, WITH MY SHORTNESS OF BREATH, IT'S ALSO NO GOOD TO BE NEAR...
BUT IF ANYWAY YOU'RE SMOKING, PLEASE DON'T USE FROM ME MY WOODEN MATCHES. I DON'T HAVE LEFT SO MANY, AND ALREADY TO MAKE COFFEE YOU USED ONE.
ONLY TO LIGHT THE OVEN I USE THEM. THESE WOOD MATCHES I HAVE TO BUY! THE PAPER MATCHES I CAN HAVE FREE FROM THE LOBBY OF THE PINES HOTEL.
JEEZ! I'LL BUY YOU A WHOLE BOX OF WOODEN MATCHES!
IT ISN'T NECESSARY... AT HOME OUR OVEN IS AUTOMATIC, AND HERE I'M STAYING ONLY 15 MORE DAYS.
AND I HAVE STILL 50 MATCHES LEFT. HOW MANY MATCHES CAN I USE?...
WHAT A MISER! I CAN'T TAKE ANY MORE. I'M GOING OUT FOR AIR!
ALWAYS ARTIE IS NERVOUS- SO LIKE HIS MOTHER- SHE ALSO WAS NERVOUS.
BAH.
PSST.

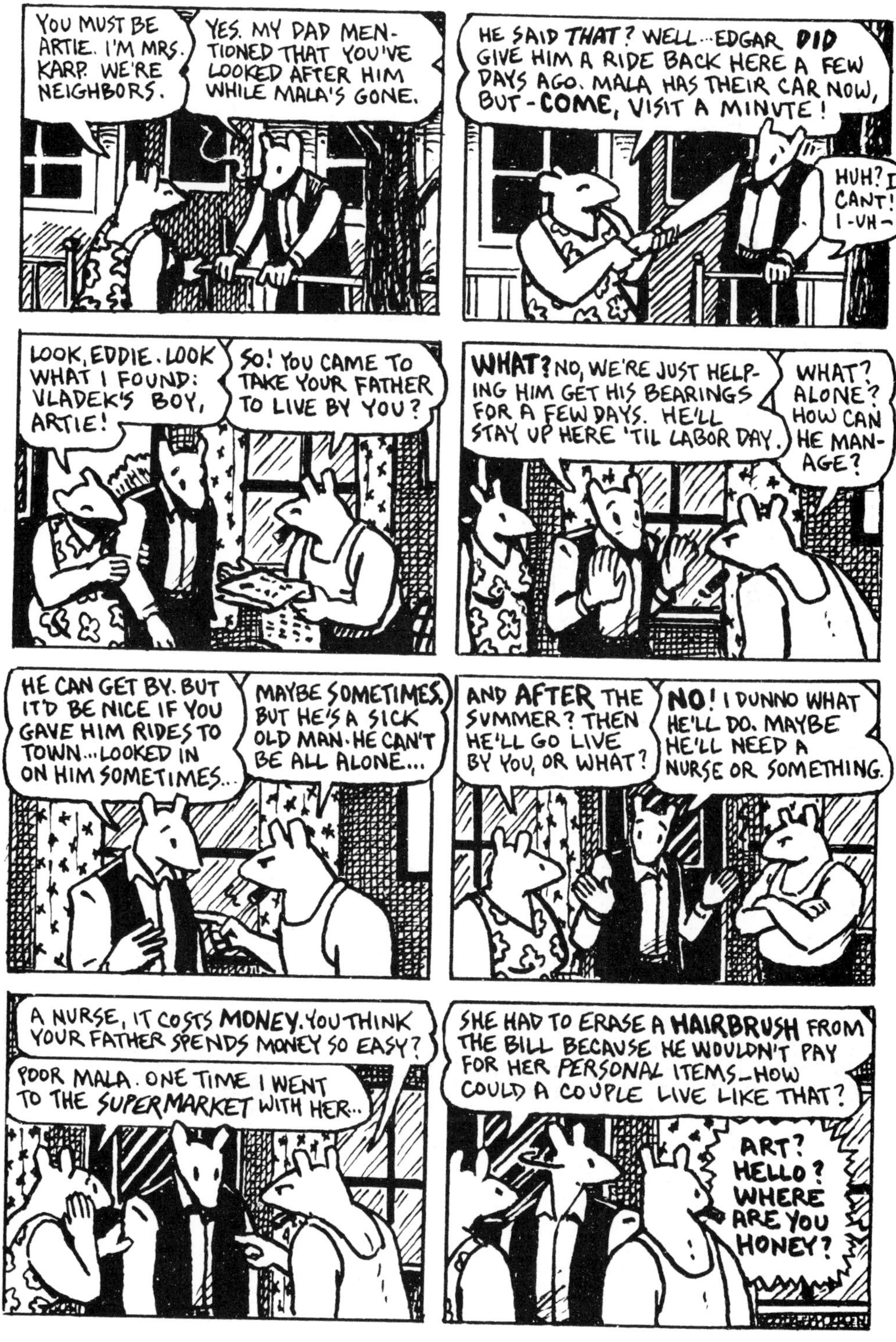
YOU MUST BE ARTIE. I'M MRS. KARP. WE'RE NEIGHBORS.
YES. MY DAD MENTIONED THAT YOU'VE LOOKED AFTER HIM WHILE MALA'S GONE.
HE SAID THAT? WELL... EDGAR DID GIVE HIM A RIDE BACK HERE A FEW DAYS AGO. MALA HAS THEIR CAR NOW, BUT - COME, VISIT A MINUTE!
HUH? I CAN'T! I-UH-
LOOK, EDDIE. LOOK WHAT I FOUND: VLADEK'S BOY, ARTIE!
SO! YOU CAME TO TAKE YOUR FATHER TO LIVE BY YOU?
WHAT? NO, WE'RE JUST HELPING HIM GET HIS BEARINGS FOR A FEW DAYS. HE'LL STAY UP HERE 'TIL LABOR DAY.
WHAT? ALONE? HOW CAN HE MANAGE?
HE CAN GET BY. BUT IT'D BE NICE IF YOU GAVE HIM RIDES TO TOWN... LOOKED IN ON HIM SOMETIMES...
MAYBE SOMETIMES, BUT HE'S A SICK OLD MAN. HE CAN'T BE ALL ALONE...
AND AFTER THE SUMMER? THEN HE'LL GO LIVE BY YOU, OR WHAT?
NO! I DUNNO WHAT HE'LL DO. MAYBE HE'LL NEED A NURSE OR SOMETHING.
A NURSE, IT COSTS MONEY. YOU THINK YOUR FATHER SPENDS MONEY SO EASY?
POOR MALA. ONE TIME I WENT TO THE SUPERMARKET WITH HER...
SHE HAD TO ERASE A HAIRBRUSH FROM THE BILL BECAUSE HE WOULDN'T PAY FOR HER PERSONAL ITEMS_HOW COULD A COUPLE LIVE LIKE THAT?
ART? HELLO? WHERE ARE YOU HONEY?

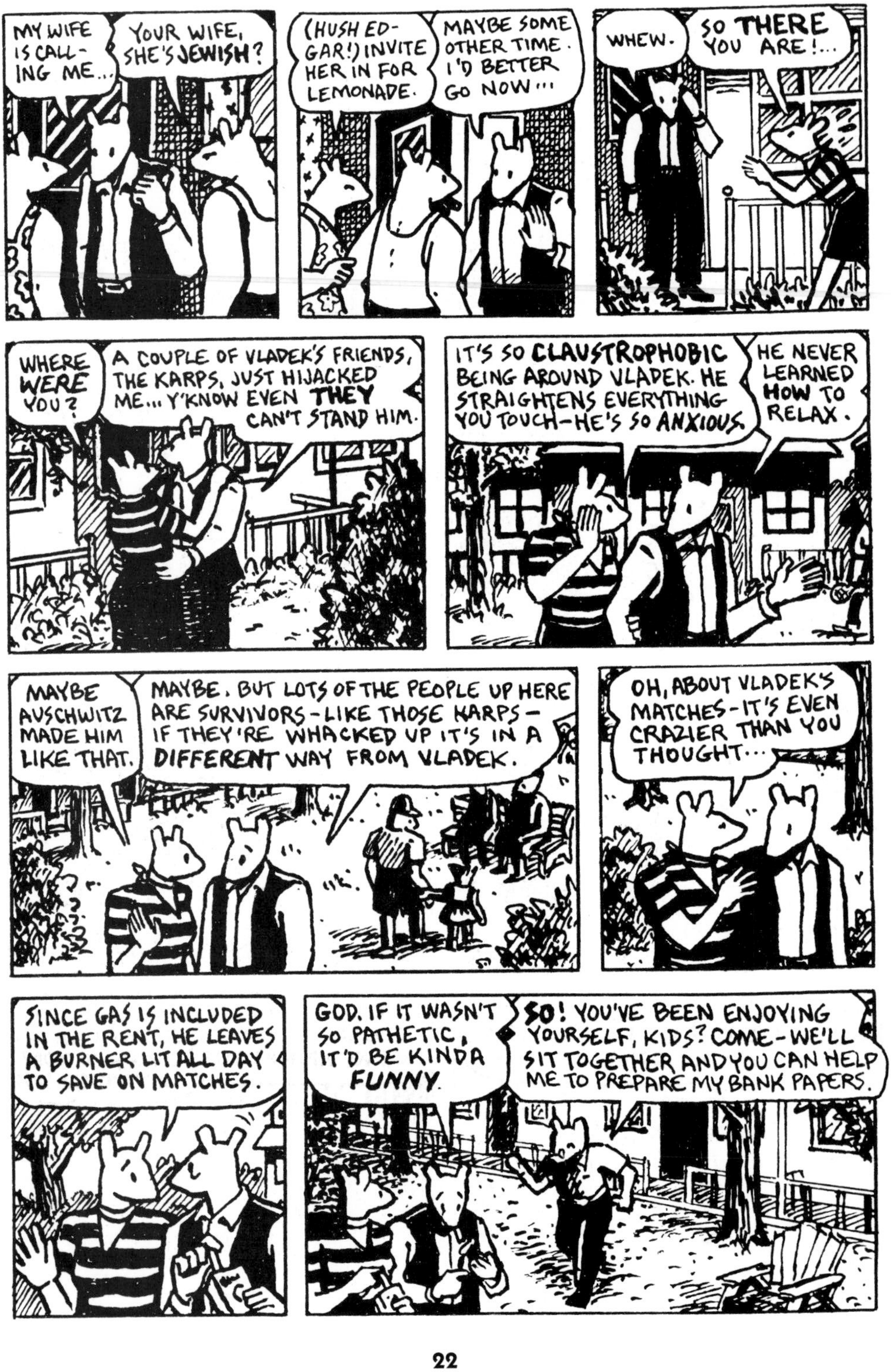
MY WIFE IS CALLING ME...
YOUR WIFE, SHE'S JEWISH?
(HUSH EDGAR!) INVITE HER IN FOR LEMONADE.
MAYBE SOME OTHER TIME. I'D BETTER GO NOW...
WHEW.
SO THERE YOU ARE!...
WHERE WERE YOU?
A COUPLE OF VLADEK'S FRIENDS, THE KARPS, JUST HIJACKED ME... Y'KNOW EVEN THEY CAN'T STAND HIM.
IT'S SO CLAUSTROPHOBIC BEING AROUND VLADEK. HE STRAIGHTENS EVERYTHING YOU TOUCH—HE'S SO ANXIOUS.
HE NEVER LEARNED HOW TO RELAX.
MAYBE AUSCHWITZ MADE HIM LIKE THAT.
MAYBE. BUT LOTS OF THE PEOPLE UP HERE ARE SURVIVORS—LIKE THOSE KARPS—IF THEY'RE WHACKED UP IT'S IN A DIFFERENT WAY FROM VLADEK.
OH, ABOUT VLADEK'S MATCHES—IT'S EVEN CRAZIER THAN YOU THOUGHT...
SINCE GAS IS INCLUDED IN THE RENT, HE LEAVES A BURNER LIT ALL DAY TO SAVE ON MATCHES.
GOD. IF IT WASN'T SO PATHETIC, IT'D BE KINDA FUNNY.
SO! YOU'VE BEEN ENJOYING YOURSELF, KIDS? COME—WE'LL SIT TOGETHER AND YOU CAN HELP ME TO PREPARE MY BANK PAPERS.

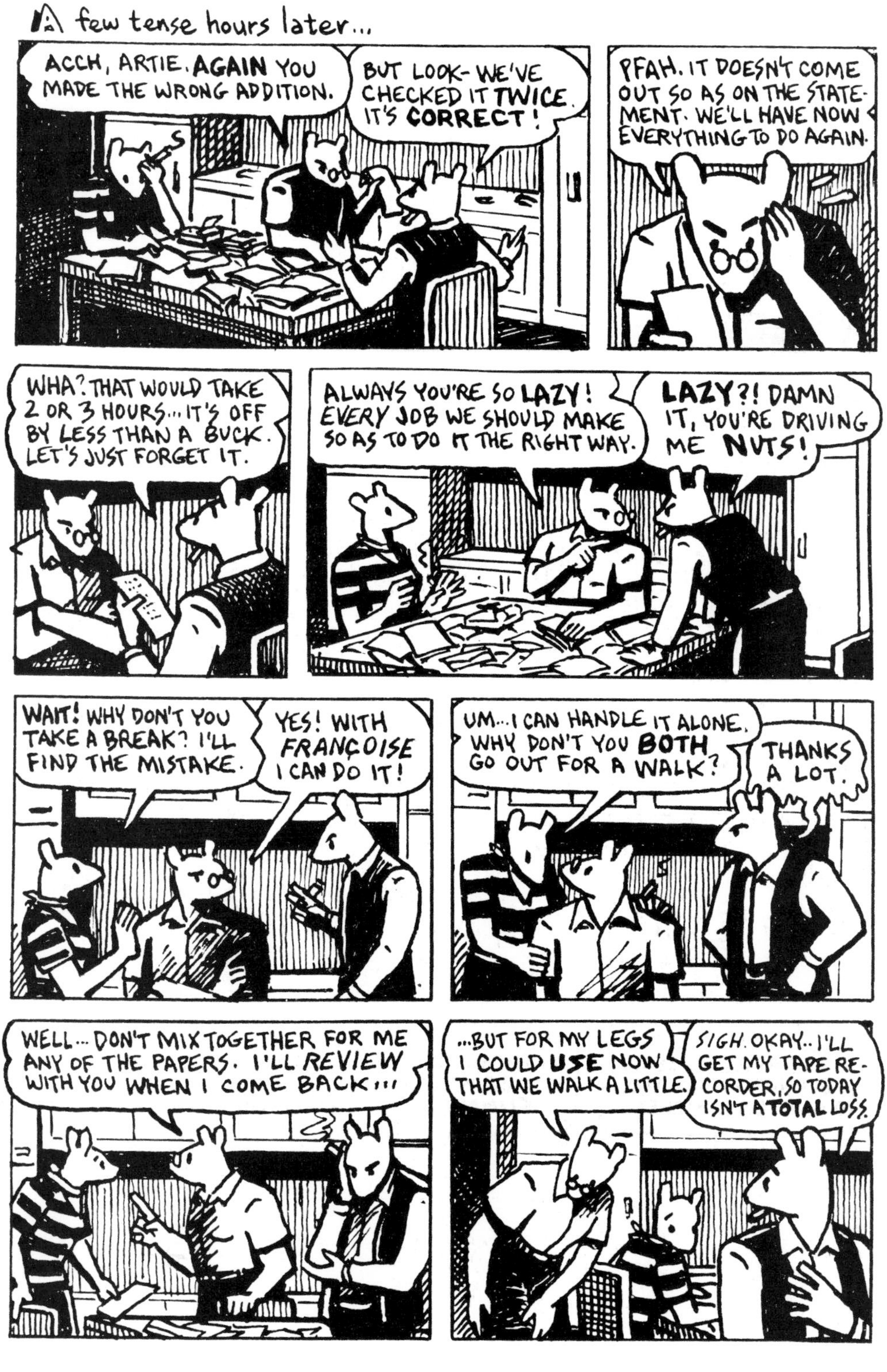
A few tense hours later...
ACCH, ARTIE. AGAIN YOU MADE THE WRONG ADDITION.
BUT LOOK- WE'VE CHECKED IT TWICE. IT'S CORRECT!
PFAH. IT DOESN'T COME OUT SO AS ON THE STATEMENT. WE'LL HAVE NOW EVERYTHING TO DO AGAIN.
WHA? THAT WOULD TAKE 2 OR 3 HOURS... IT'S OFF BY LESS THAN A BUCK. LET'S JUST FORGET IT.
ALWAYS YOU'RE SO LAZY! EVERY JOB WE SHOULD MAKE SO AS TO DO IT THE RIGHT WAY.
LAZY?! DAMN IT, YOU'RE DRIVING ME NUTS!
WAIT! WHY DON'T YOU TAKE A BREAK? I'LL FIND THE MISTAKE.
YES! WITH FRANÇOISE I CAN DO IT!
UM... I CAN HANDLE IT ALONE. WHY DON'T YOU BOTH GO OUT FOR A WALK?
THANKS A LOT.
WELL... DON'T MIX TOGETHER FOR ME ANY OF THE PAPERS. I'LL REVIEW WITH YOU WHEN I COME BACK...
...BUT FOR MY LEGS I COULD USE NOW THAT WE WALK A LITTLE.
SIGH. OKAY.. I'LL GET MY TAPE RECORDER, SO TODAY ISN'T A TOTAL LOSS.

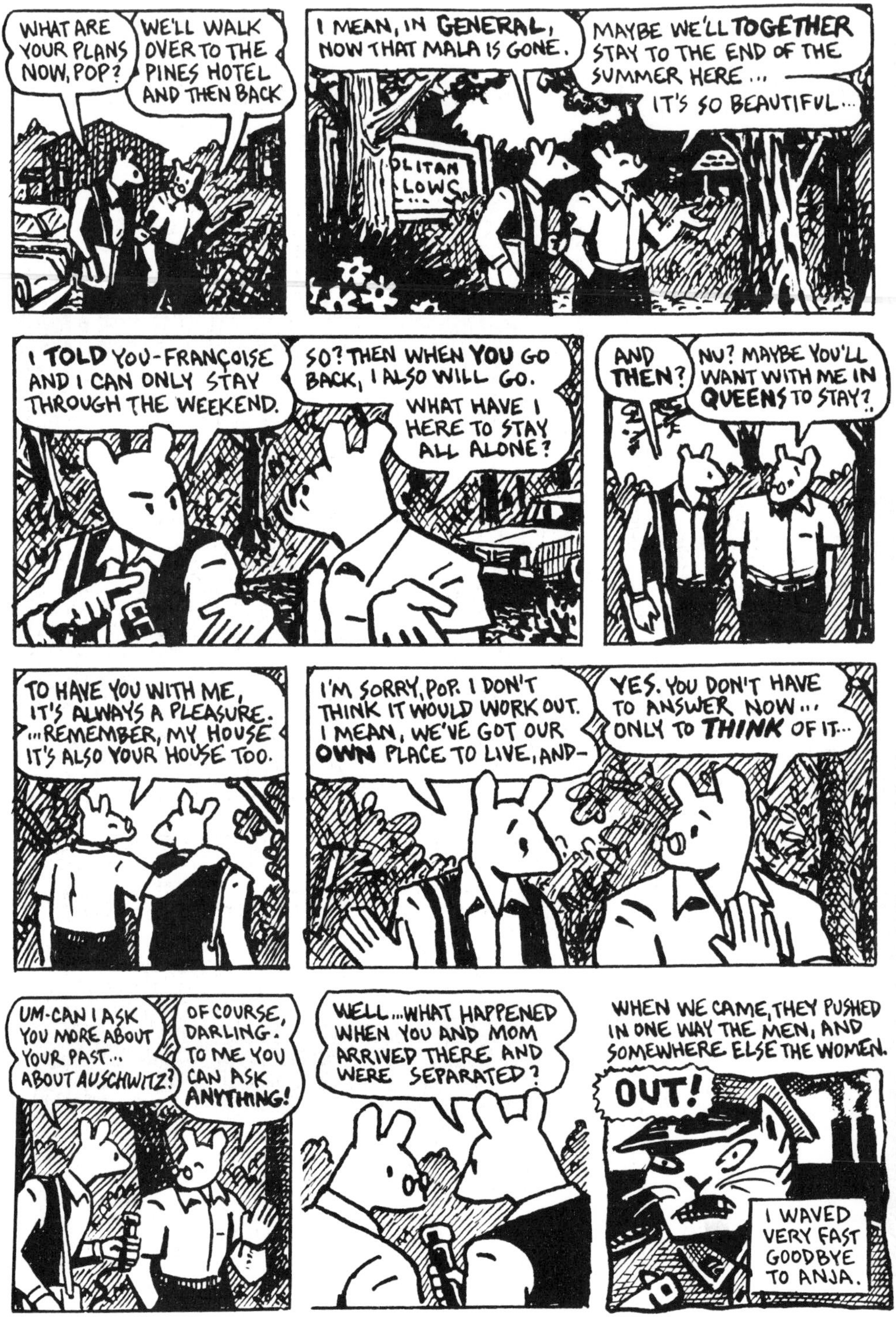

WHAT ARE YOUR PLANS NOW, POP?
WE'LL WALK OVER TO THE PINES HOTEL AND THEN BACK
I MEAN, IN GENERAL, NOW THAT MALA IS GONE.
MAYBE WE'LL TOGETHER STAY TO THE END OF THE SUMMER HERE...
IT'S SO BEAUTIFUL...
I TOLD YOU- FRANÇOISE AND I CAN ONLY STAY THROUGH THE WEEKEND.
SO? THEN WHEN YOU GO BACK, I ALSO WILL GO.
WHAT HAVE I HERE TO STAY ALL ALONE?
AND THEN?
NU? MAYBE YOU'LL WANT WITH ME IN QUEENS TO STAY?
TO HAVE YOU WITH ME, IT'S ALWAYS A PLEASURE. ...REMEMBER, MY HOUSE IT'S ALSO YOUR HOUSE TOO.
I'M SORRY, POP. I DON'T THINK IT WOULD WORK OUT. I MEAN, WE'VE GOT OUR OWN PLACE TO LIVE, AND-
YES. YOU DON'T HAVE TO ANSWER NOW... ONLY TO THINK OF IT...
UM- CAN I ASK YOU MORE ABOUT YOUR PAST... ABOUT AUSCHWITZ?
OF COURSE, DARLING. TO ME YOU CAN ASK ANYTHING!
WELL...WHAT HAPPENED WHEN YOU AND MOM ARRIVED THERE AND WERE SEPARATED?
WHEN WE CAME, THEY PUSHED IN ONE WAY THE MEN, AND SOMEWHERE ELSE THE WOMEN.
OUT!
I WAVED VERY FAST GOODBYE TO ANJA.

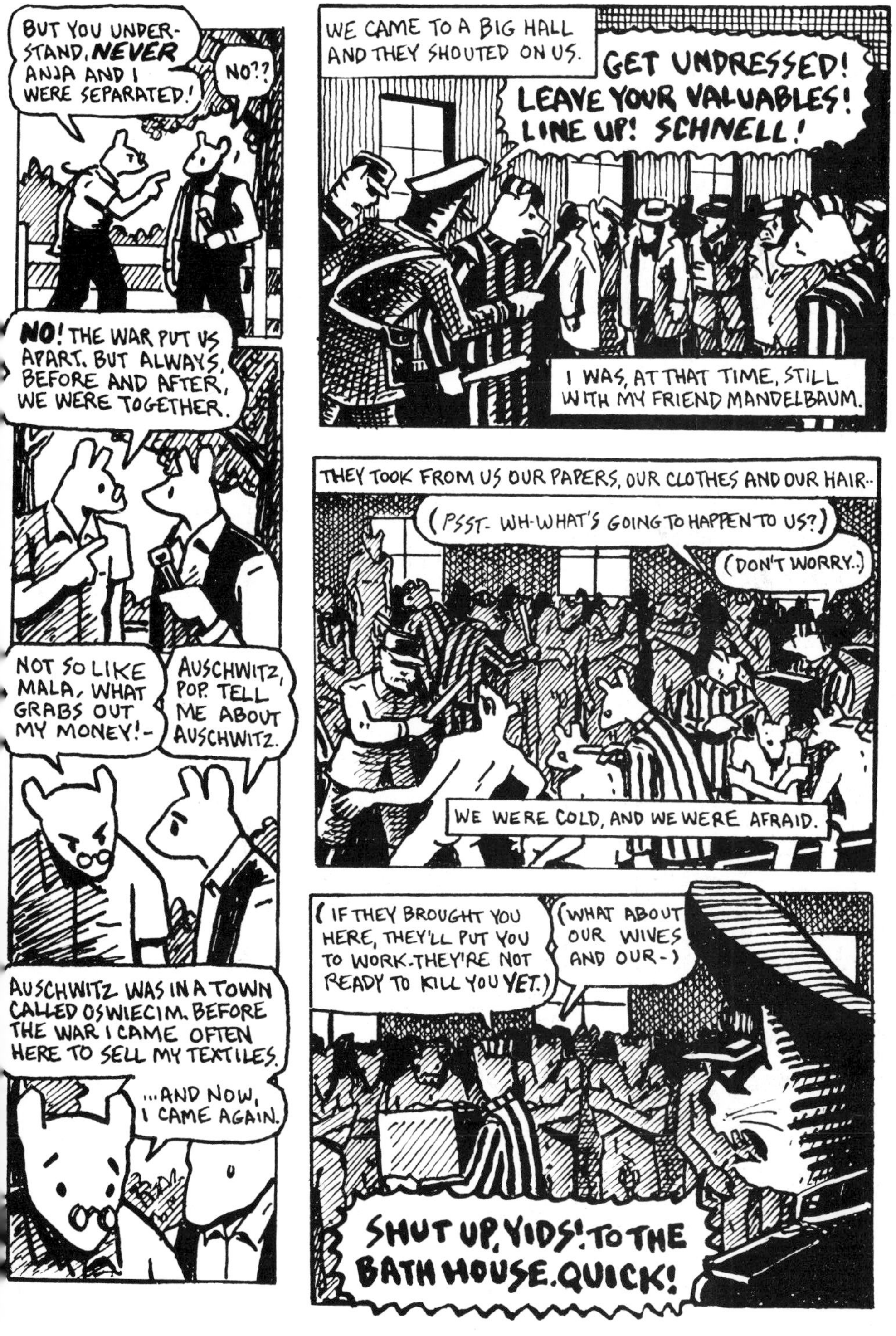

BUT YOU UNDERSTAND, NEVER ANJA AND I WERE SEPARATED!
NO??
NO! THE WAR PUT US APART. BUT ALWAYS, BEFORE AND AFTER, WE WERE TOGETHER.
NOT SO LIKE MALA, WHAT GRABS OUT MY MONEY!-
AUSCHWITZ, POP. TELL ME ABOUT AUSCHWITZ.
AUSCHWITZ WAS IN A TOWN CALLED OSWIECIM. BEFORE THE WAR I CAME OFTEN HERE TO SELL MY TEXTILES.
...AND NOW, I CAME AGAIN.
WE CAME TO A BIG HALL AND THEY SHOUTED ON US.
GET UNDRESSED! LEAVE YOUR VALUABLES! LINE UP! SCHNELL!
I WAS, AT THAT TIME, STILL WITH MY FRIEND MANDELBAUM.
THEY TOOK FROM US OUR PAPERS, OUR CLOTHES AND OUR HAIR..
(PSST- WH-WHAT'S GOING TO HAPPEN TO US?)
(DON'T WORRY..)
WE WERE COLD, AND WE WERE AFRAID.
(IF THEY BROUGHT YOU HERE, THEY'LL PUT YOU TO WORK. THEY'RE NOT READY TO KILL YOU YET.)
(WHAT ABOUT OUR WIVES AND OUR-)
SHUT UP, YIDS! TO THE BATH HOUSE. QUICK!

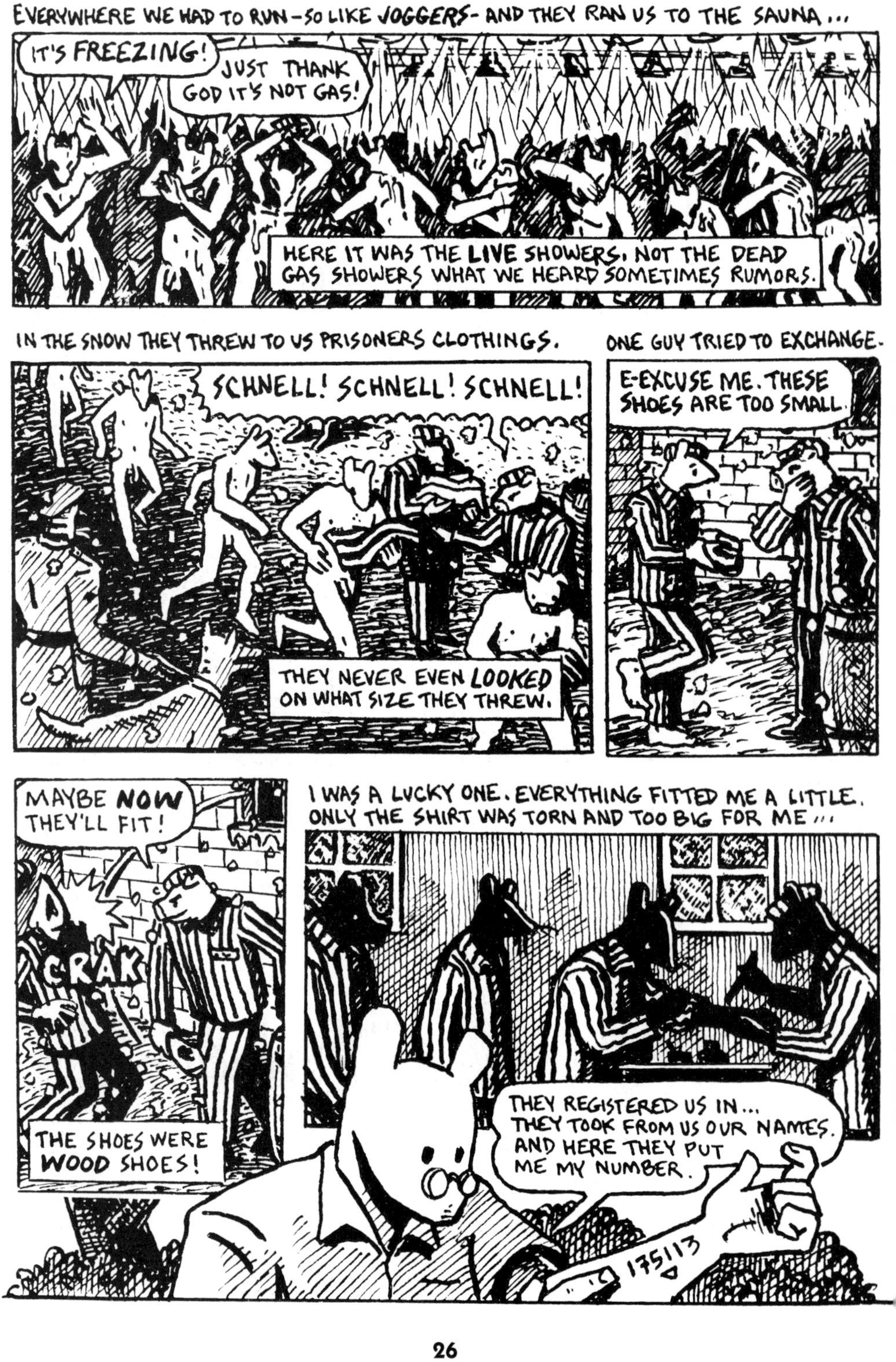
EVERYWHERE WE HAD TO RUN - SO LIKE JOGGERS - AND THEY RAN US TO THE SAUNA...
IT'S FREEZING!
JUST THANK GOD IT'S NOT GAS!
HERE IT WAS THE LIVE SHOWERS, NOT THE DEAD GAS SHOWERS WHAT WE HEARD SOMETIMES RUMORS.
IN THE SNOW THEY THREW TO US PRISONERS CLOTHINGS.
SCHNELL! SCHNELL! SCHNELL!
THEY NEVER EVEN LOOKED ON WHAT SIZE THEY THREW.
ONE GUY TRIED TO EXCHANGE.
E-EXCUSE ME. THESE SHOES ARE TOO SMALL.
MAYBE NOW THEY'LL FIT!
CRAK
THE SHOES WERE WOOD SHOES!
I WAS A LUCKY ONE. EVERYTHING FITTED ME A LITTLE. ONLY THE SHIRT WAS TORN AND TOO BIG FOR ME...
THEY REGISTERED US IN... THEY TOOK FROM US OUR NAMES. AND HERE THEY PUT ME MY NUMBER.
175113

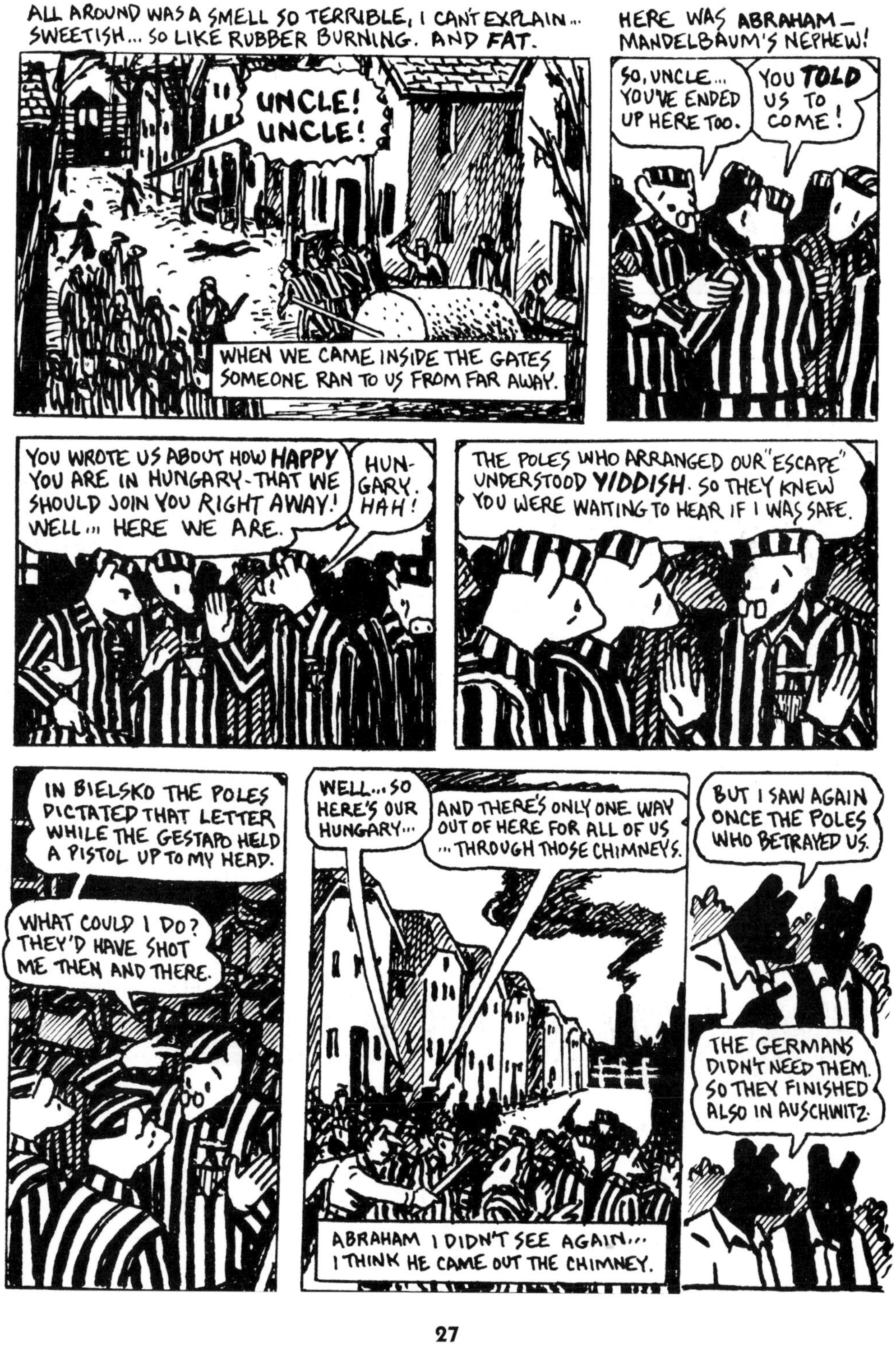
ALL AROUND WAS A SMELL SO TERRIBLE, I CAN'T EXPLAIN... SWEETISH... SO LIKE RUBBER BURNING. AND FAT.
UNCLE! UNCLE!
WHEN WE CAME INSIDE THE GATES SOMEONE RAN TO US FROM FAR AWAY.
HERE WAS ABRAHAM — MANDELBAUM'S NEPHEW!
SO, UNCLE... YOU'VE ENDED UP HERE TOO.
YOU TOLD US TO COME!
YOU WROTE US ABOUT HOW HAPPY YOU ARE IN HUNGARY - THAT WE SHOULD JOIN YOU RIGHT AWAY! WELL... HERE WE ARE.
HUN-GARY. HAH!
THE POLES WHO ARRANGED OUR "ESCAPE" UNDERSTOOD YIDDISH. SO THEY KNEW YOU WERE WAITING TO HEAR IF I WAS SAFE.
IN BIELSKO THE POLES DICTATED THAT LETTER WHILE THE GESTAPO HELD A PISTOL UP TO MY HEAD.
WHAT COULD I DO? THEY'D HAVE SHOT ME THEN AND THERE.
WELL... SO HERE'S OUR HUNGARY...
AND THERE'S ONLY ONE WAY OUT OF HERE FOR ALL OF US ... THROUGH THOSE CHIMNEYS.
ABRAHAM I DIDN'T SEE AGAIN... I THINK HE CAME OUT THE CHIMNEY.
BUT I SAW AGAIN ONCE THE POLES WHO BETRAYED US.
THE GERMANS DIDN'T NEED THEM. SO THEY FINISHED ALSO IN AUSCHWITZ.

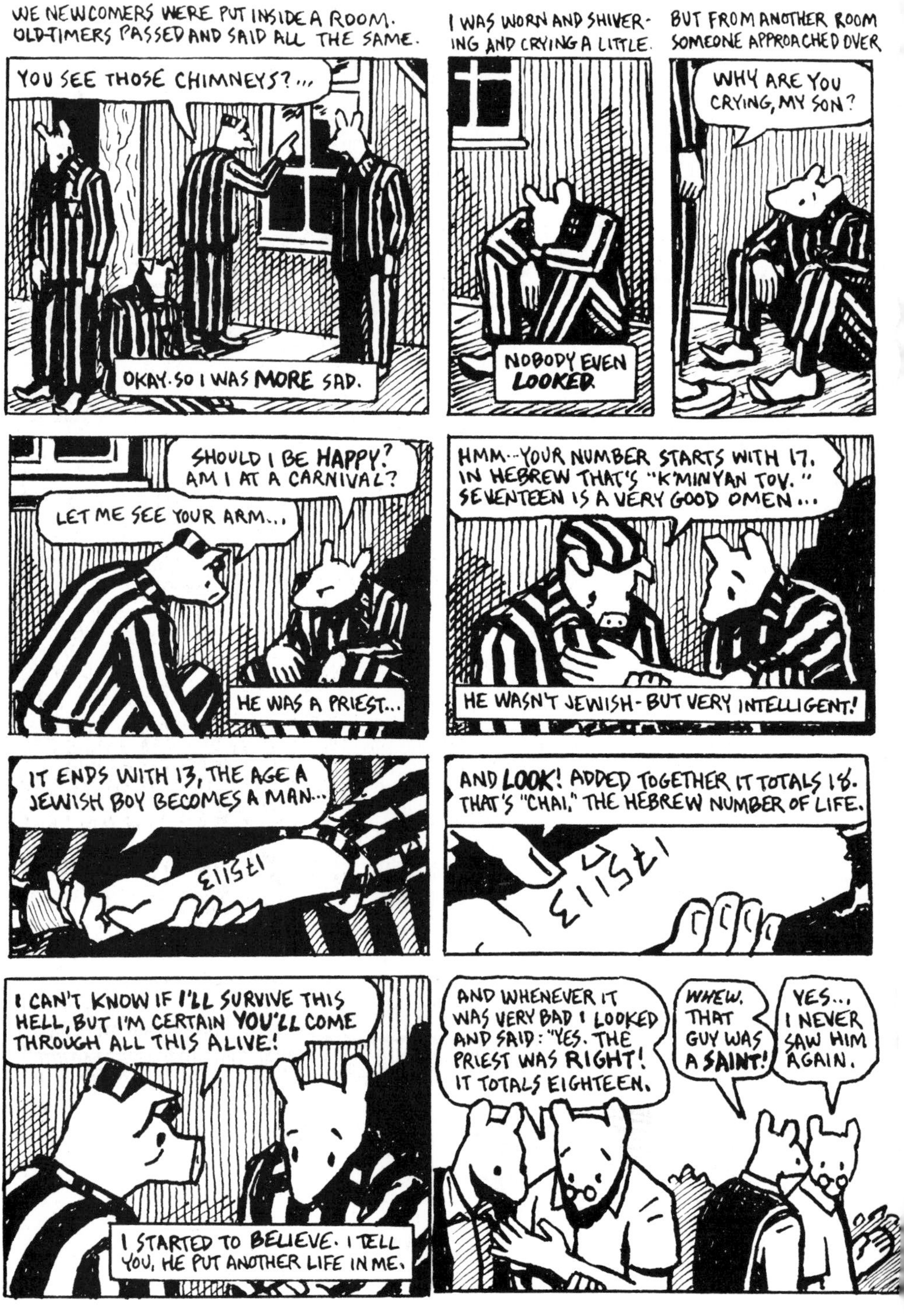
WE NEWCOMERS WERE PUT INSIDE A ROOM. OLD-TIMERS PASSED AND SAID ALL THE SAME.
YOU SEE THOSE CHIMNEYS?...
OKAY. SO I WAS MORE SAD.
I WAS WORN AND SHIVERING AND CRYING A LITTLE.
NOBODY EVEN LOOKED.
BUT FROM ANOTHER ROOM SOMEONE APPROACHED OVER
WHY ARE YOU CRYING, MY SON?
SHOULD I BE HAPPY? AM I AT A CARNIVAL?
LET ME SEE YOUR ARM...
HE WAS A PRIEST...
HMM... YOUR NUMBER STARTS WITH 17. IN HEBREW THAT'S "K'MINYAN TOV." SEVENTEEN IS A VERY GOOD OMEN...
HE WASN'T JEWISH - BUT VERY INTELLIGENT!
IT ENDS WITH 13, THE AGE A JEWISH BOY BECOMES A MAN...
175113
AND LOOK! ADDED TOGETHER IT TOTALS 18. THAT'S "CHAI," THE HEBREW NUMBER OF LIFE.
175113
I CAN'T KNOW IF I'LL SURVIVE THIS HELL, BUT I'M CERTAIN YOU'LL COME THROUGH ALL THIS ALIVE!
I STARTED TO BELIEVE. I TELL YOU, HE PUT ANOTHER LIFE IN ME.
AND WHENEVER IT WAS VERY BAD I LOOKED AND SAID: "YES. THE PRIEST WAS RIGHT! IT TOTALS EIGHTEEN.
WHEW. THAT GUY WAS A SAINT!
YES... I NEVER SAW HIM AGAIN.

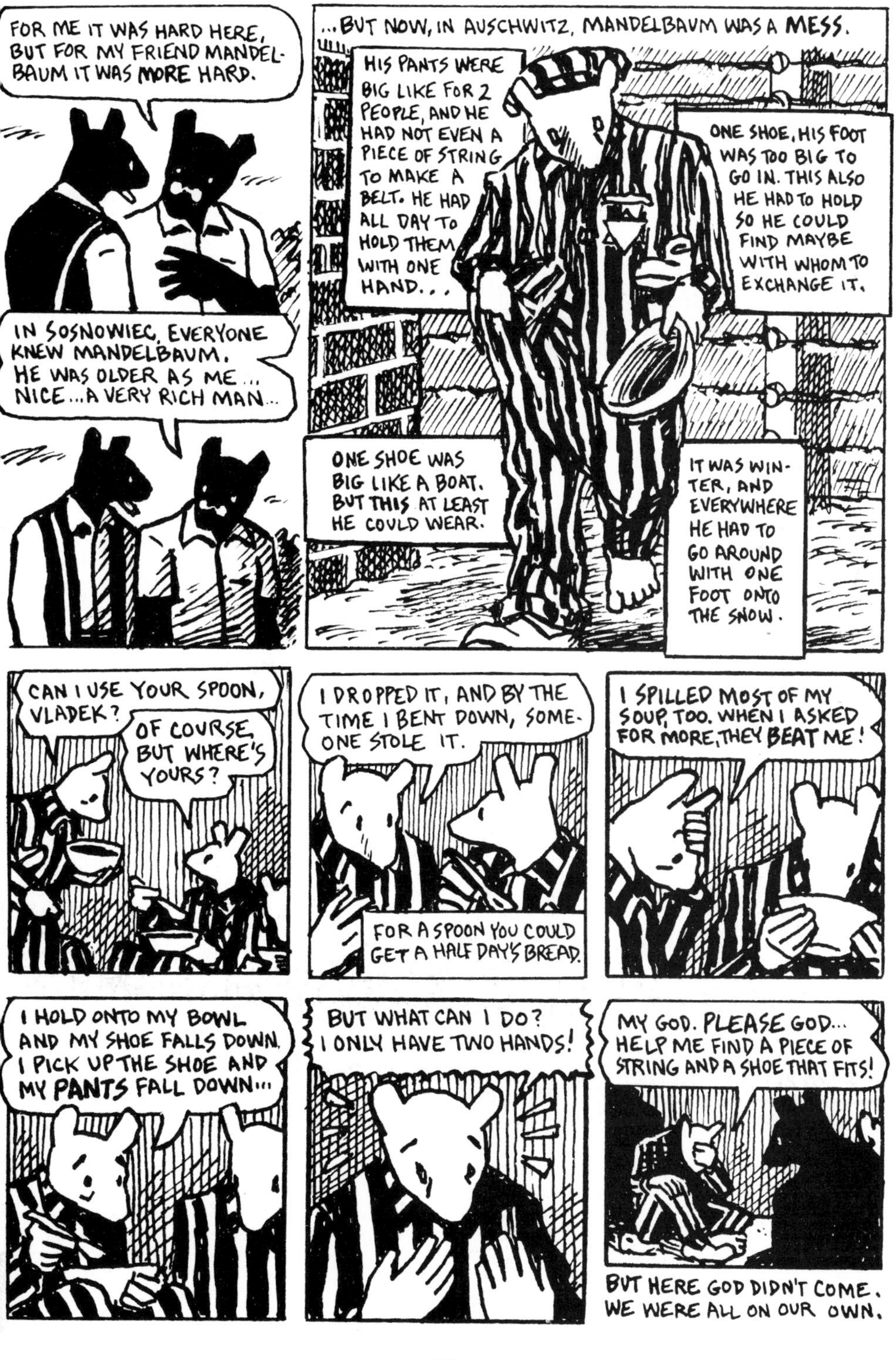
FOR ME IT WAS HARD HERE, BUT FOR MY FRIEND MANDELBAUM IT WAS MORE HARD.
IN SOSNOWIEC, EVERYONE KNEW MANDELBAUM. HE WAS OLDER AS ME... NICE...A VERY RICH MAN...
...BUT NOW, IN AUSCHWITZ, MANDELBAUM WAS A MESS.
HIS PANTS WERE BIG LIKE FOR 2 PEOPLE, AND HE HAD NOT EVEN A PIECE OF STRING TO MAKE A BELT. HE HAD ALL DAY TO HOLD THEM WITH ONE HAND...
ONE SHOE, HIS FOOT WAS TOO BIG TO GO IN. THIS ALSO HE HAD TO HOLD SO HE COULD FIND MAYBE WITH WHOM TO EXCHANGE IT.
ONE SHOE WAS BIG LIKE A BOAT. BUT THIS AT LEAST HE COULD WEAR.
IT WAS WINTER, AND EVERYWHERE HE HAD TO GO AROUND WITH ONE FOOT ONTO THE SNOW.
CAN I USE YOUR SPOON, VLADEK?
OF COURSE, BUT WHERE'S YOURS?
I DROPPED IT, AND BY THE TIME I BENT DOWN, SOMEONE STOLE IT.
FOR A SPOON YOU COULD GET A HALF DAY'S BREAD.
I SPILLED MOST OF MY SOUP, TOO. WHEN I ASKED FOR MORE, THEY BEAT ME!
I HOLD ONTO MY BOWL AND MY SHOE FALLS DOWN. I PICK UP THE SHOE AND MY PANTS FALL DOWN...
BUT WHAT CAN I DO? I ONLY HAVE TWO HANDS!
MY GOD. PLEASE GOD... HELP ME FIND A PIECE OF STRING AND A SHOE THAT FITS!
BUT HERE GOD DIDN'T COME. WE WERE ALL ON OUR OWN.

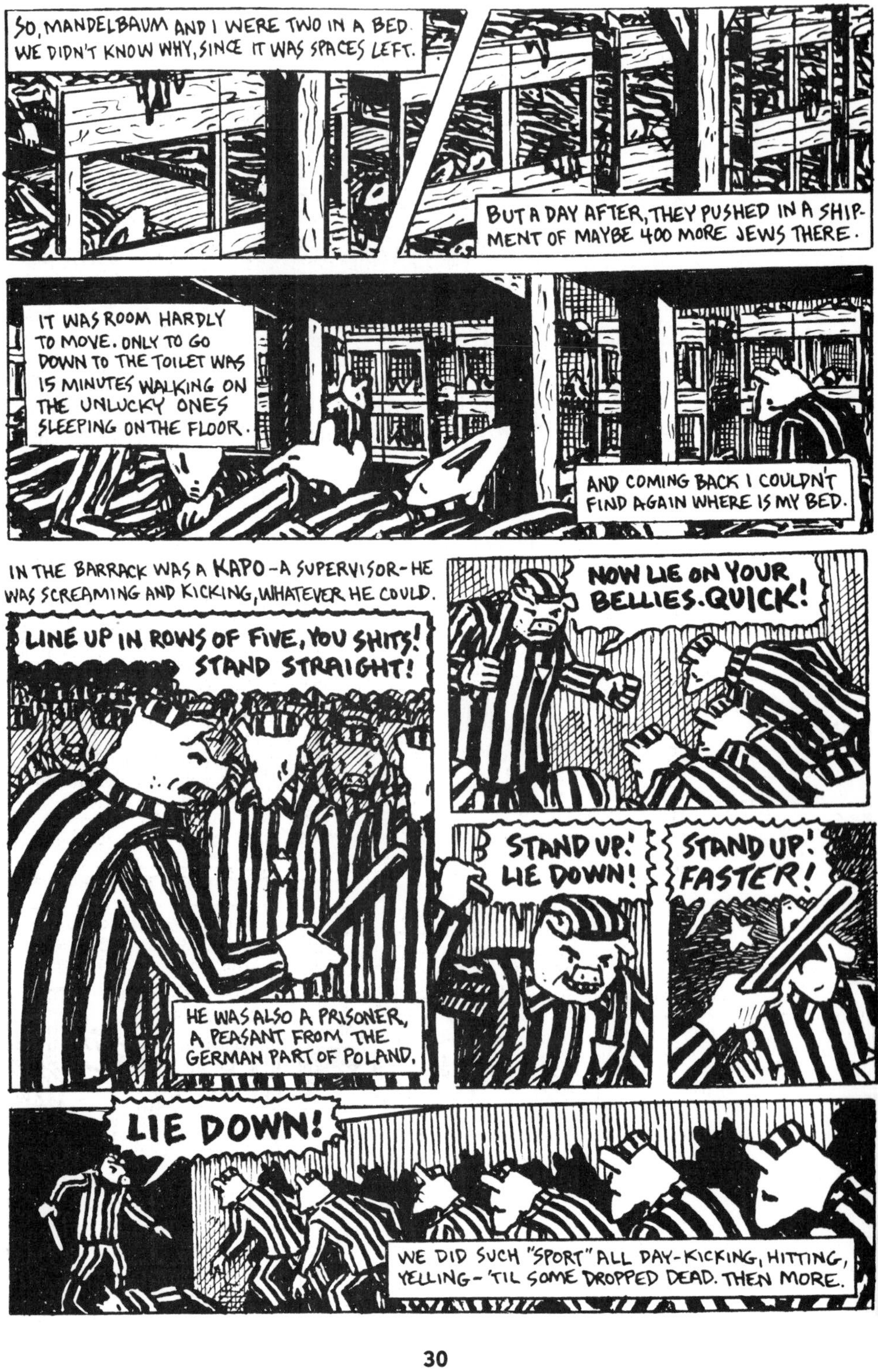
SO, MANDELBAUM AND I WERE TWO IN A BED. WE DIDN'T KNOW WHY, SINCE IT WAS SPACES LEFT.
BUT A DAY AFTER, THEY PUSHED IN A SHIPMENT OF MAYBE 400 MORE JEWS THERE.
IT WAS ROOM HARDLY TO MOVE. ONLY TO GO DOWN TO THE TOILET WAS 15 MINUTES WALKING ON THE UNLUCKY ONES SLEEPING ON THE FLOOR.
AND COMING BACK I COULDN'T FIND AGAIN WHERE IS MY BED.
IN THE BARRACK WAS A KAPO - A SUPERVISOR - HE WAS SCREAMING AND KICKING, WHATEVER HE COULD.
LINE UP IN ROWS OF FIVE, YOU SHITS! STAND STRAIGHT!
HE WAS ALSO A PRISONER, A PEASANT FROM THE GERMAN PART OF POLAND.
NOW LIE ON YOUR BELLIES. QUICK!
STAND UP! LIE DOWN!
STAND UP! FASTER!
LIE DOWN!
WE DID SUCH "SPORT" ALL DAY - KICKING, HITTING, YELLING - 'TIL SOME DROPPED DEAD. THEN MORE.

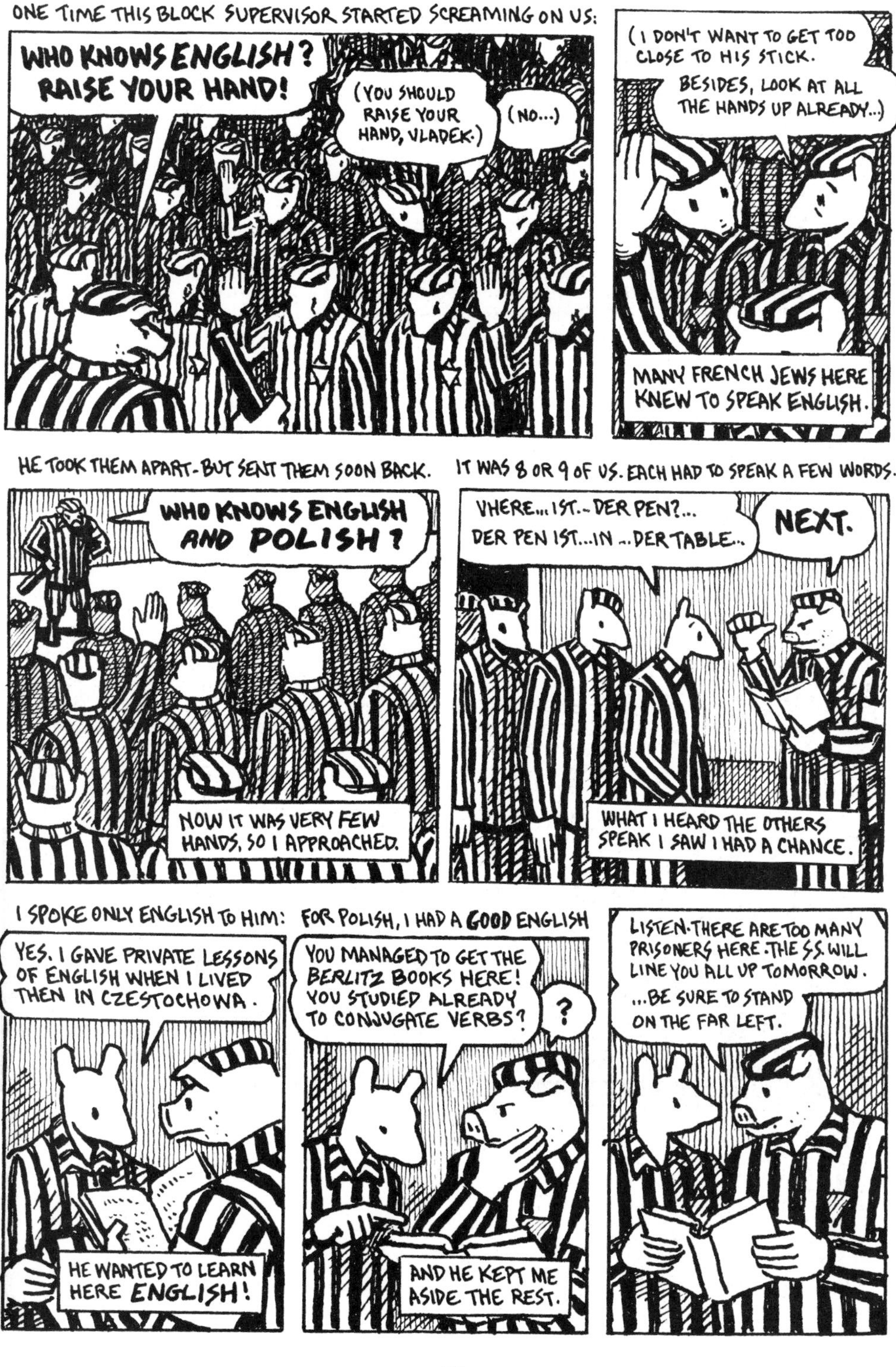
ONE TIME THIS BLOCK SUPERVISOR STARTED SCREAMING ON US:
WHO KNOWS ENGLISH? RAISE YOUR HAND!
(YOU SHOULD RAISE YOUR HAND, VLADEK.)
(NO...)
(I DON'T WANT TO GET TOO CLOSE TO HIS STICK.
BESIDES, LOOK AT ALL THE HANDS UP ALREADY...)
MANY FRENCH JEWS HERE KNEW TO SPEAK ENGLISH.
HE TOOK THEM APART- BUT SENT THEM SOON BACK.
WHO KNOWS ENGLISH AND POLISH?
NOW IT WAS VERY FEW HANDS, SO I APPROACHED.
IT WAS 8 OR 9 OF US. EACH HAD TO SPEAK A FEW WORDS.
VHERE... IST.. DER PEN?... DER PEN IST... IN .. DER TABLE..
NEXT.
WHAT I HEARD THE OTHERS SPEAK I SAW I HAD A CHANCE.
I SPOKE ONLY ENGLISH TO HIM:
YES. I GAVE PRIVATE LESSONS OF ENGLISH WHEN I LIVED THEN IN CZESTOCHOWA.
HE WANTED TO LEARN HERE ENGLISH!
FOR POLISH, I HAD A GOOD ENGLISH
YOU MANAGED TO GET THE BERLITZ BOOKS HERE! YOU STUDIED ALREADY TO CONJUGATE VERBS?
?
AND HE KEPT ME ASIDE THE REST.
LISTEN. THERE ARE TOO MANY PRISONERS HERE. THE S.S. WILL LINE YOU ALL UP TOMORROW.
...BE SURE TO STAND ON THE FAR LEFT.

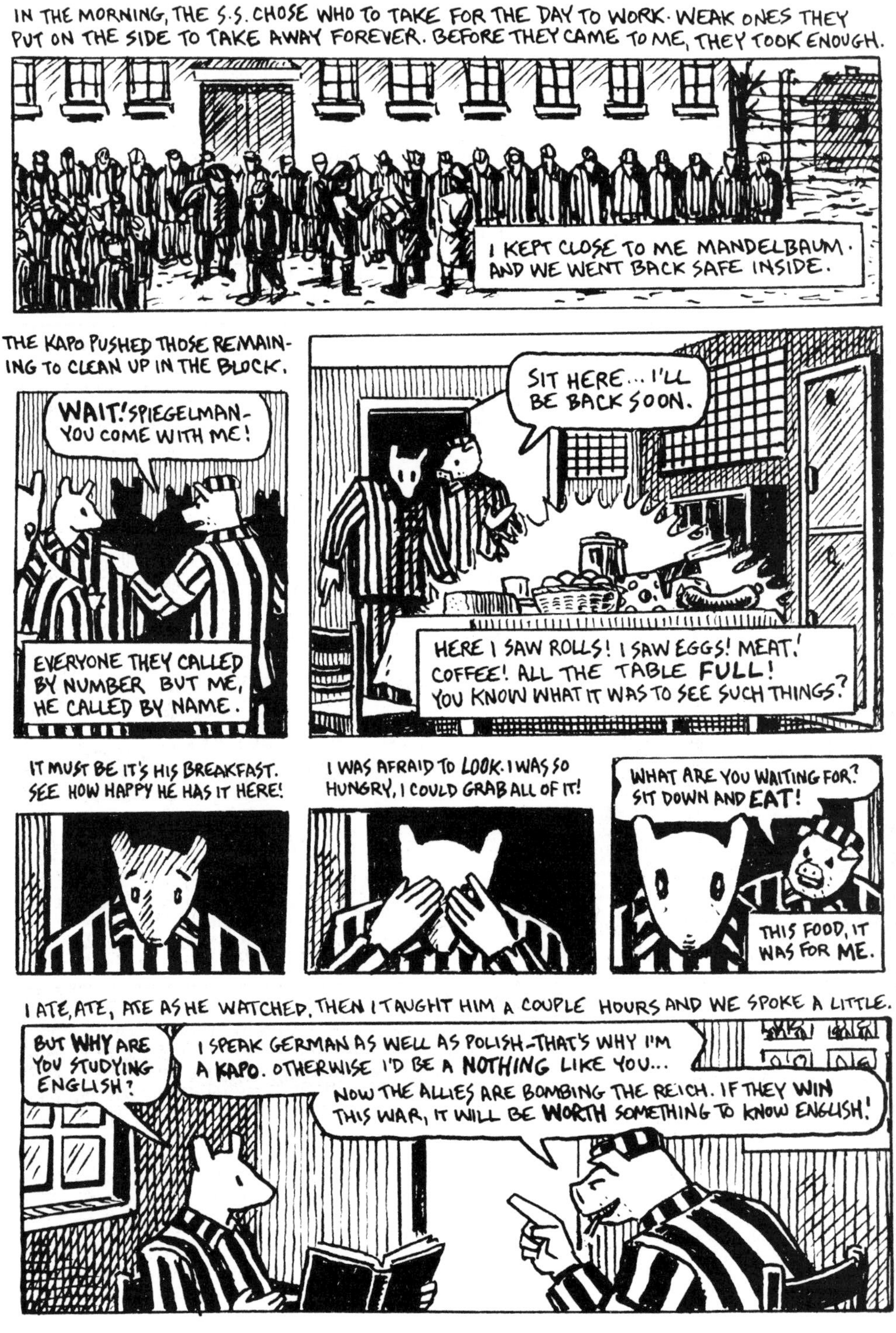

IN THE MORNING, THE S.S. CHOSE WHO TO TAKE FOR THE DAY TO WORK. WEAK ONES THEY PUT ON THE SIDE TO TAKE AWAY FOREVER. BEFORE THEY CAME TO ME, THEY TOOK ENOUGH.
I KEPT CLOSE TO ME MANDELBAUM. AND WE WENT BACK SAFE INSIDE.
THE KAPO PUSHED THOSE REMAINING TO CLEAN UP IN THE BLOCK.
WAIT! SPIEGELMAN- YOU COME WITH ME!
EVERYONE THEY CALLED BY NUMBER BUT ME, HE CALLED BY NAME.
SIT HERE... I'LL BE BACK SOON.
HERE I SAW ROLLS! I SAW EGGS! MEAT! COFFEE! ALL THE TABLE FULL! YOU KNOW WHAT IT WAS TO SEE SUCH THINGS?
IT MUST BE IT'S HIS BREAKFAST. SEE HOW HAPPY HE HAS IT HERE!
I WAS AFRAID TO LOOK. I WAS SO HUNGRY, I COULD GRAB ALL OF IT!
WHAT ARE YOU WAITING FOR? SIT DOWN AND EAT!
THIS FOOD, IT WAS FOR ME.
I ATE, ATE, ATE AS HE WATCHED. THEN I TAUGHT HIM A COUPLE HOURS AND WE SPOKE A LITTLE.
BUT WHY ARE YOU STUDYING ENGLISH?
I SPEAK GERMAN AS WELL AS POLISH-THAT'S WHY I'M A KAPO. OTHERWISE I'D BE A NOTHING LIKE YOU...
NOW THE ALLIES ARE BOMBING THE REICH. IF THEY WIN THIS WAR, IT WILL BE WORTH SOMETHING TO KNOW ENGLISH!

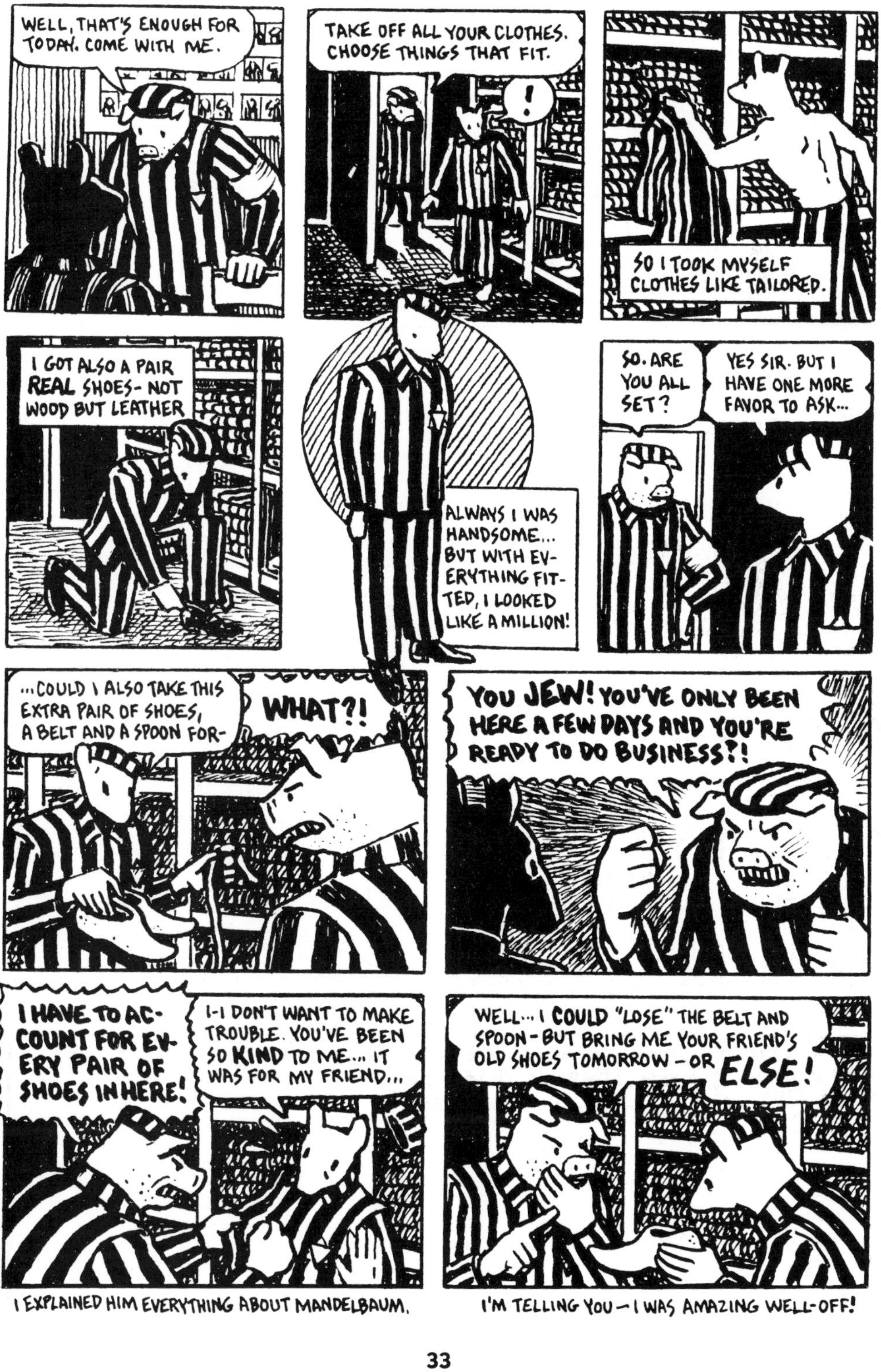
WELL, THAT'S ENOUGH FOR TODAY. COME WITH ME.
TAKE OFF ALL YOUR CLOTHES. CHOOSE THINGS THAT FIT.
!
SO I TOOK MYSELF CLOTHES LIKE TAILORED.
I GOT ALSO A PAIR REAL SHOES - NOT WOOD BUT LEATHER
ALWAYS I WAS HANDSOME... BUT WITH EVERYTHING FITTED, I LOOKED LIKE A MILLION!
SO. ARE YOU ALL SET?
YES SIR. BUT I HAVE ONE MORE FAVOR TO ASK...
...COULD I ALSO TAKE THIS EXTRA PAIR OF SHOES, A BELT AND A SPOON FOR-
WHAT?!
YOU JEW! YOU'VE ONLY BEEN HERE A FEW DAYS AND YOU'RE READY TO DO BUSINESS?!
I HAVE TO ACCOUNT FOR EVERY PAIR OF SHOES IN HERE!
I-I DON'T WANT TO MAKE TROUBLE. YOU'VE BEEN SO KIND TO ME... IT WAS FOR MY FRIEND...
I EXPLAINED HIM EVERYTHING ABOUT MANDELBAUM.
WELL... I COULD "LOSE" THE BELT AND SPOON - BUT BRING ME YOUR FRIEND'S OLD SHOES TOMORROW - OR ELSE!
I'M TELLING YOU - I WAS AMAZING WELL-OFF!

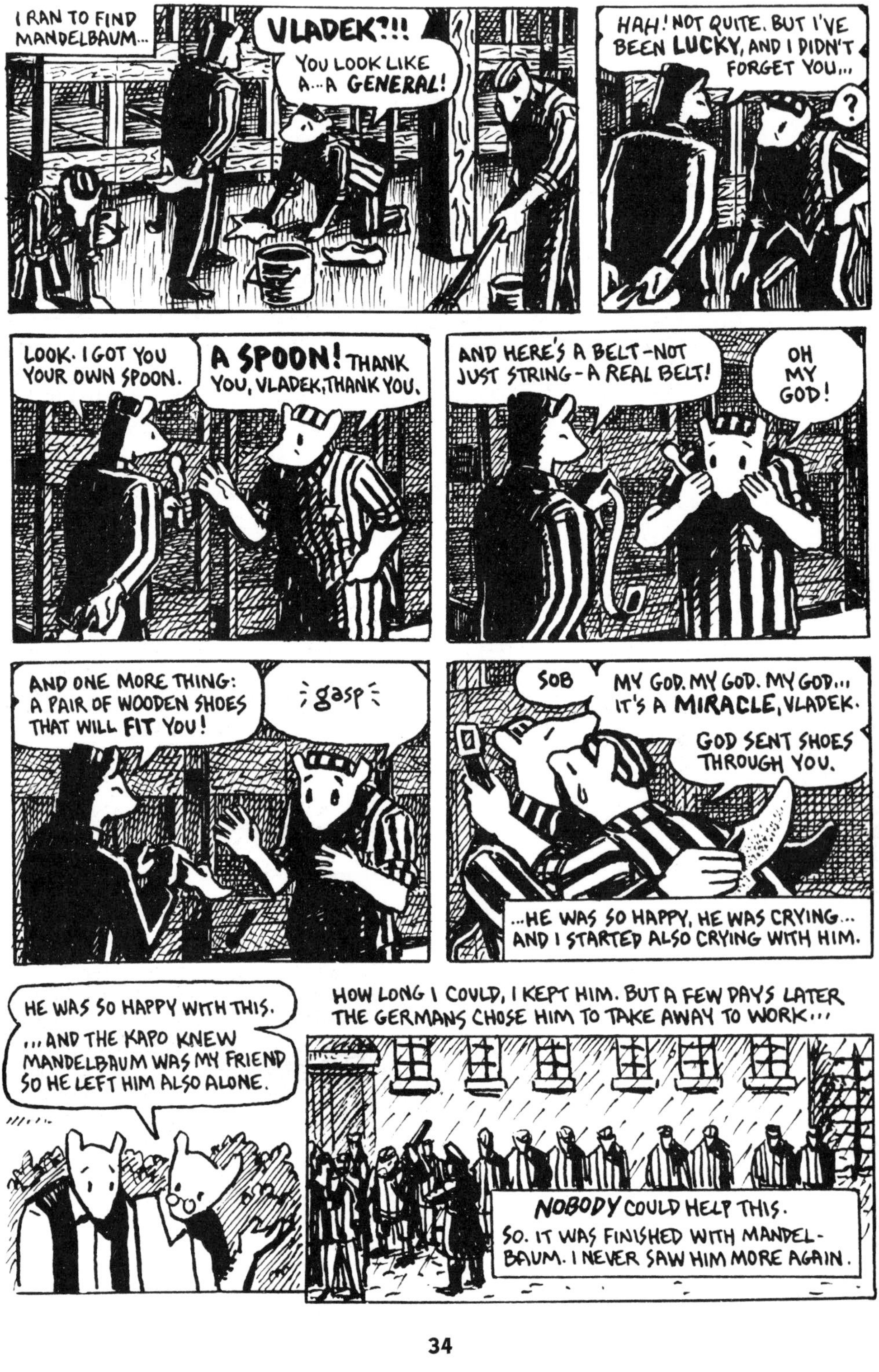
I RAN TO FIND MANDELBAUM...
VLADEK?!!
YOU LOOK LIKE A...A GENERAL!
HAH! NOT QUITE. BUT I'VE BEEN LUCKY, AND I DIDN'T FORGET YOU...
?
LOOK. I GOT YOU YOUR OWN SPOON.
A SPOON! THANK YOU, VLADEK, THANK YOU.
AND HERE'S A BELT-NOT JUST STRING-A REAL BELT!
OH MY GOD!
AND ONE MORE THING: A PAIR OF WOODEN SHOES THAT WILL FIT YOU!
gasp
SOB
MY GOD. MY GOD. MY GOD... IT'S A MIRACLE, VLADEK.
GOD SENT SHOES THROUGH YOU.
...HE WAS SO HAPPY, HE WAS CRYING... AND I STARTED ALSO CRYING WITH HIM.
HE WAS SO HAPPY WITH THIS.
...AND THE KAPO KNEW MANDELBAUM WAS MY FRIEND SO HE LEFT HIM ALSO ALONE.
HOW LONG I COULD, I KEPT HIM. BUT A FEW DAYS LATER THE GERMANS CHOSE HIM TO TAKE AWAY TO WORK...
NOBODY COULD HELP THIS.
SO. IT WAS FINISHED WITH MANDEL-BAUM. I NEVER SAW HIM MORE AGAIN.

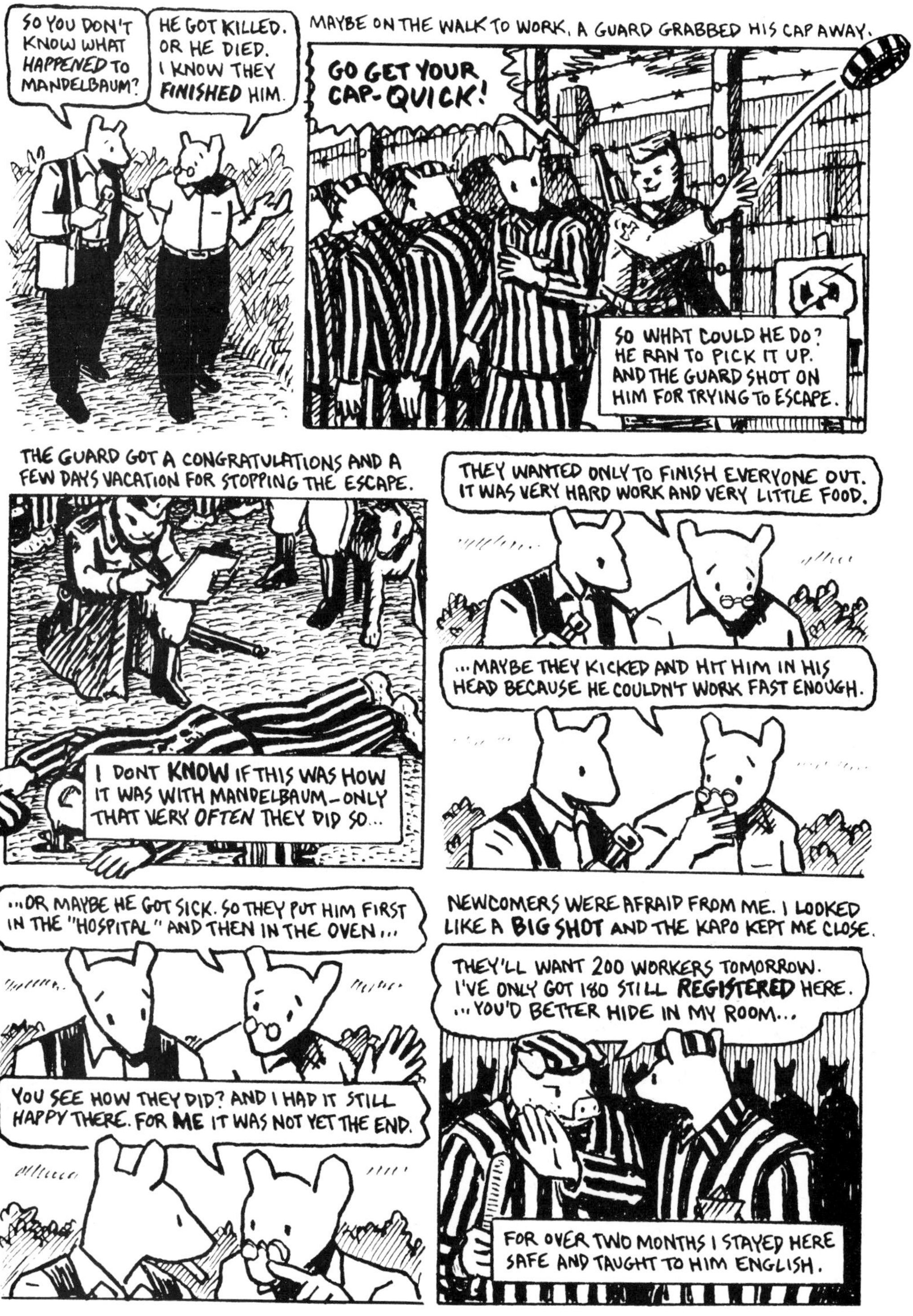
SO YOU DON'T KNOW WHAT HAPPENED TO MANDELBAUM?
HE GOT KILLED. OR HE DIED. I KNOW THEY FINISHED HIM.
MAYBE ON THE WALK TO WORK, A GUARD GRABBED HIS CAP AWAY.
GO GET YOUR CAP-QUICK!
SO WHAT COULD HE DO? HE RAN TO PICK IT UP. AND THE GUARD SHOT ON HIM FOR TRYING TO ESCAPE.
THE GUARD GOT A CONGRATULATIONS AND A FEW DAYS VACATION FOR STOPPING THE ESCAPE.
I DONT KNOW IF THIS WAS HOW IT WAS WITH MANDELBAUM—ONLY THAT VERY OFTEN THEY DID SO...
THEY WANTED ONLY TO FINISH EVERYONE OUT. IT WAS VERY HARD WORK AND VERY LITTLE FOOD.
...MAYBE THEY KICKED AND HIT HIM IN HIS HEAD BECAUSE HE COULDN'T WORK FAST ENOUGH.
...OR MAYBE HE GOT SICK. SO THEY PUT HIM FIRST IN THE "HOSPITAL" AND THEN IN THE OVEN...
YOU SEE HOW THEY DID? AND I HAD IT STILL HAPPY THERE. FOR ME IT WAS NOT YET THE END.
NEWCOMERS WERE AFRAID FROM ME. I LOOKED LIKE A BIG SHOT AND THE KAPO KEPT ME CLOSE.
THEY'LL WANT 200 WORKERS TOMORROW. I'VE ONLY GOT 180 STILL REGISTERED HERE. ...YOU'D BETTER HIDE IN MY ROOM...
FOR OVER TWO MONTHS I STAYED HERE SAFE AND TAUGHT TO HIM ENGLISH.

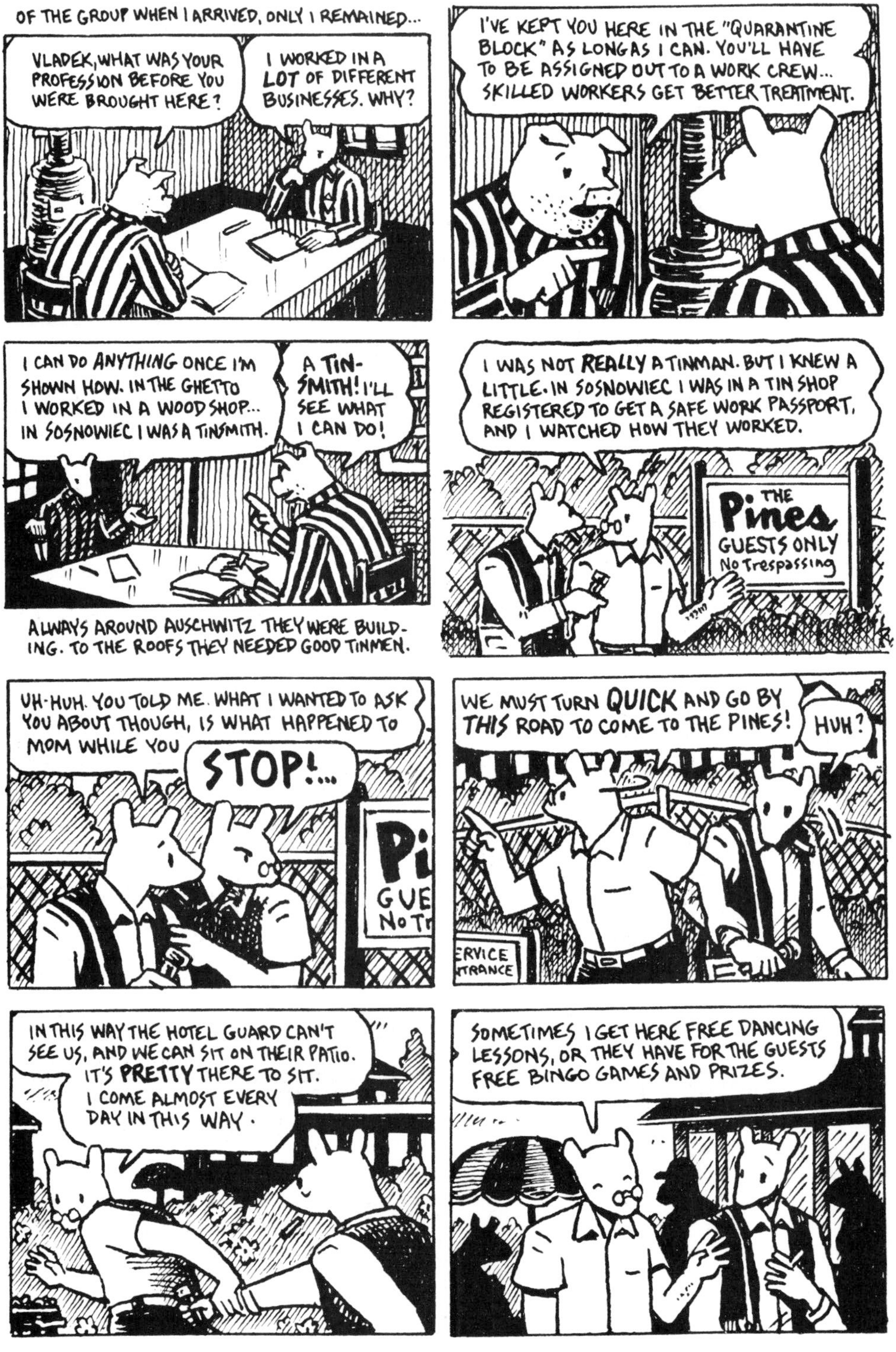

OF THE GROUP WHEN I ARRIVED, ONLY I REMAINED...
VLADEK, WHAT WAS YOUR PROFESSION BEFORE YOU WERE BROUGHT HERE?
I WORKED IN A LOT OF DIFFERENT BUSINESSES. WHY?
I'VE KEPT YOU HERE IN THE "QUARANTINE BLOCK" AS LONG AS I CAN. YOU'LL HAVE TO BE ASSIGNED OUT TO A WORK CREW... SKILLED WORKERS GET BETTER TREATMENT.
I CAN DO ANYTHING ONCE I'M SHOWN HOW. IN THE GHETTO I WORKED IN A WOOD SHOP... IN SOSNOWIEC I WAS A TINSMITH.
A TIN-SMITH! I'LL SEE WHAT I CAN DO!
ALWAYS AROUND AUSCHWITZ THEY WERE BUILDING. TO THE ROOFS THEY NEEDED GOOD TINMEN.
I WAS NOT REALLY A TINMAN. BUT I KNEW A LITTLE. IN SOSNOWIEC I WAS IN A TIN SHOP REGISTERED TO GET A SAFE WORK PASSPORT, AND I WATCHED HOW THEY WORKED.
THE Pines
GUESTS ONLY
No Trespassing
UH-HUH. YOU TOLD ME. WHAT I WANTED TO ASK YOU ABOUT THOUGH, IS WHAT HAPPENED TO MOM WHILE YOU
STOP!...
WE MUST TURN QUICK AND GO BY THIS ROAD TO COME TO THE PINES!
HUH?
ERVICE
NTRANCE
IN THIS WAY THE HOTEL GUARD CAN'T SEE US, AND WE CAN SIT ON THEIR PATIO. IT'S PRETTY THERE TO SIT. I COME ALMOST EVERY DAY IN THIS WAY.
SOMETIMES I GET HERE FREE DANCING LESSONS, OR THEY HAVE FOR THE GUESTS FREE BINGO GAMES AND PRIZES.

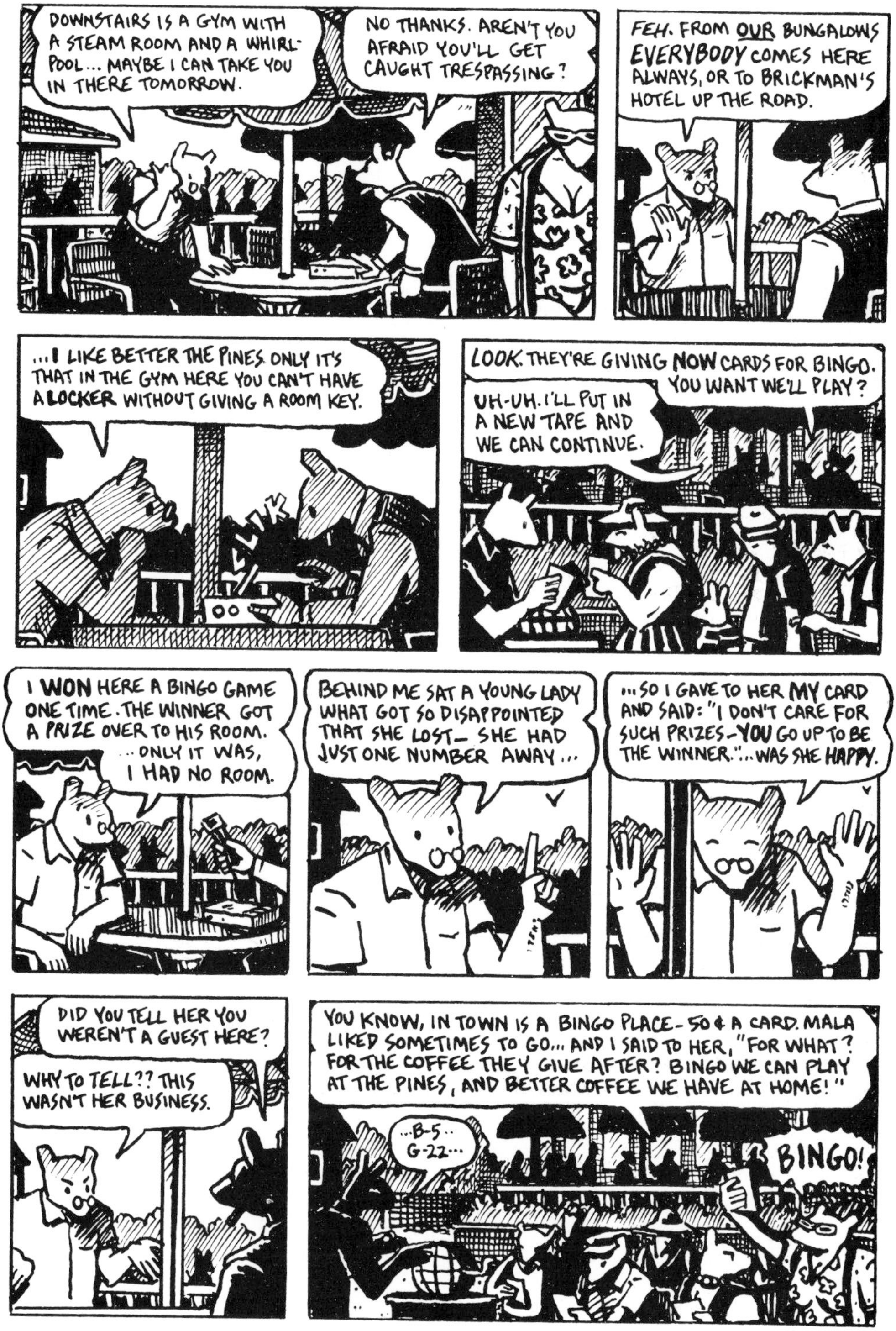
DOWNSTAIRS IS A GYM WITH A STEAM ROOM AND A WHIRL-POOL... MAYBE I CAN TAKE YOU IN THERE TOMORROW.
NO THANKS. AREN'T YOU AFRAID YOU'LL GET CAUGHT TRESPASSING?
FEH. FROM OUR BUNGALOWS EVERYBODY COMES HERE ALWAYS, OR TO BRICKMAN'S HOTEL UP THE ROAD.
...I LIKE BETTER THE PINES. ONLY IT'S THAT IN THE GYM HERE YOU CAN'T HAVE A LOCKER WITHOUT GIVING A ROOM KEY.
KLIK
LOOK. THEY'RE GIVING NOW CARDS FOR BINGO. YOU WANT WE'LL PLAY?
UH-UH. I'LL PUT IN A NEW TAPE AND WE CAN CONTINUE.
I WON HERE A BINGO GAME ONE TIME. THE WINNER GOT A PRIZE OVER TO HIS ROOM.
...ONLY IT WAS, I HAD NO ROOM.
BEHIND ME SAT A YOUNG LADY WHAT GOT SO DISAPPOINTED THAT SHE LOST– SHE HAD JUST ONE NUMBER AWAY...
...SO I GAVE TO HER MY CARD AND SAID: "I DON'T CARE FOR SUCH PRIZES–YOU GO UP TO BE THE WINNER."...WAS SHE HAPPY.
DID YOU TELL HER YOU WEREN'T A GUEST HERE?
WHY TO TELL?? THIS WASN'T HER BUSINESS.
YOU KNOW, IN TOWN IS A BINGO PLACE- 50¢ A CARD. MALA LIKED SOMETIMES TO GO... AND I SAID TO HER, "FOR WHAT? FOR THE COFFEE THEY GIVE AFTER? BINGO WE CAN PLAY AT THE PINES, AND BETTER COFFEE WE HAVE AT HOME!"
...B-5 G-22...
BINGO!

CHAPTER TWO

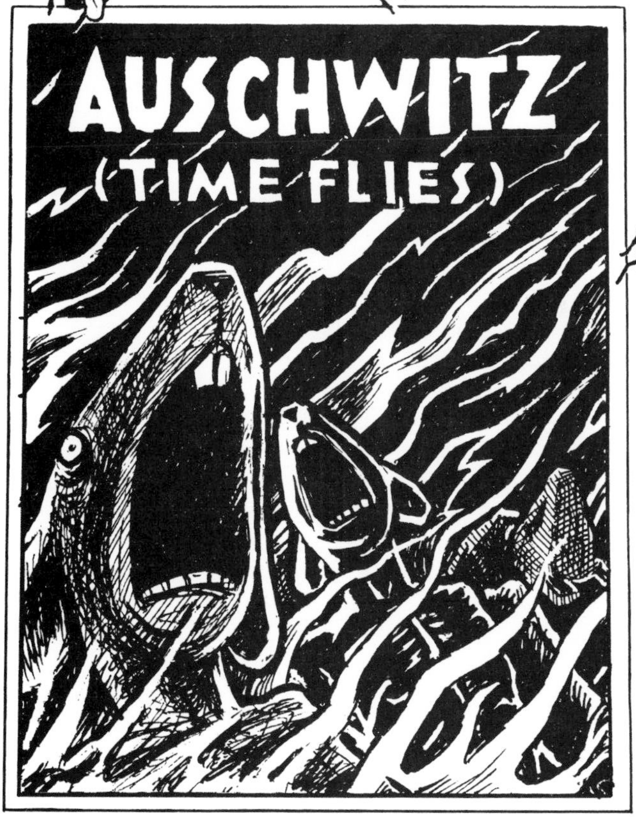
AUSCHWITZ
(TIME FLIES)

Time flies...

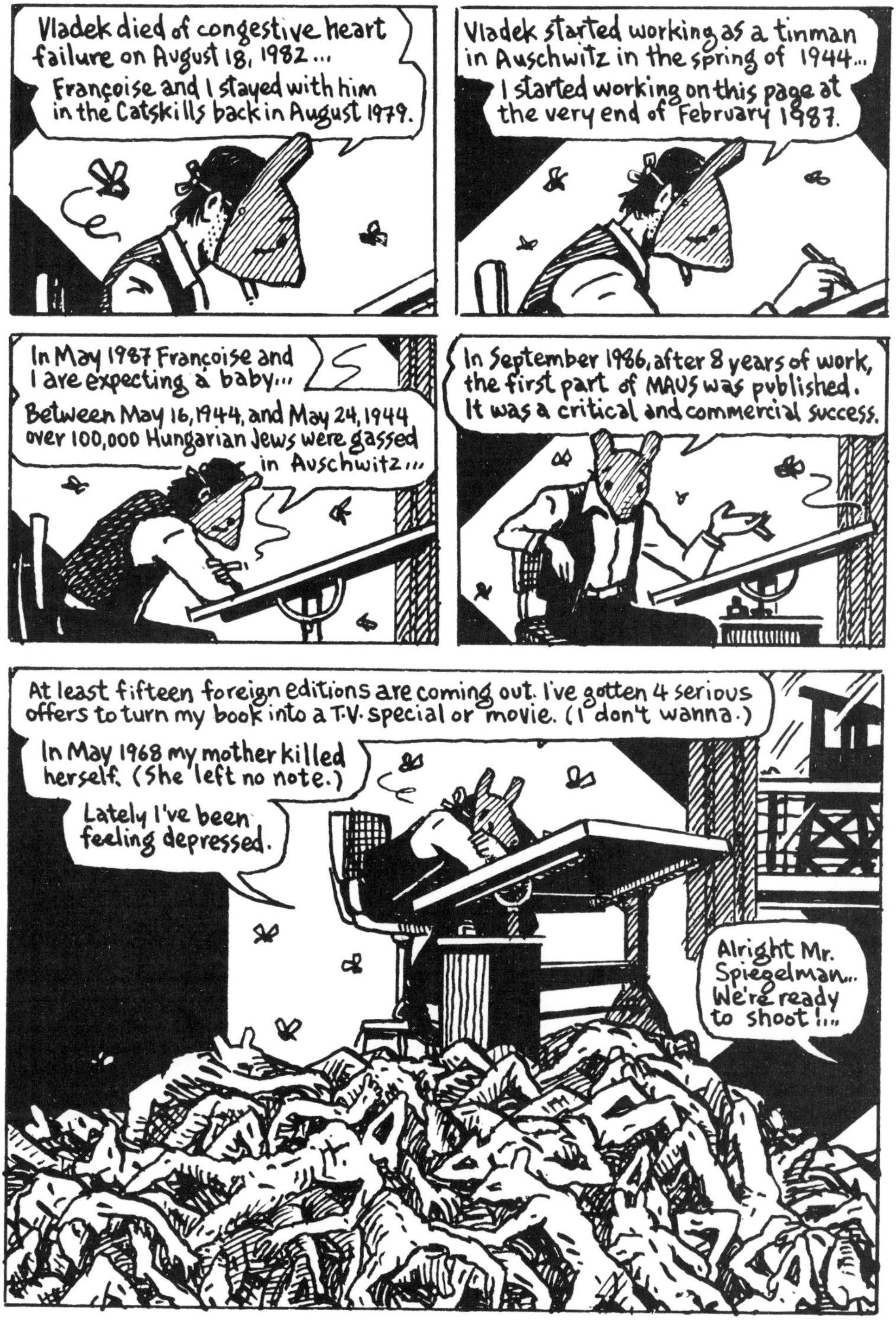

Vladek died of congestive heart failure on August 18, 1982...
Françoise and I stayed with him in the Catskills back in August 1979.
Vladek started working as a tinman in Auschwitz in the spring of 1944...
I started working on this page at the very end of February 1987.
In May 1987 Françoise and I are expecting a baby...
Between May 16, 1944, and May 24, 1944 over 100,000 Hungarian Jews were gassed in Auschwitz...
In September 1986, after 8 years of work, the first part of MAUS was published. It was a critical and commercial success.
At least fifteen foreign editions are coming out. I've gotten 4 serious offers to turn my book into a T.V. special or movie. (I don't wanna.)
In May 1968 my mother killed herself. (She left no note.)
Lately I've been feeling depressed.
Alright Mr. Spiegelman... We're ready to shoot!...

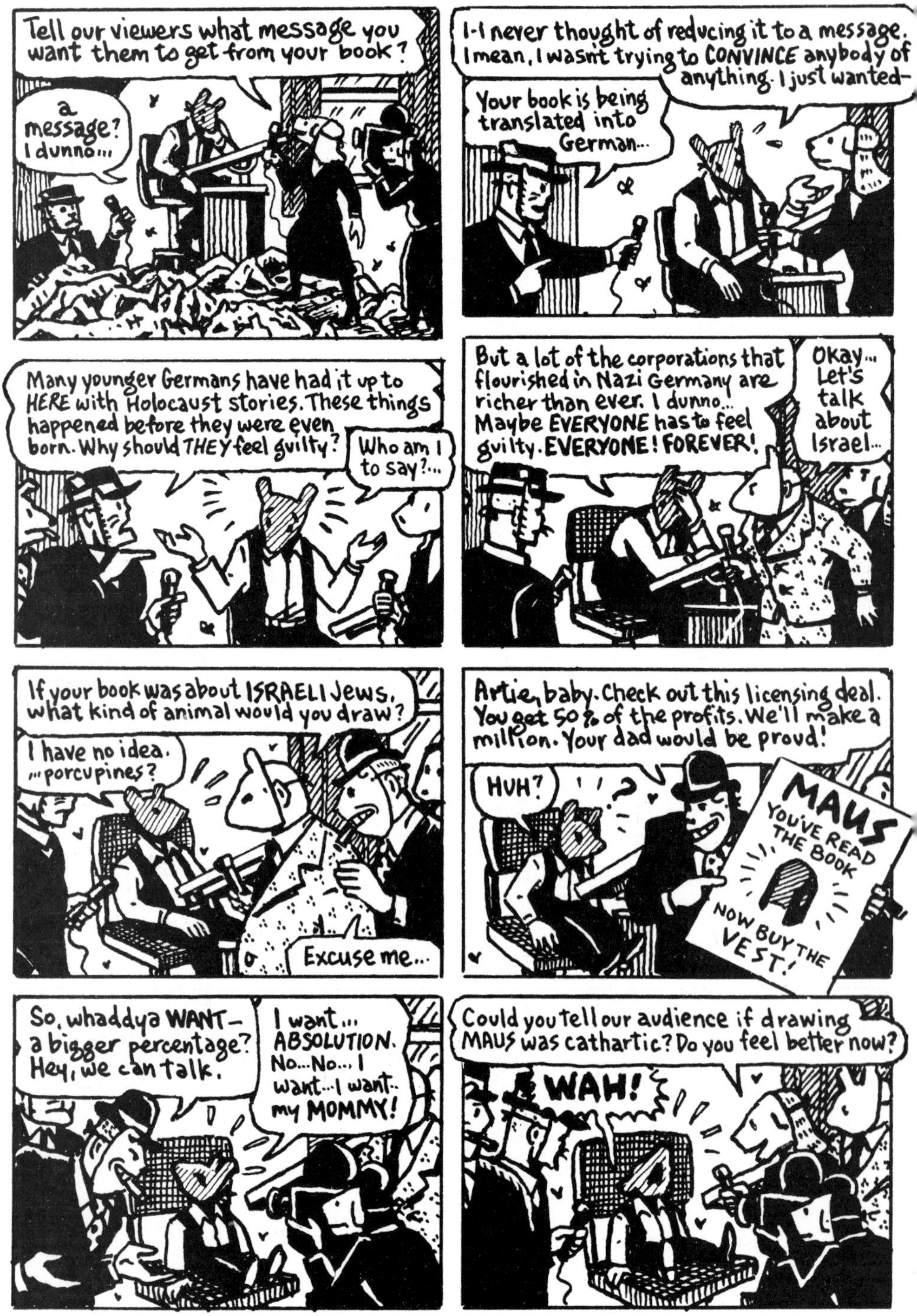
Tell our viewers what message you want them to get from your book?
a message? I dunno...
I-I never thought of reducing it to a message. I mean, I wasn't trying to CONVINCE anybody of anything. I just wanted–
Your book is being translated into German...
Many younger Germans have had it up to HERE with Holocaust stories. These things happened before they were even born. Why should THEY feel guilty?
Who am I to say?...
But a lot of the corporations that flourished in Nazi Germany are richer than ever. I dunno... Maybe EVERYONE has to feel guilty. EVERYONE! FOREVER!
Okay... Let's talk about Israel...
If your book was about ISRAELI Jews, what kind of animal would you draw?
I have no idea. ...porcupines?
Excuse me...
Artie, baby. Check out this licensing deal. You get 50% of the profits. We'll make a million. Your dad would be proud!
HUH?
MAUS
YOU'VE READ THE BOOK
NOW BUY THE VEST!
So, whaddya WANT– a bigger percentage? Hey, we can talk.
I want... ABSOLUTION. No...No... I want...I want.. my MOMMY!
Could you tell our audience if drawing MAUS was cathartic? Do you feel better now?
WAH!

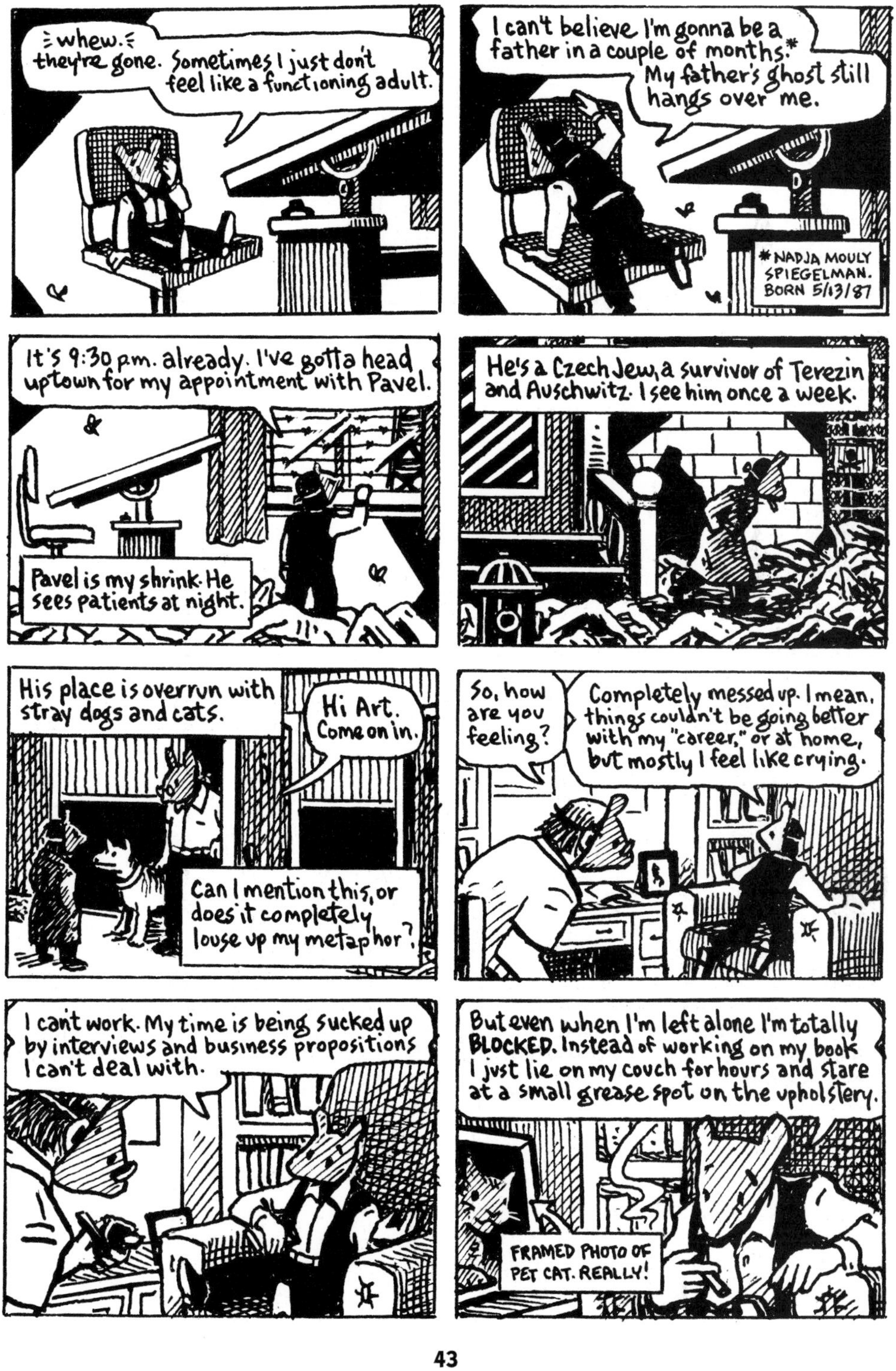
whew. they're gone.
Sometimes I just don't feel like a functioning adult.
I can't believe I'm gonna be a father in a couple of months.* My father's ghost still hangs over me.
*NADJA MOULY SPIEGELMAN. BORN 5/13/87
It's 9:30 p.m. already. I've gotta head uptown for my appointment with Pavel.
Pavel is my shrink. He sees patients at night.
He's a Czech Jew, a survivor of Terezin and Auschwitz. I see him once a week.
His place is overrun with stray dogs and cats.
Hi Art. Come on in.
Can I mention this, or does it completely louse up my metaphor?
So, how are you feeling?
Completely messed up. I mean, things couldn't be going better with my "career," or at home, but mostly I feel like crying.
I can't work. My time is being sucked up by interviews and business propositions I can't deal with.
But even when I'm left alone I'm totally BLOCKED. Instead of working on my book I just lie on my couch for hours and stare at a small grease spot on the upholstery.
FRAMED PHOTO OF PET CAT. REALLY!

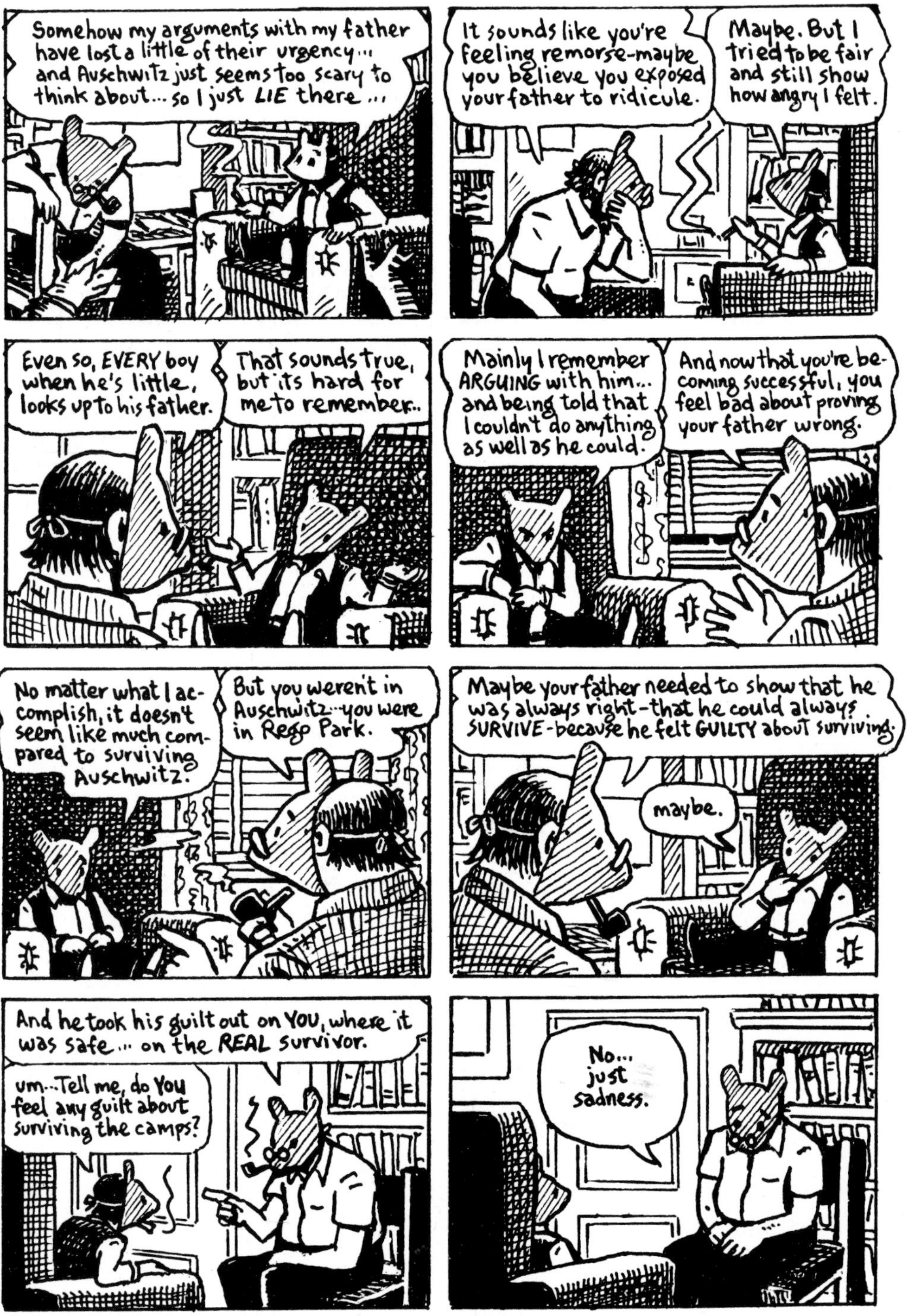
Somehow my arguments with my father have lost a little of their urgency... and Auschwitz just seems too scary to think about... so I just LIE there...
It sounds like you're feeling remorse-maybe you believe you exposed your father to ridicule.
Maybe. But I tried to be fair and still show how angry I felt.
Even so, EVERY boy when he's little, looks up to his father.
That sounds true, but its hard for me to remember..
Mainly I remember ARGUING with him... and being told that I couldn't do anything as well as he could.
And now that you're becoming successful, you feel bad about proving your father wrong.
No matter what I accomplish, it doesn't seem like much compared to surviving Auschwitz.
But you weren't in Auschwitz... you were in Rego Park.
Maybe your father needed to show that he was always right-that he could always SURVIVE-because he felt GUILTY about surviving.
maybe.
And he took his guilt out on YOU, where it was safe... on the REAL survivor.
um...Tell me, do YOU feel any guilt about surviving the camps?
No... just sadness.

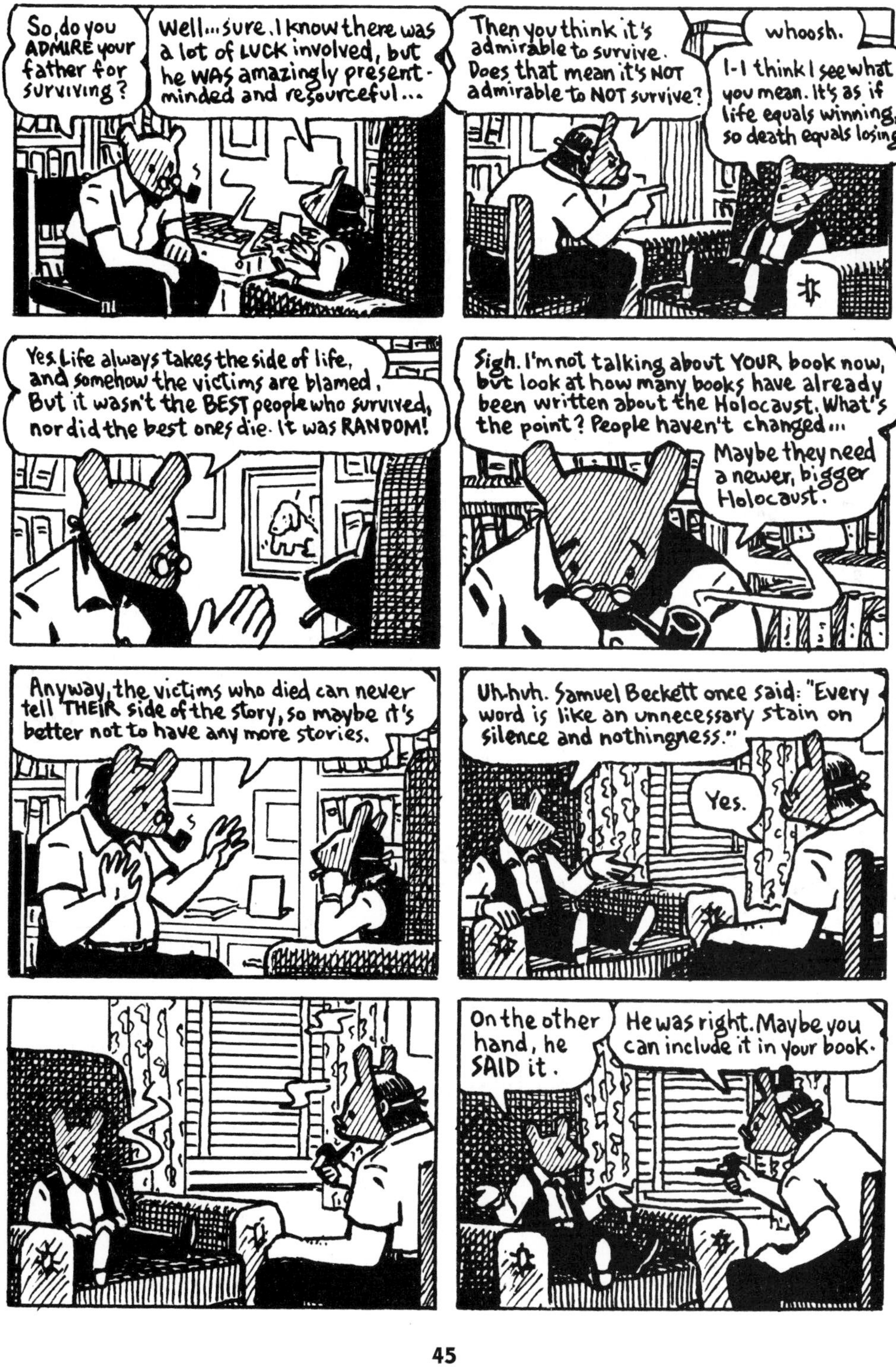
So, do you ADMIRE your father for surviving?
Well... sure. I know there was a lot of LUCK involved, but he WAS amazingly present-minded and resourceful...
Then you think it's admirable to survive. Does that mean it's NOT admirable to NOT survive?
whoosh.
I-I think I see what you mean. It's as if life equals winning, so death equals losing.
Yes. Life always takes the side of life, and somehow the victims are blamed. But it wasn't the BEST people who survived, nor did the best ones die. It was RANDOM!
Sigh. I'm not talking about YOUR book now, but look at how many books have already been written about the Holocaust. What's the point? People haven't changed...
Maybe they need a newer, bigger Holocaust.
Anyway, the victims who died can never tell THEIR side of the story, so maybe it's better not to have any more stories.
Uh-huh. Samuel Beckett once said: "Every word is like an unnecessary stain on silence and nothingness."
Yes.
On the other hand, he SAID it.
He was right. Maybe you can include it in your book.

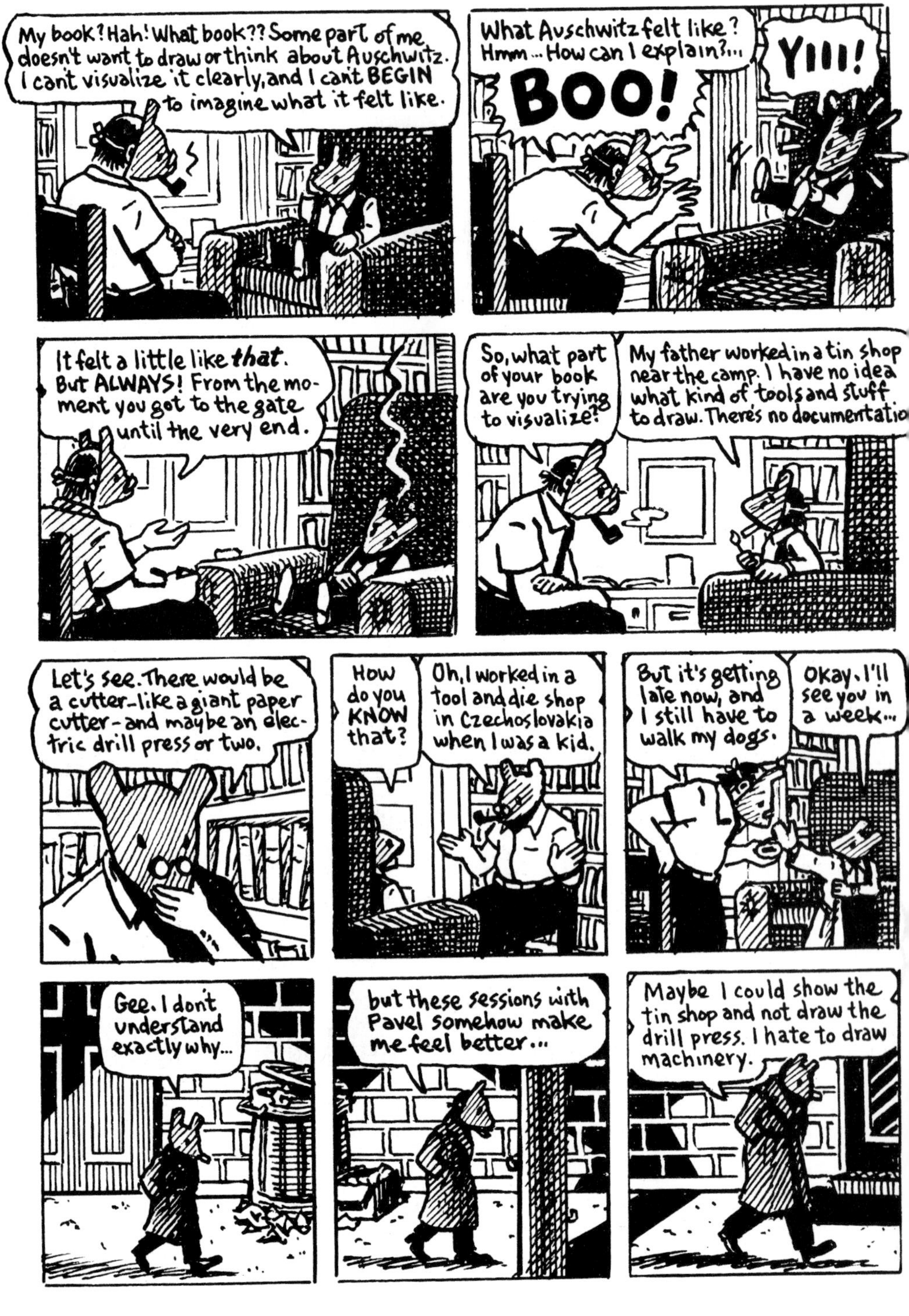

My book? Hah! What book?? Some part of me doesn't want to draw or think about Auschwitz. I can't visualize it clearly, and I can't BEGIN to imagine what it felt like.
What Auschwitz felt like? Hmm... How can I explain?...
BOO!
YIII!
It felt a little like *that*. But ALWAYS! From the moment you got to the gate until the very end.
So, what part of your book are you trying to visualize?
My father worked in a tin shop near the camp. I have no idea what kind of tools and stuff to draw. There's no documentatio
Let's see. There would be a cutter-like a giant paper cutter-and maybe an electric drill press or two.
How do you KNOW that?
Oh, I worked in a tool and die shop in Czechoslovakia when I was a kid.
But it's getting late now, and I still have to walk my dogs.
Okay. I'll see you in a week...
Gee. I don't understand exactly why...
but these sessions with Pavel somehow make me feel better...
Maybe I could show the tin shop and not draw the drill press. I hate to draw machinery.

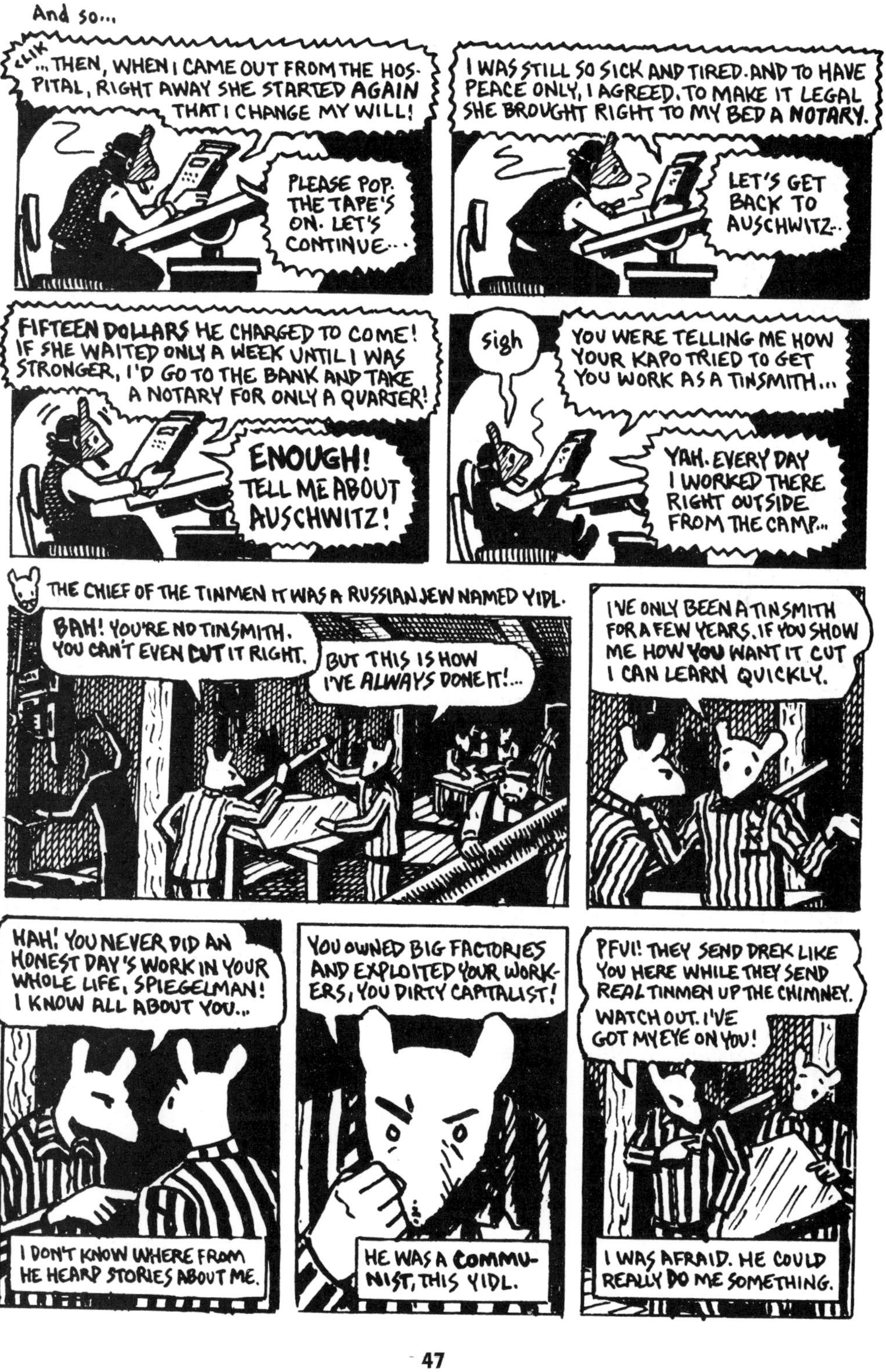
And so...
CLIK
...THEN, WHEN I CAME OUT FROM THE HOSPITAL, RIGHT AWAY SHE STARTED AGAIN THAT I CHANGE MY WILL!
PLEASE POP. THE TAPE'S ON. LET'S CONTINUE...
I WAS STILL SO SICK AND TIRED. AND TO HAVE PEACE ONLY, I AGREED. TO MAKE IT LEGAL SHE BROUGHT RIGHT TO MY BED A NOTARY.
LET'S GET BACK TO AUSCHWITZ...
FIFTEEN DOLLARS HE CHARGED TO COME! IF SHE WAITED ONLY A WEEK UNTIL I WAS STRONGER, I'D GO TO THE BANK AND TAKE A NOTARY FOR ONLY A QUARTER!
ENOUGH! TELL ME ABOUT AUSCHWITZ!
Sigh
YOU WERE TELLING ME HOW YOUR KAPO TRIED TO GET YOU WORK AS A TINSMITH...
YAH. EVERY DAY I WORKED THERE RIGHT OUTSIDE FROM THE CAMP...
THE CHIEF OF THE TINMEN IT WAS A RUSSIAN JEW NAMED YIDL.
BAH! YOU'RE NO TINSMITH. YOU CAN'T EVEN CUT IT RIGHT.
BUT THIS IS HOW I'VE ALWAYS DONE IT!...
I'VE ONLY BEEN A TINSMITH FOR A FEW YEARS. IF YOU SHOW ME HOW YOU WANT IT CUT I CAN LEARN QUICKLY.
HAH! YOU NEVER DID AN HONEST DAY'S WORK IN YOUR WHOLE LIFE, SPIEGELMAN! I KNOW ALL ABOUT YOU...
I DON'T KNOW WHERE FROM HE HEARD STORIES ABOUT ME.
YOU OWNED BIG FACTORIES AND EXPLOITED YOUR WORKERS, YOU DIRTY CAPITALIST!
HE WAS A COMMUNIST, THIS YIDL.
PFUI! THEY SEND DREK LIKE YOU HERE WHILE THEY SEND REAL TINMEN UP THE CHIMNEY.
WATCH OUT. I'VE GOT MY EYE ON YOU!
I WAS AFRAID. HE COULD REALLY DO ME SOMETHING.

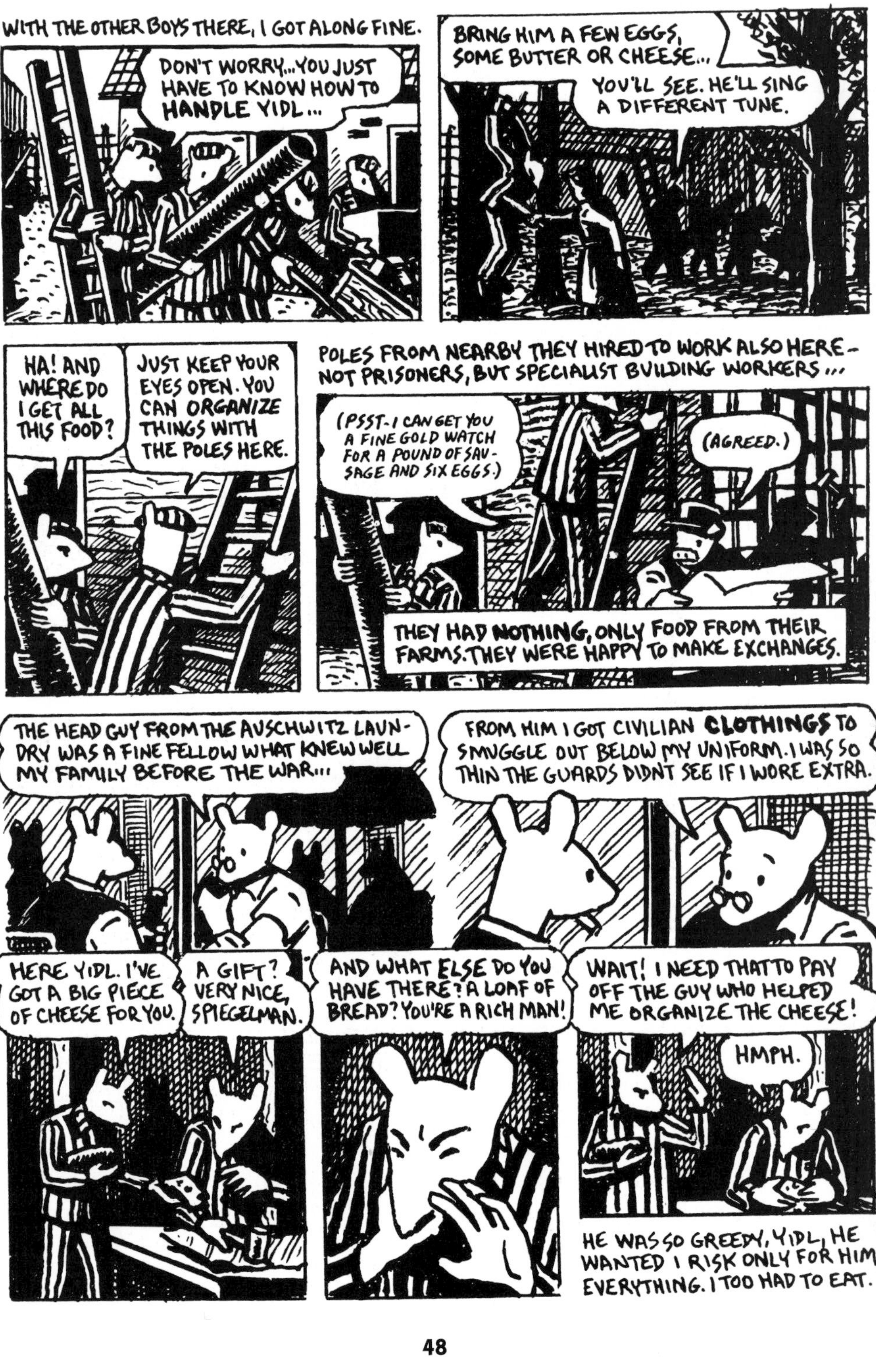
WITH THE OTHER BOYS THERE, I GOT ALONG FINE.
DON'T WORRY... YOU JUST HAVE TO KNOW HOW TO HANDLE YIDL...
BRING HIM A FEW EGGS, SOME BUTTER OR CHEESE...
YOU'LL SEE. HE'LL SING A DIFFERENT TUNE.
HA! AND WHERE DO I GET ALL THIS FOOD?
JUST KEEP YOUR EYES OPEN. YOU CAN ORGANIZE THINGS WITH THE POLES HERE.
POLES FROM NEARBY THEY HIRED TO WORK ALSO HERE - NOT PRISONERS, BUT SPECIALIST BUILDING WORKERS...
(PSST - I CAN GET YOU A FINE GOLD WATCH FOR A POUND OF SAUSAGE AND SIX EGGS.)
(AGREED.)
THEY HAD NOTHING, ONLY FOOD FROM THEIR FARMS. THEY WERE HAPPY TO MAKE EXCHANGES.
THE HEAD GUY FROM THE AUSCHWITZ LAUNDRY WAS A FINE FELLOW WHAT KNEW WELL MY FAMILY BEFORE THE WAR...
FROM HIM I GOT CIVILIAN CLOTHINGS TO SMUGGLE OUT BELOW MY UNIFORM. I WAS SO THIN THE GUARDS DIDN'T SEE IF I WORE EXTRA.
HERE YIDL. I'VE GOT A BIG PIECE OF CHEESE FOR YOU.
A GIFT? VERY NICE, SPIEGELMAN.
AND WHAT ELSE DO YOU HAVE THERE? A LOAF OF BREAD? YOU'RE A RICH MAN!
WAIT! I NEED THAT TO PAY OFF THE GUY WHO HELPED ME ORGANIZE THE CHEESE!
HMPH.
HE WAS SO GREEDY, YIDL, HE WANTED I RISK ONLY FOR HIM EVERYTHING. I TOO HAD TO EAT.

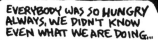

EVERYBODY WAS SO HUNGRY ALWAYS, WE DIDN'T KNOW EVEN WHAT WE ARE DOING...

IN THE MORNING FOR BREAKFAST WE GOT ONLY A BITTER DRINK MADE FROM ROOTS.

I WOKE BEFORE EVERYBODY TO HAVE TIME TO THE TOILET AND FIND STILL SOME TEA LEFT.

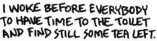

ONE TIME A DAY THEY GAVE A SOUP FROM TURNIPS. TO STAND NEAR THE FIRST OF THE LINE WAS NO GOOD. YOU GOT ONLY WATER.

MIX IT! MIX IT!

NEAR THE END WAS BETTER - SOLID THINGS TO THE BOTTOM FLOATED.

BUT TOO FAR TO THE END IT WAS ALSO NO GOOD

...BECAUSE MANY TIMES IT COULD BE NO SOUP ANYMORE.

THE FLOUR THEY MIXED WITH SAWDUST TOGETHER - WE GOT ONE LITTLE BRICK OF THIS WHAT HAD TO LAST THE FULL DAY.

MOST GOBBLED IT RIGHT AWAY, BUT ALWAYS I SAVED A HALF FOR LATER.

AND ONE TIME EACH DAY THEY GAVE TO US A SMALL BREAD, CRUNCHY LIKE GLASS.

AND IN THE EVENING WE GOT A SPOILED CHEESE OR JAM. IF WE WERE LUCKY A COUPLE TIMES A WEEK WE GOT A SAUSAGE BIG LIKE TWO OF MY FINGERS. ONLY THIS MUCH WE GOT

IF YOU ATE HOW THEY GAVE YOU, IT WAS JUST ENOUGH TO DIE MORE SLOWLY.

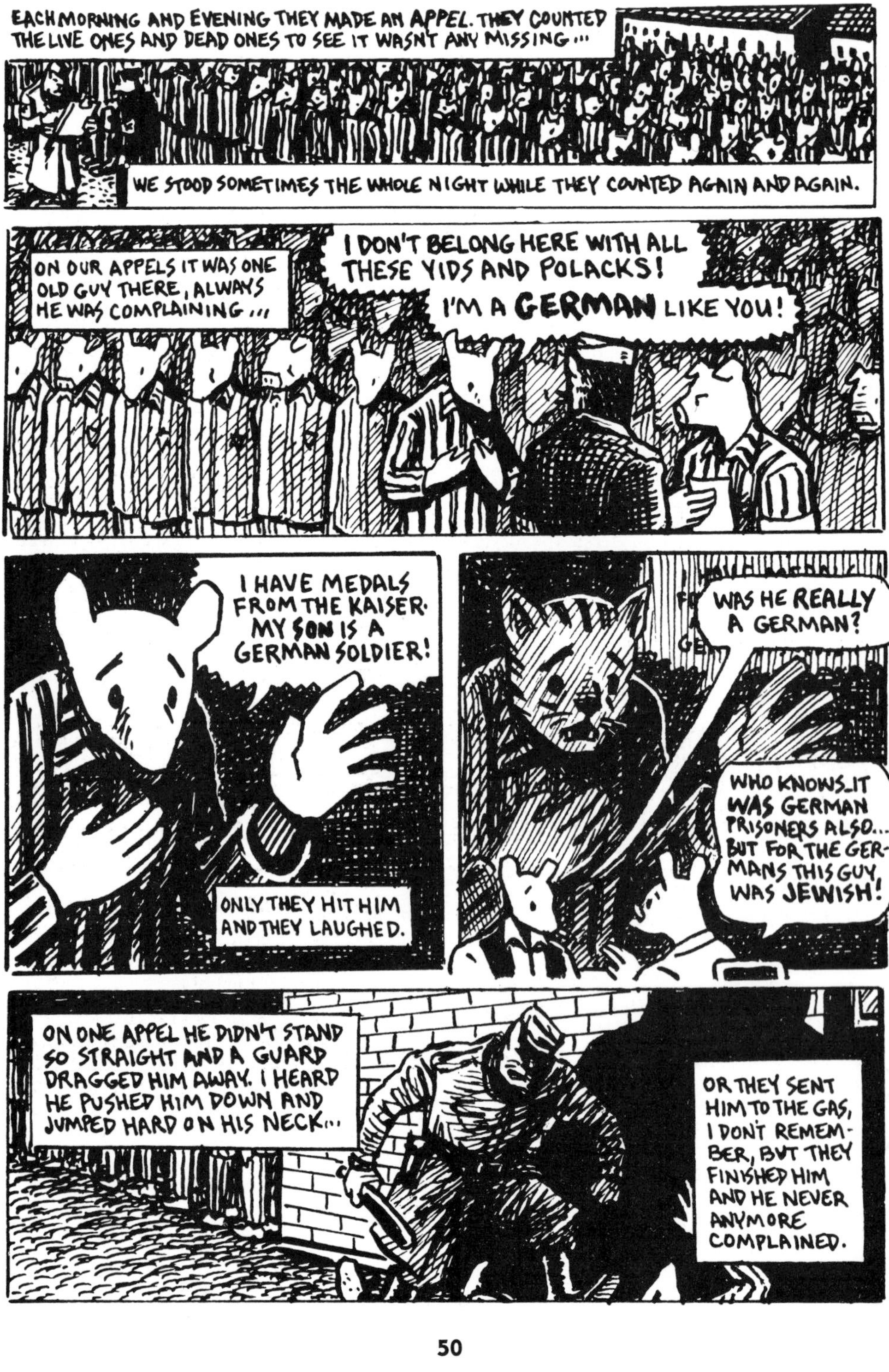
EACH MORNING AND EVENING THEY MADE AN APPEL. THEY COUNTED THE LIVE ONES AND DEAD ONES TO SEE IT WASN'T ANY MISSING...
WE STOOD SOMETIMES THE WHOLE NIGHT WHILE THEY COUNTED AGAIN AND AGAIN.
ON OUR APPELS IT WAS ONE OLD GUY THERE, ALWAYS HE WAS COMPLAINING...
I DON'T BELONG HERE WITH ALL THESE YIDS AND POLACKS!
I'M A GERMAN LIKE YOU!
I HAVE MEDALS FROM THE KAISER. MY SON IS A GERMAN SOLDIER!
ONLY THEY HIT HIM AND THEY LAUGHED.
WAS HE REALLY A GERMAN?
WHO KNOWS. IT WAS GERMAN PRISONERS ALSO... BUT FOR THE GERMANS THIS GUY WAS JEWISH!
ON ONE APPEL HE DIDN'T STAND SO STRAIGHT AND A GUARD DRAGGED HIM AWAY. I HEARD HE PUSHED HIM DOWN AND JUMPED HARD ON HIS NECK...
OR THEY SENT HIM TO THE GAS, I DON'T REMEMBER, BUT THEY FINISHED HIM AND HE NEVER ANYMORE COMPLAINED.

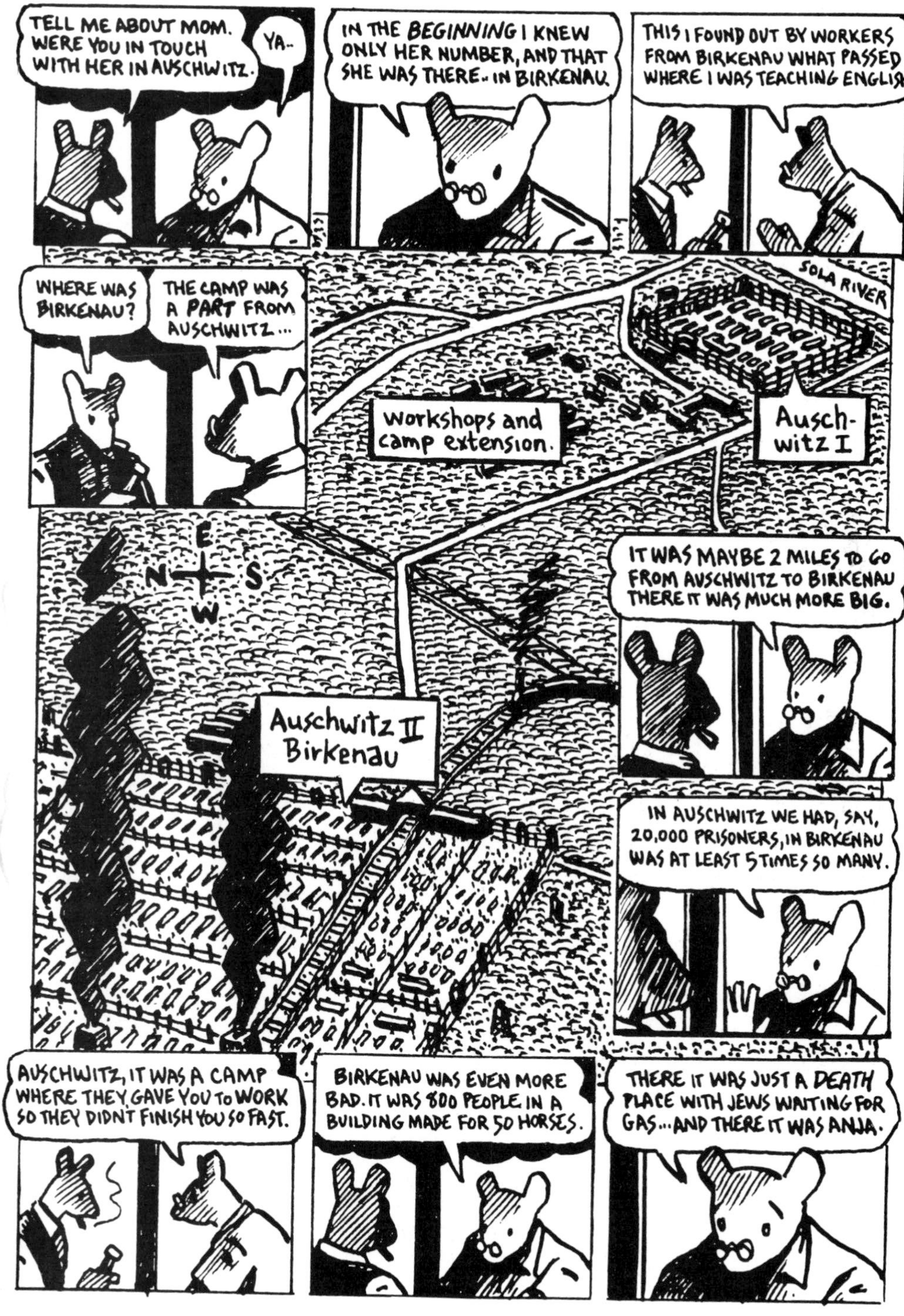

TELL ME ABOUT MOM. WERE YOU IN TOUCH WITH HER IN AUSCHWITZ.
YA..
IN THE BEGINNING I KNEW ONLY HER NUMBER, AND THAT SHE WAS THERE.. IN BIRKENAU.
THIS I FOUND OUT BY WORKERS FROM BIRKENAU WHAT PASSED WHERE I WAS TEACHING ENGLISH.
WHERE WAS BIRKENAU?
THE CAMP WAS A PART FROM AUSCHWITZ...
SOLA RIVER
workshops and camp extension.
Ausch-witz I
E
N
S
W
IT WAS MAYBE 2 MILES TO GO FROM AUSCHWITZ TO BIRKENAU THERE IT WAS MUCH MORE BIG.
Auschwitz II Birkenau
IN AUSCHWITZ WE HAD, SAY, 20,000 PRISONERS, IN BIRKENAU WAS AT LEAST 5 TIMES SO MANY.
AUSCHWITZ, IT WAS A CAMP WHERE THEY GAVE YOU TO WORK SO THEY DIDN'T FINISH YOU SO FAST.
BIRKENAU WAS EVEN MORE BAD. IT WAS 800 PEOPLE IN A BUILDING MADE FOR 50 HORSES.
THERE IT WAS JUST A DEATH PLACE WITH JEWS WAITING FOR GAS... AND THERE IT WAS ANJA.

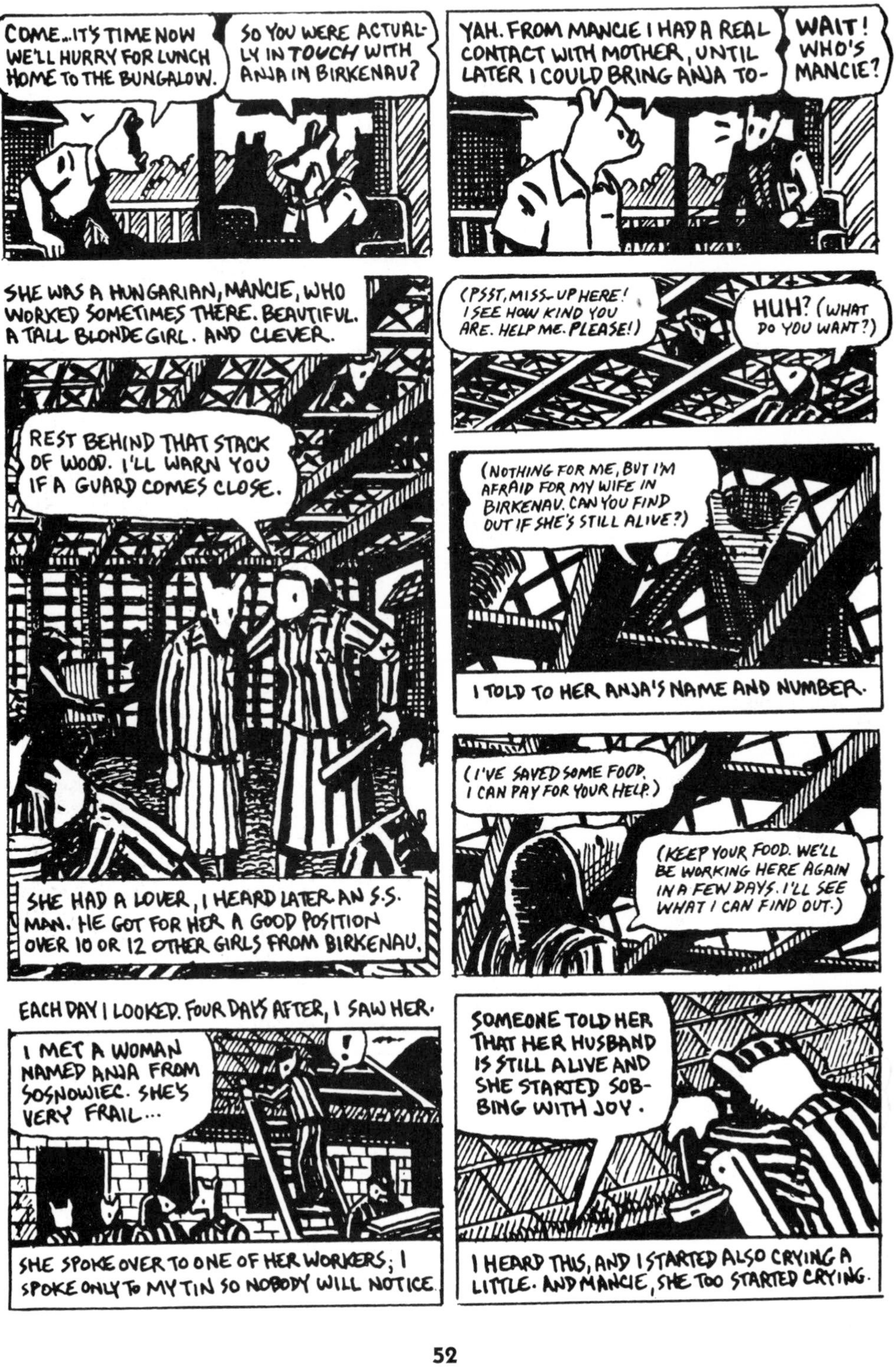
COME...IT'S TIME NOW WE'LL HURRY FOR LUNCH HOME TO THE BUNGALOW.
SO YOU WERE ACTUALLY IN TOUCH WITH ANJA IN BIRKENAU?
YAH. FROM MANCIE I HAD A REAL CONTACT WITH MOTHER, UNTIL LATER I COULD BRING ANJA TO-
WAIT! WHO'S MANCIE?
SHE WAS A HUNGARIAN, MANCIE, WHO WORKED SOMETIMES THERE. BEAUTIFUL. A TALL BLONDE GIRL. AND CLEVER.
REST BEHIND THAT STACK OF WOOD. I'LL WARN YOU IF A GUARD COMES CLOSE.
SHE HAD A LOVER, I HEARD LATER AN S.S. MAN. HE GOT FOR HER A GOOD POSITION OVER 10 OR 12 OTHER GIRLS FROM BIRKENAU.
(PSST, MISS- UP HERE! I SEE HOW KIND YOU ARE. HELP ME. PLEASE!)
HUH? (WHAT DO YOU WANT?)
(NOTHING FOR ME, BUT I'M AFRAID FOR MY WIFE IN BIRKENAU. CAN YOU FIND OUT IF SHE'S STILL ALIVE?)
I TOLD TO HER ANJA'S NAME AND NUMBER.
(I'VE SAVED SOME FOOD. I CAN PAY FOR YOUR HELP.)
(KEEP YOUR FOOD. WE'LL BE WORKING HERE AGAIN IN A FEW DAYS. I'LL SEE WHAT I CAN FIND OUT.)
EACH DAY I LOOKED. FOUR DAYS AFTER, I SAW HER.
I MET A WOMAN NAMED ANJA FROM SOSNOWIEC. SHE'S VERY FRAIL...
!
SHE SPOKE OVER TO ONE OF HER WORKERS; I SPOKE ONLY TO MY TIN SO NOBODY WILL NOTICE.
SOMEONE TOLD HER THAT HER HUSBAND IS STILL ALIVE AND SHE STARTED SOBBING WITH JOY.
I HEARD THIS, AND I STARTED ALSO CRYING A LITTLE. AND MANCIE, SHE TOO STARTED CRYING.

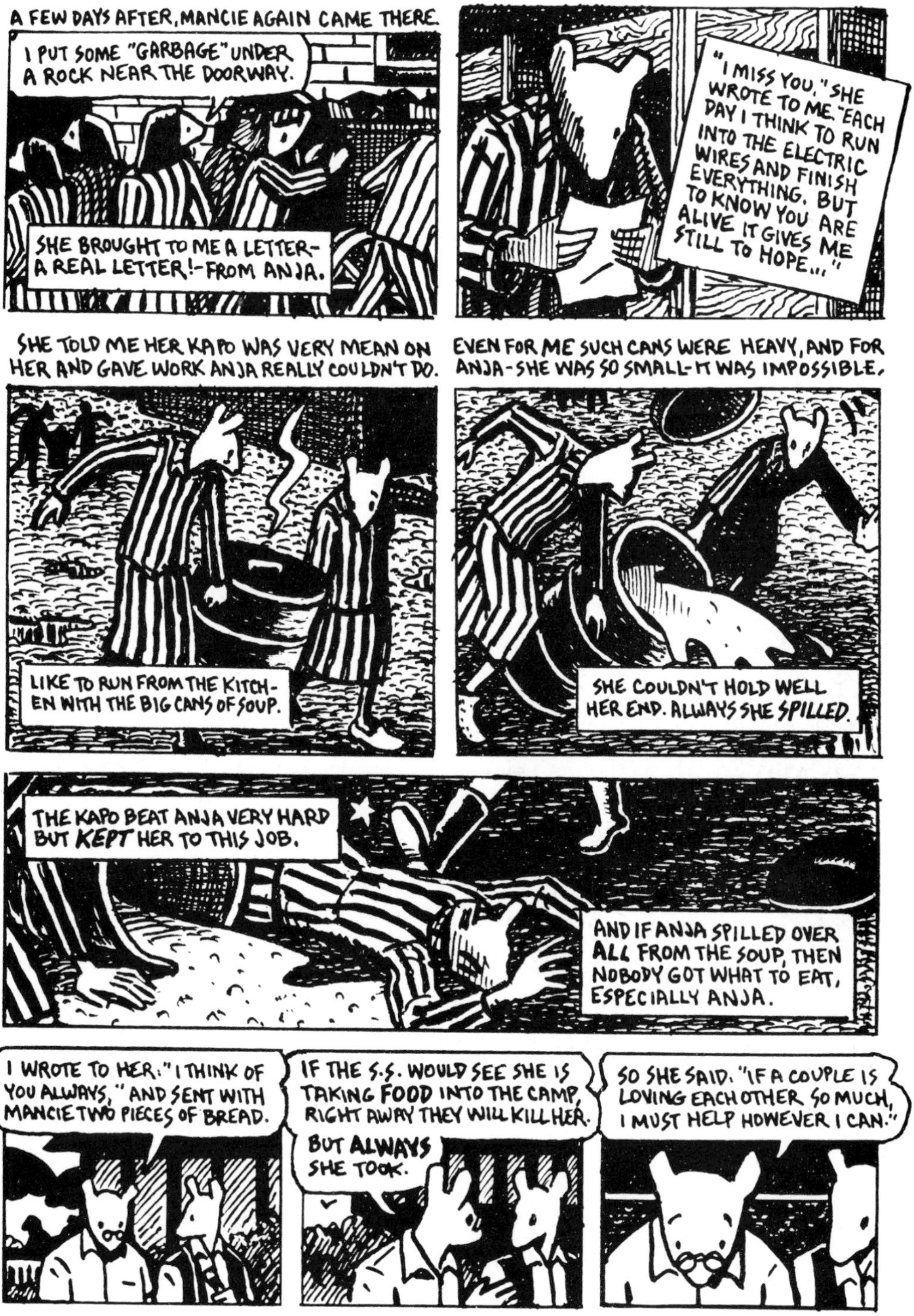
A FEW DAYS AFTER, MANCIE AGAIN CAME THERE.
I PUT SOME "GARBAGE" UNDER A ROCK NEAR THE DOORWAY.
SHE BROUGHT TO ME A LETTER- A REAL LETTER!- FROM ANJA.
"I MISS YOU," SHE WROTE TO ME. "EACH DAY I THINK TO RUN INTO THE ELECTRIC WIRES AND FINISH EVERYTHING. BUT TO KNOW YOU ARE ALIVE IT GIVES ME STILL TO HOPE..."
SHE TOLD ME HER KAPO WAS VERY MEAN ON HER AND GAVE WORK ANJA REALLY COULDN'T DO.
LIKE TO RUN FROM THE KITCHEN WITH THE BIG CANS OF SOUP.
EVEN FOR ME SUCH CANS WERE HEAVY, AND FOR ANJA- SHE WAS SO SMALL- IT WAS IMPOSSIBLE.
SHE COULDN'T HOLD WELL HER END. ALWAYS SHE SPILLED.
THE KAPO BEAT ANJA VERY HARD BUT KEPT HER TO THIS JOB.
AND IF ANJA SPILLED OVER ALL FROM THE SOUP, THEN NOBODY GOT WHAT TO EAT, ESPECIALLY ANJA.
I WROTE TO HER: "I THINK OF YOU ALWAYS," AND SENT WITH MANCIE TWO PIECES OF BREAD.
IF THE S.S. WOULD SEE SHE IS TAKING FOOD INTO THE CAMP, RIGHT AWAY THEY WILL KILL HER.
BUT ALWAYS SHE TOOK.
SO SHE SAID: "IF A COUPLE IS LOVING EACH OTHER SO MUCH, I MUST HELP HOWEVER I CAN."

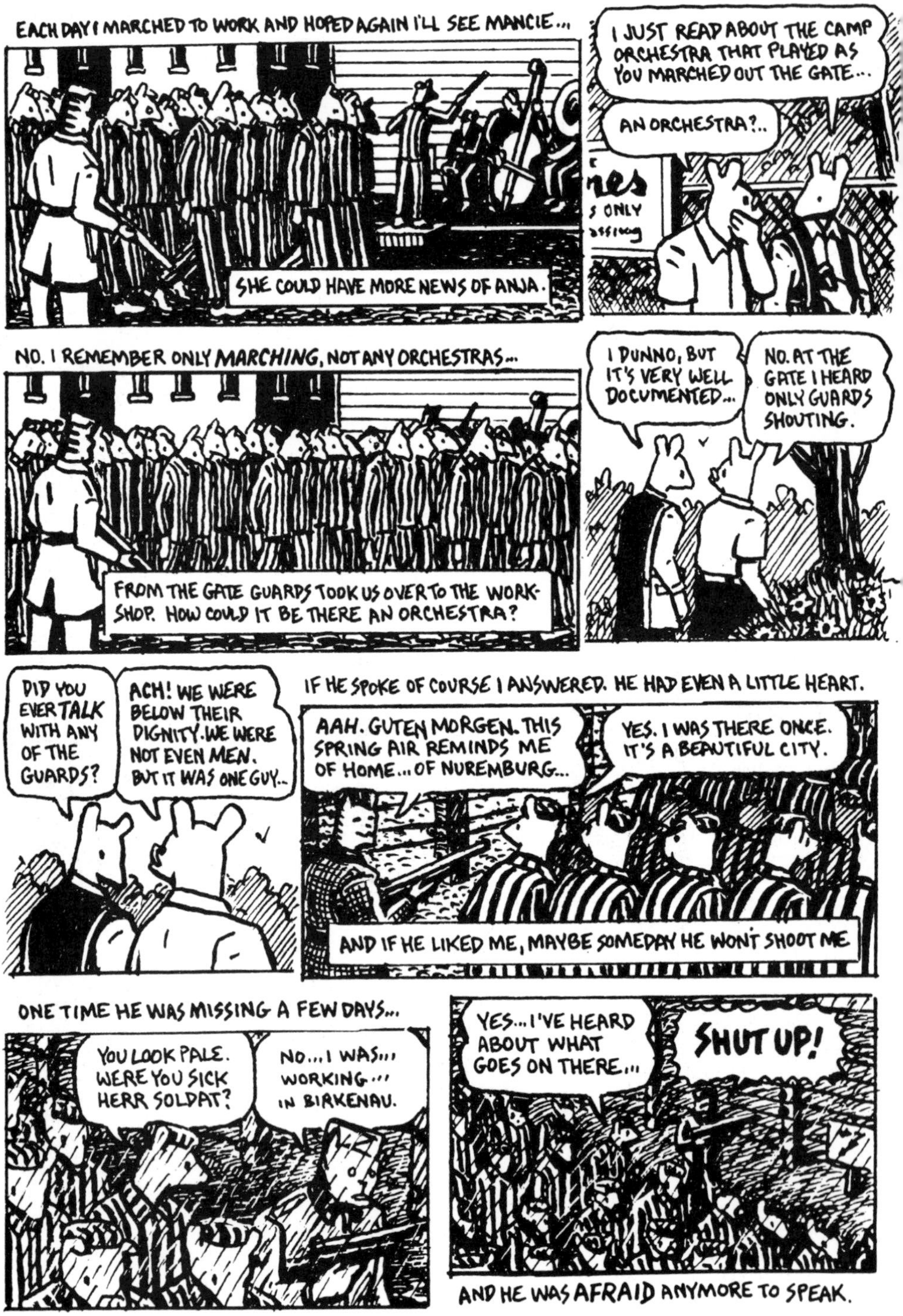
EACH DAY I MARCHED TO WORK AND HOPED AGAIN I'LL SEE MANCIE...
SHE COULD HAVE MORE NEWS OF ANJA.
I JUST READ ABOUT THE CAMP ORCHESTRA THAT PLAYED AS YOU MARCHED OUT THE GATE...
AN ORCHESTRA?..
NO. I REMEMBER ONLY MARCHING, NOT ANY ORCHESTRAS...
FROM THE GATE GUARDS TOOK US OVER TO THE WORK-SHOP. HOW COULD IT BE THERE AN ORCHESTRA?
I DUNNO, BUT IT'S VERY WELL DOCUMENTED...
NO. AT THE GATE I HEARD ONLY GUARDS SHOUTING.
DID YOU EVER TALK WITH ANY OF THE GUARDS?
ACH! WE WERE BELOW THEIR DIGNITY. WE WERE NOT EVEN MEN. BUT IT WAS ONE GUY...
IF HE SPOKE OF COURSE I ANSWERED. HE HAD EVEN A LITTLE HEART.
AAH. GUTEN MORGEN. THIS SPRING AIR REMINDS ME OF HOME... OF NUREMBURG...
YES. I WAS THERE ONCE. IT'S A BEAUTIFUL CITY.
AND IF HE LIKED ME, MAYBE SOMEDAY HE WON'T SHOOT ME
ONE TIME HE WAS MISSING A FEW DAYS...
YOU LOOK PALE. WERE YOU SICK HERR SOLDAT?
NO... I WAS... WORKING... IN BIRKENAU.
YES... I'VE HEARD ABOUT WHAT GOES ON THERE...
SHUT UP!
AND HE WAS AFRAID ANYMORE TO SPEAK.

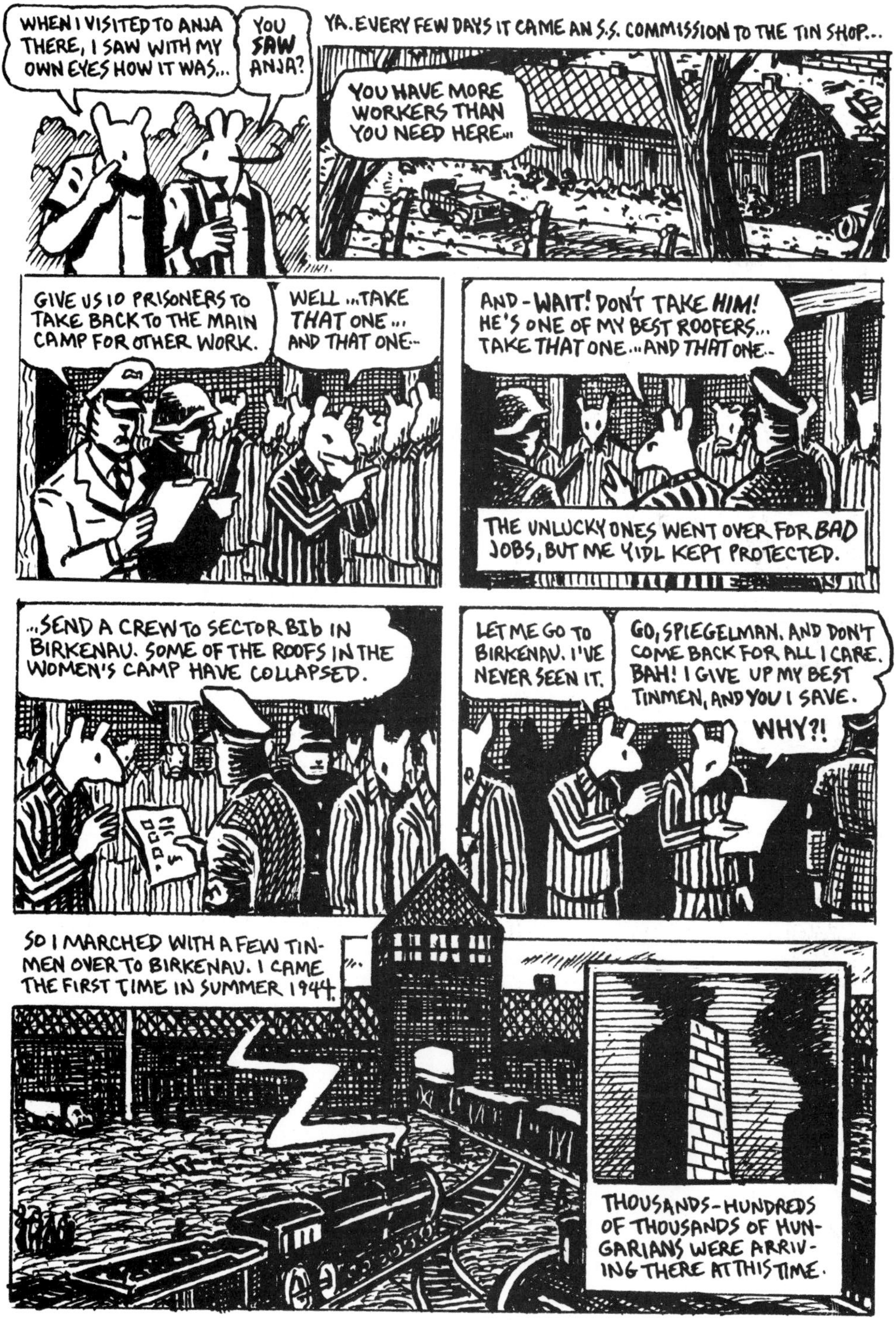
WHEN I VISITED TO ANJA THERE, I SAW WITH MY OWN EYES HOW IT WAS...
YOU SAW ANJA?
YA. EVERY FEW DAYS IT CAME AN S.S. COMMISSION TO THE TIN SHOP...
YOU HAVE MORE WORKERS THAN YOU NEED HERE...
GIVE US 10 PRISONERS TO TAKE BACK TO THE MAIN CAMP FOR OTHER WORK.
WELL ...TAKE THAT ONE... AND THAT ONE..
AND - WAIT! DON'T TAKE HIM! HE'S ONE OF MY BEST ROOFERS... TAKE THAT ONE... AND THAT ONE..
THE UNLUCKY ONES WENT OVER FOR BAD JOBS, BUT ME YIDL KEPT PROTECTED.
...SEND A CREW TO SECTOR BIb IN BIRKENAU. SOME OF THE ROOFS IN THE WOMEN'S CAMP HAVE COLLAPSED.
LET ME GO TO BIRKENAU. I'VE NEVER SEEN IT.
GO, SPIEGELMAN. AND DON'T COME BACK FOR ALL I CARE. BAH! I GIVE UP MY BEST TINMEN, AND YOU I SAVE.
WHY?!
SO I MARCHED WITH A FEW TINMEN OVER TO BIRKENAU. I CAME THE FIRST TIME IN SUMMER 1944.
THOUSANDS - HUNDREDS OF THOUSANDS OF HUNGARIANS WERE ARRIVING THERE AT THIS TIME.

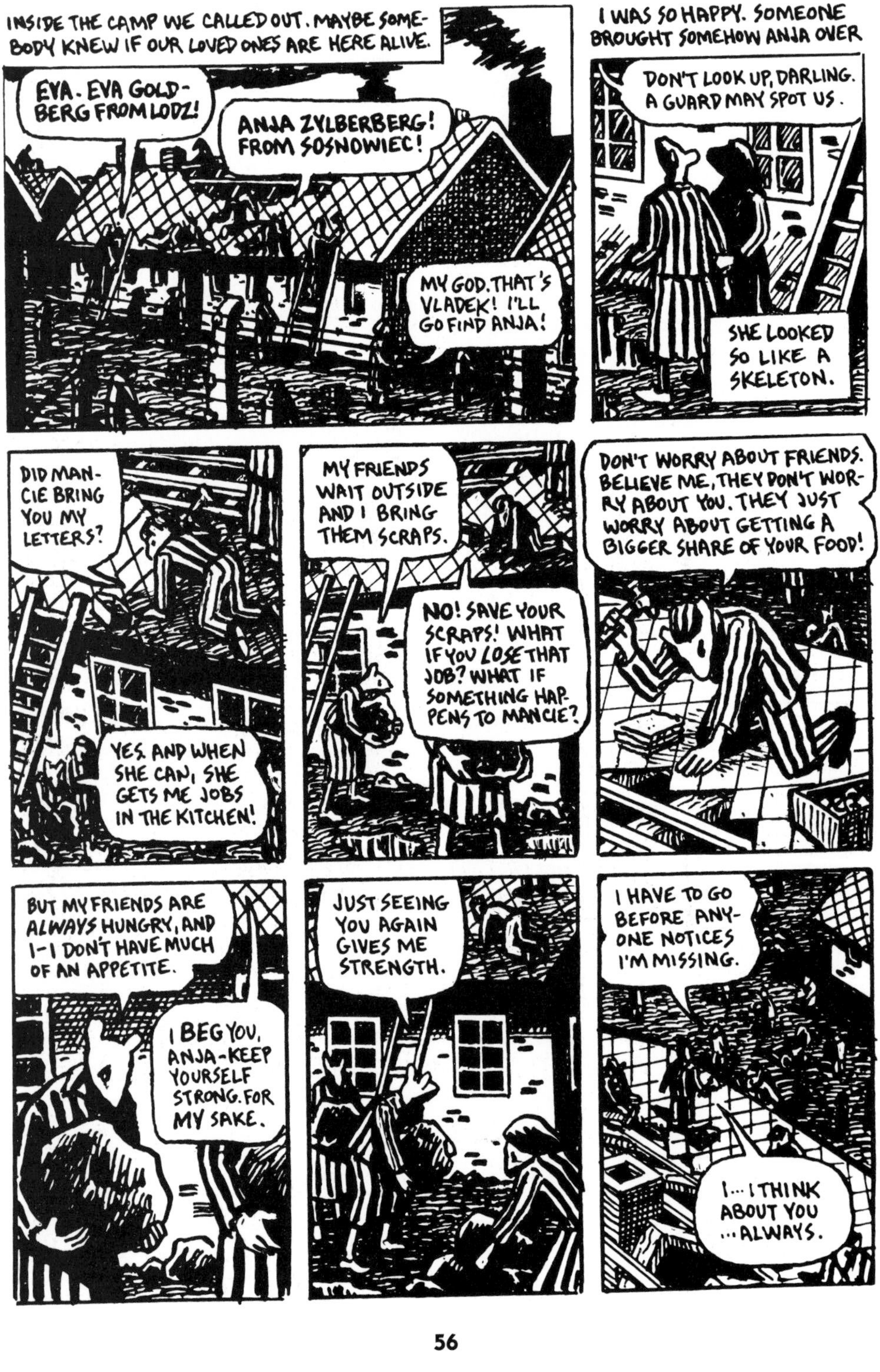
INSIDE THE CAMP WE CALLED OUT. MAYBE SOMEBODY KNEW IF OUR LOVED ONES ARE HERE ALIVE.
EVA. EVA GOLDBERG FROM LODZ!
ANJA ZYLBERBERG! FROM SOSNOWIEC!
MY GOD. THAT'S VLADEK! I'LL GO FIND ANJA!
I WAS SO HAPPY. SOMEONE BROUGHT SOMEHOW ANJA OVER
DON'T LOOK UP, DARLING. A GUARD MAY SPOT US.
SHE LOOKED SO LIKE A SKELETON.
DID MANCIE BRING YOU MY LETTERS?
YES. AND WHEN SHE CAN, SHE GETS ME JOBS IN THE KITCHEN!
MY FRIENDS WAIT OUTSIDE AND I BRING THEM SCRAPS.
NO! SAVE YOUR SCRAPS! WHAT IF YOU *LOSE* THAT JOB? WHAT IF SOMETHING HAPPENS TO MANCIE?
DON'T WORRY ABOUT FRIENDS. BELIEVE ME, THEY DON'T WORRY ABOUT YOU. THEY JUST WORRY ABOUT GETTING A BIGGER SHARE OF YOUR FOOD!
BUT MY FRIENDS ARE ALWAYS HUNGRY, AND I-I DON'T HAVE MUCH OF AN APPETITE.
I BEG YOU, ANJA-KEEP YOURSELF STRONG. FOR MY SAKE.
JUST SEEING YOU AGAIN GIVES ME STRENGTH.
I HAVE TO GO BEFORE ANYONE NOTICES I'M MISSING.
I... I THINK ABOUT YOU ...ALWAYS.

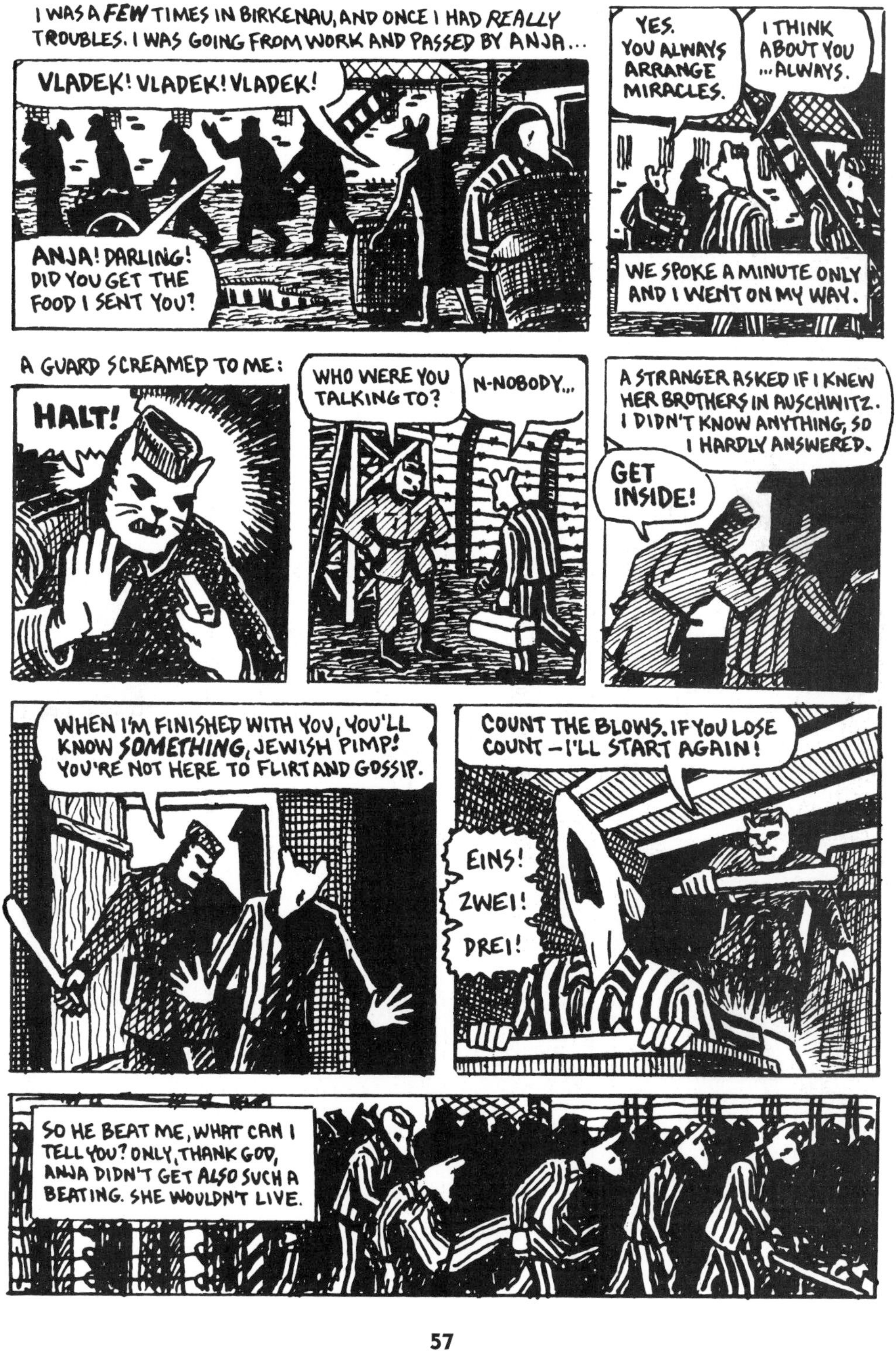
I WAS A FEW TIMES IN BIRKENAU, AND ONCE I HAD REALLY TROUBLES. I WAS GOING FROM WORK AND PASSED BY ANJA...
VLADEK! VLADEK! VLADEK!
ANJA! DARLING! DID YOU GET THE FOOD I SENT YOU?
YES. YOU ALWAYS ARRANGE MIRACLES.
I THINK ABOUT YOU ...ALWAYS.
WE SPOKE A MINUTE ONLY AND I WENT ON MY WAY.
A GUARD SCREAMED TO ME:
HALT!
WHO WERE YOU TALKING TO?
N-NOBODY...
A STRANGER ASKED IF I KNEW HER BROTHERS IN AUSCHWITZ. I DIDN'T KNOW ANYTHING, SO I HARDLY ANSWERED.
GET INSIDE!
WHEN I'M FINISHED WITH YOU, YOU'LL KNOW SOMETHING, JEWISH PIMP! YOU'RE NOT HERE TO FLIRT AND GOSSIP.
COUNT THE BLOWS. IF YOU LOSE COUNT – I'LL START AGAIN!
EINS!
ZWEI!
DREI!
SO HE BEAT ME, WHAT CAN I TELL YOU? ONLY, THANK GOD, ANJA DIDN'T GET ALSO SUCH A BEATING. SHE WOULDN'T LIVE.

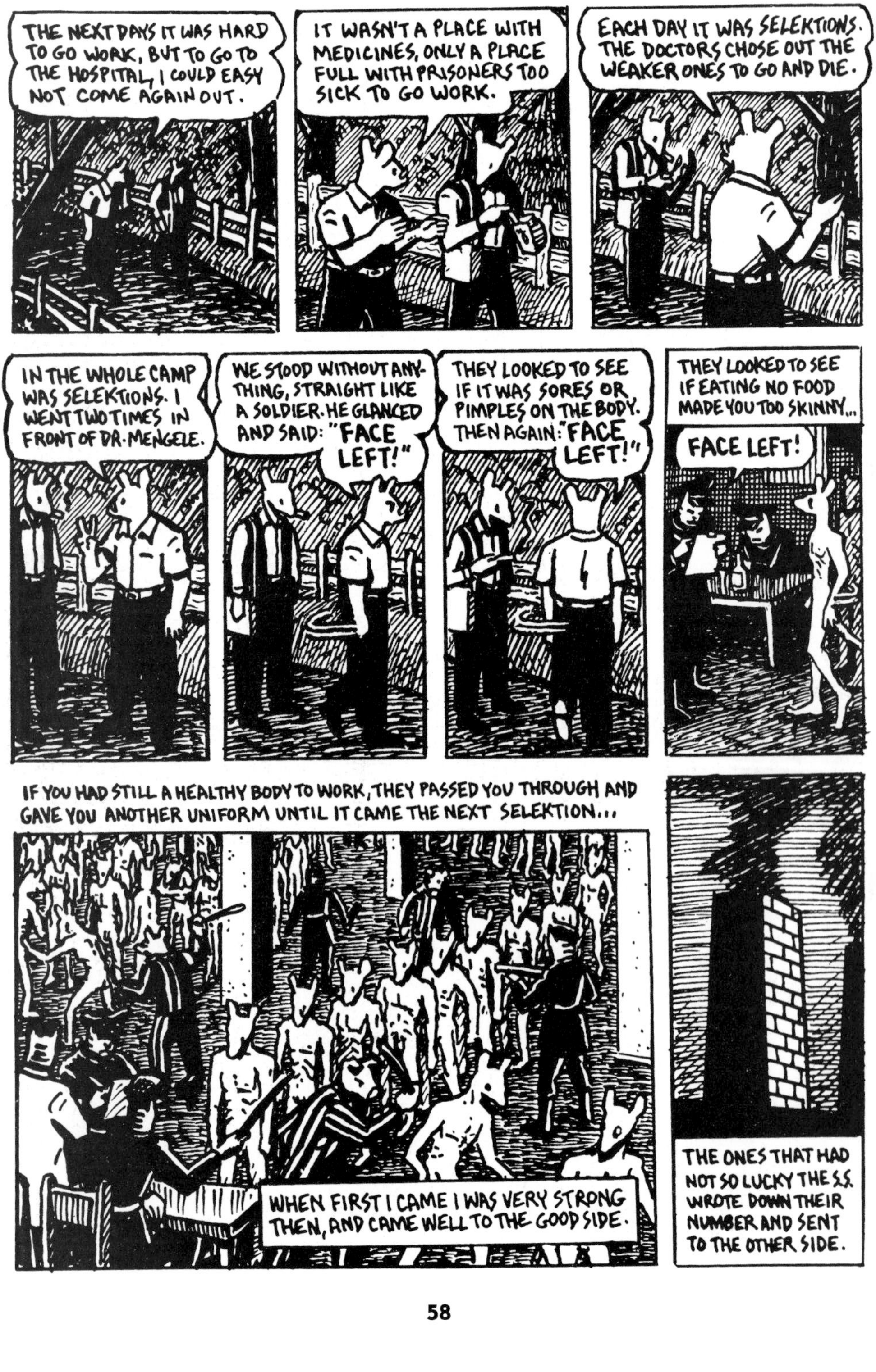
THE NEXT DAYS IT WAS HARD TO GO WORK, BUT TO GO TO THE HOSPITAL, I COULD EASY NOT COME AGAIN OUT.
IT WASN'T A PLACE WITH MEDICINES, ONLY A PLACE FULL WITH PRISONERS TOO SICK TO GO WORK.
EACH DAY IT WAS SELEKTIONS. THE DOCTORS CHOSE OUT THE WEAKER ONES TO GO AND DIE.
IN THE WHOLE CAMP WAS SELEKTIONS. I WENT TWO TIMES IN FRONT OF DR. MENGELE.
WE STOOD WITHOUT ANYTHING, STRAIGHT LIKE A SOLDIER. HE GLANCED AND SAID: "FACE LEFT!"
THEY LOOKED TO SEE IF IT WAS SORES OR PIMPLES ON THE BODY. THEN AGAIN: "FACE LEFT!"
THEY LOOKED TO SEE IF EATING NO FOOD MADE YOU TOO SKINNY...
FACE LEFT!
IF YOU HAD STILL A HEALTHY BODY TO WORK, THEY PASSED YOU THROUGH AND GAVE YOU ANOTHER UNIFORM UNTIL IT CAME THE NEXT SELEKTION...
WHEN FIRST I CAME I WAS VERY STRONG THEN, AND CAME WELL TO THE GOOD SIDE.
THE ONES THAT HAD NOT SO LUCKY THE S.S. WROTE DOWN THEIR NUMBER AND SENT TO THE OTHER SIDE.

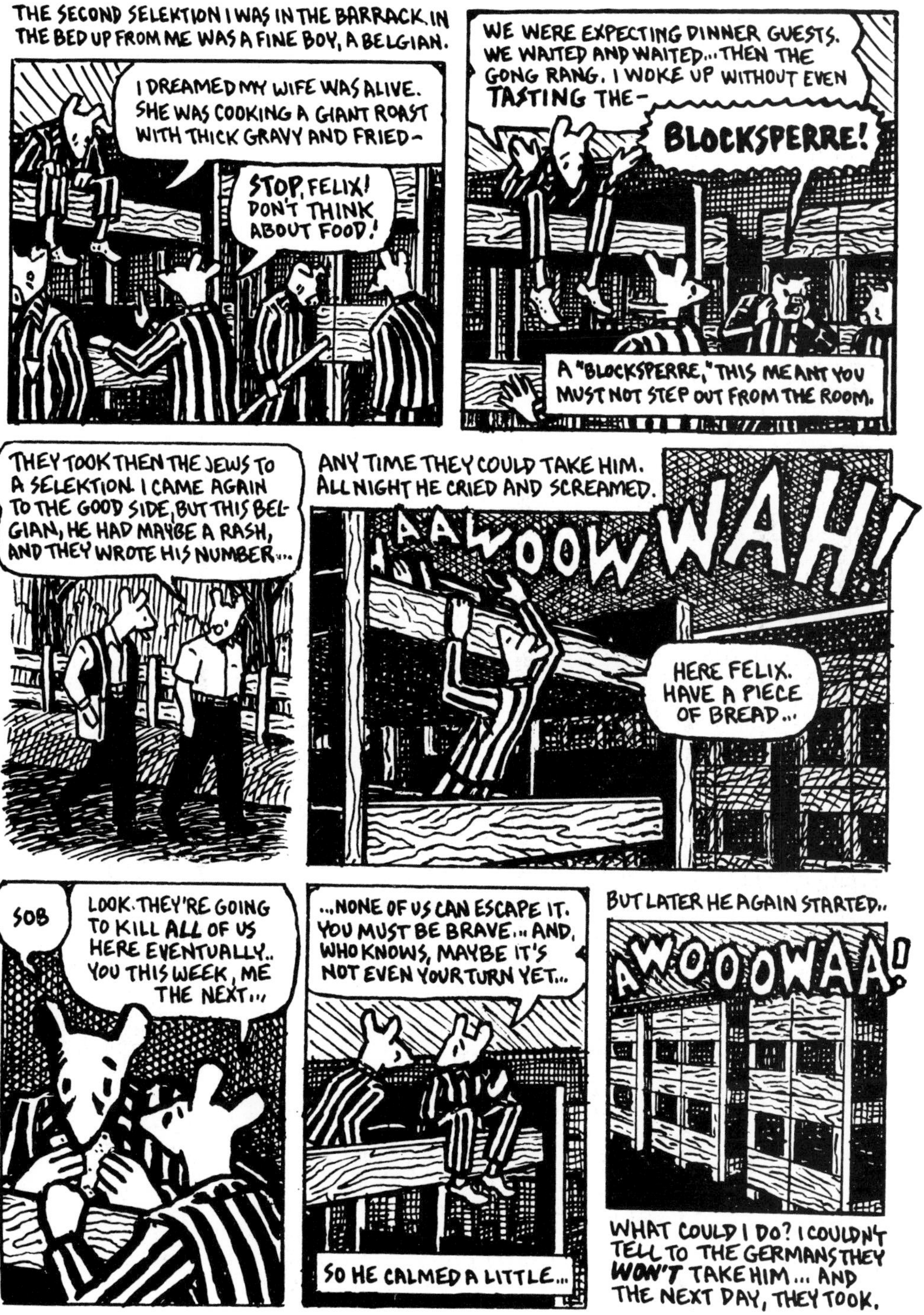
THE SECOND SELEKTION I WAS IN THE BARRACK. IN THE BED UP FROM ME WAS A FINE BOY, A BELGIAN.
I DREAMED MY WIFE WAS ALIVE. SHE WAS COOKING A GIANT ROAST WITH THICK GRAVY AND FRIED-
STOP, FELIX! DON'T THINK ABOUT FOOD!
WE WERE EXPECTING DINNER GUESTS. WE WAITED AND WAITED... THEN THE GONG RANG. I WOKE UP WITHOUT EVEN TASTING THE-
BLOCKSPERRE!
A "BLOCKSPERRE," THIS MEANT YOU MUST NOT STEP OUT FROM THE ROOM.
THEY TOOK THEN THE JEWS TO A SELEKTION. I CAME AGAIN TO THE GOOD SIDE, BUT THIS BELGIAN, HE HAD MAYBE A RASH, AND THEY WROTE HIS NUMBER...
ANY TIME THEY COULD TAKE HIM. ALL NIGHT HE CRIED AND SCREAMED.
AAWOOOWWAH!
HERE FELIX. HAVE A PIECE OF BREAD...
SOB
LOOK. THEY'RE GOING TO KILL ALL OF US HERE EVENTUALLY.. YOU THIS WEEK, ME THE NEXT...
...NONE OF US CAN ESCAPE IT. YOU MUST BE BRAVE... AND, WHO KNOWS, MAYBE IT'S NOT EVEN YOUR TURN YET...
SO HE CALMED A LITTLE...
BUT LATER HE AGAIN STARTED..
AWOOOWAA!
WHAT COULD I DO? I COULDN'T TELL TO THE GERMANS THEY WON'T TAKE HIM... AND THE NEXT DAY, THEY TOOK.

SO... IN THE TINSHOP I HAD STILL THE SAME STORY WITH YIDL.

ONLY ONE APPLE FOR ME TODAY? IS BUSINESS BAD, MR. CAPITALIST?

WHAT HAPPENED TO THE SHOEMAKER WHO WORKED IN THERE?

A LOT OF THE POLISH PRIS-ONERS WERE SENT TO CAMPS INSIDE THE REICH. THEY TOOK SOME OF MY BOYS TOO.

I RAN TO THE KAPO IN CHARGE FROM ALL THE SHOP.

DO YOU NEED A NEW SHOEMAKER?

SURE. THE S.S. TOOK THE OLD ONE AWAY, BUT THEY'RE STILL BRINGING SHOES IN!

YOU KNOW, I'VE BEEN A SHOEMAKER SINCE CHILDHOOD.

YOU DON'T *LOOK* LIKE A SHOEMAKER TO ME... YOU'RE A **TINMAN!**

DO I HAVE TO HAVE IT WRITTEN ON MY FOREHEAD?

ALRIGHT, THEN... FIX **THIS!**

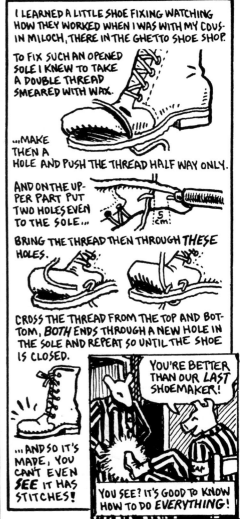

I LEARNED A LITTLE SHOE FIXING WATCHING HOW THEY WORKED WHEN I WAS WITH MY COUS-IN MILOCH, THERE IN THE GHETTO SHOE SHOP.

TO FIX SUCH AN OPENED SOLE I KNEW TO TAKE A DOUBLE THREAD SMEARED WITH WAX.

...MAKE THEN A HOLE AND PUSH THE THREAD HALF WAY ONLY.

AND ON THE UP-PER PART PUT TWO HOLES EVEN TO THE SOLE...

BRING THE THREAD THEN THROUGH *THESE* HOLES.

CROSS THE THREAD FROM THE TOP AND BOT-TOM, *BOTH* ENDS THROUGH A NEW HOLE IN THE SOLE AND REPEAT SO UNTIL THE SHOE IS CLOSED.

...AND SO IT'S MADE, YOU CAN'T EVEN *SEE* IT HAS STITCHES!

YOU'RE BETTER THAN OUR *LAST* SHOEMAKER!

YOU SEE? IT'S GOOD TO KNOW HOW TO DO EVERYTHING!

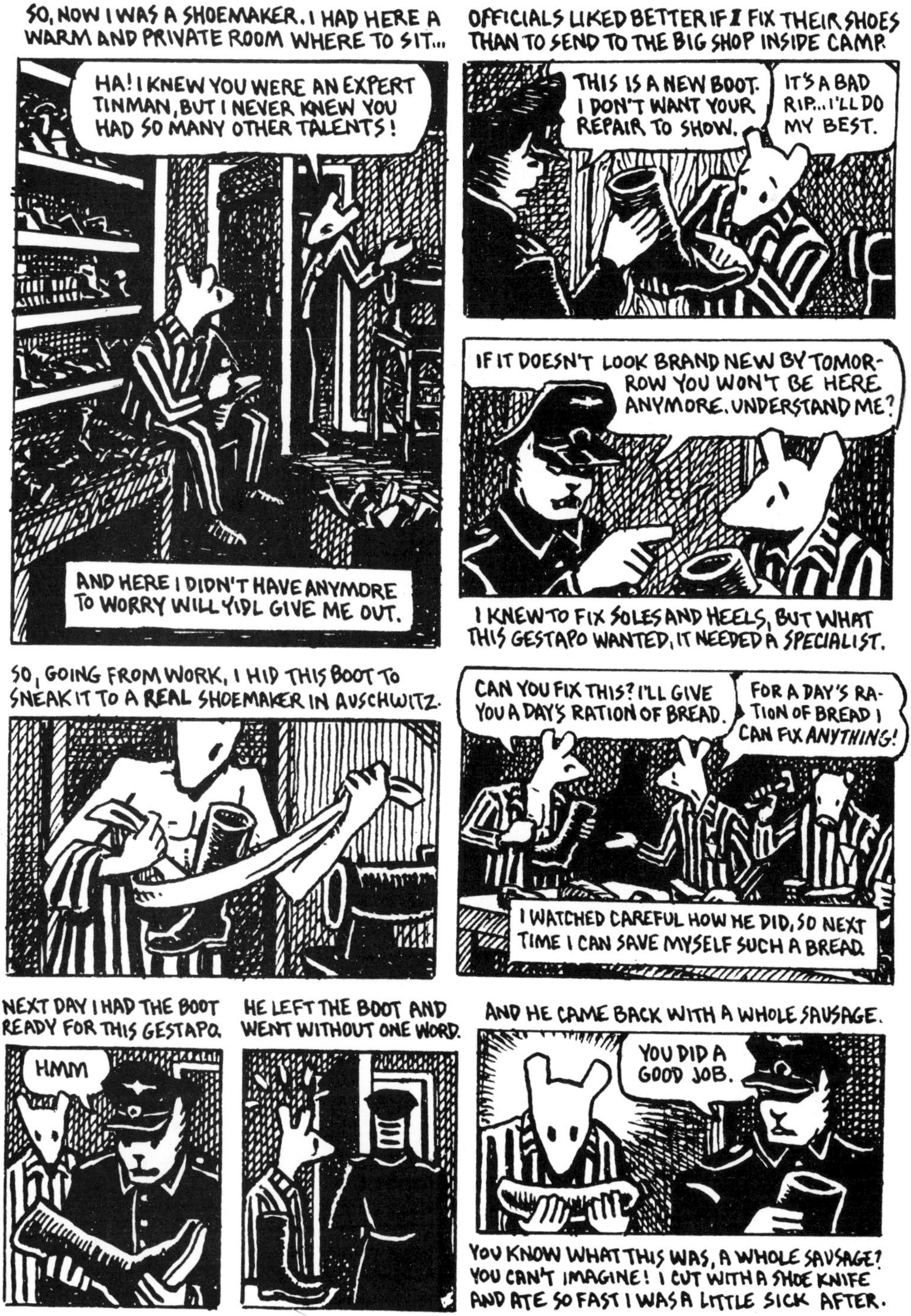
SO, NOW I WAS A SHOEMAKER. I HAD HERE A WARM AND PRIVATE ROOM WHERE TO SIT...
HA! I KNEW YOU WERE AN EXPERT TINMAN, BUT I NEVER KNEW YOU HAD SO MANY OTHER TALENTS!
AND HERE I DIDN'T HAVE ANYMORE TO WORRY WILL YIDL GIVE ME OUT.
OFFICIALS LIKED BETTER IF I FIX THEIR SHOES THAN TO SEND TO THE BIG SHOP INSIDE CAMP.
THIS IS A NEW BOOT. I DON'T WANT YOUR REPAIR TO SHOW.
IT'S A BAD RIP... I'LL DO MY BEST.
IF IT DOESN'T LOOK BRAND NEW BY TOMORROW YOU WON'T BE HERE ANYMORE. UNDERSTAND ME?
I KNEW TO FIX SOLES AND HEELS, BUT WHAT THIS GESTAPO WANTED, IT NEEDED A SPECIALIST.
SO, GOING FROM WORK, I HID THIS BOOT TO SNEAK IT TO A REAL SHOEMAKER IN AUSCHWITZ.
CAN YOU FIX THIS? I'LL GIVE YOU A DAY'S RATION OF BREAD.
FOR A DAY'S RATION OF BREAD I CAN FIX ANYTHING!
I WATCHED CAREFUL HOW HE DID, SO NEXT TIME I CAN SAVE MYSELF SUCH A BREAD.
NEXT DAY I HAD THE BOOT READY FOR THIS GESTAPO.
HMM
HE LEFT THE BOOT AND WENT WITHOUT ONE WORD.
AND HE CAME BACK WITH A WHOLE SAUSAGE.
YOU DID A GOOD JOB.
YOU KNOW WHAT THIS WAS, A WHOLE SAUSAGE? YOU CAN'T IMAGINE! I CUT WITH A SHOE KNIFE AND ATE SO FAST I WAS A LITTLE SICK AFTER.

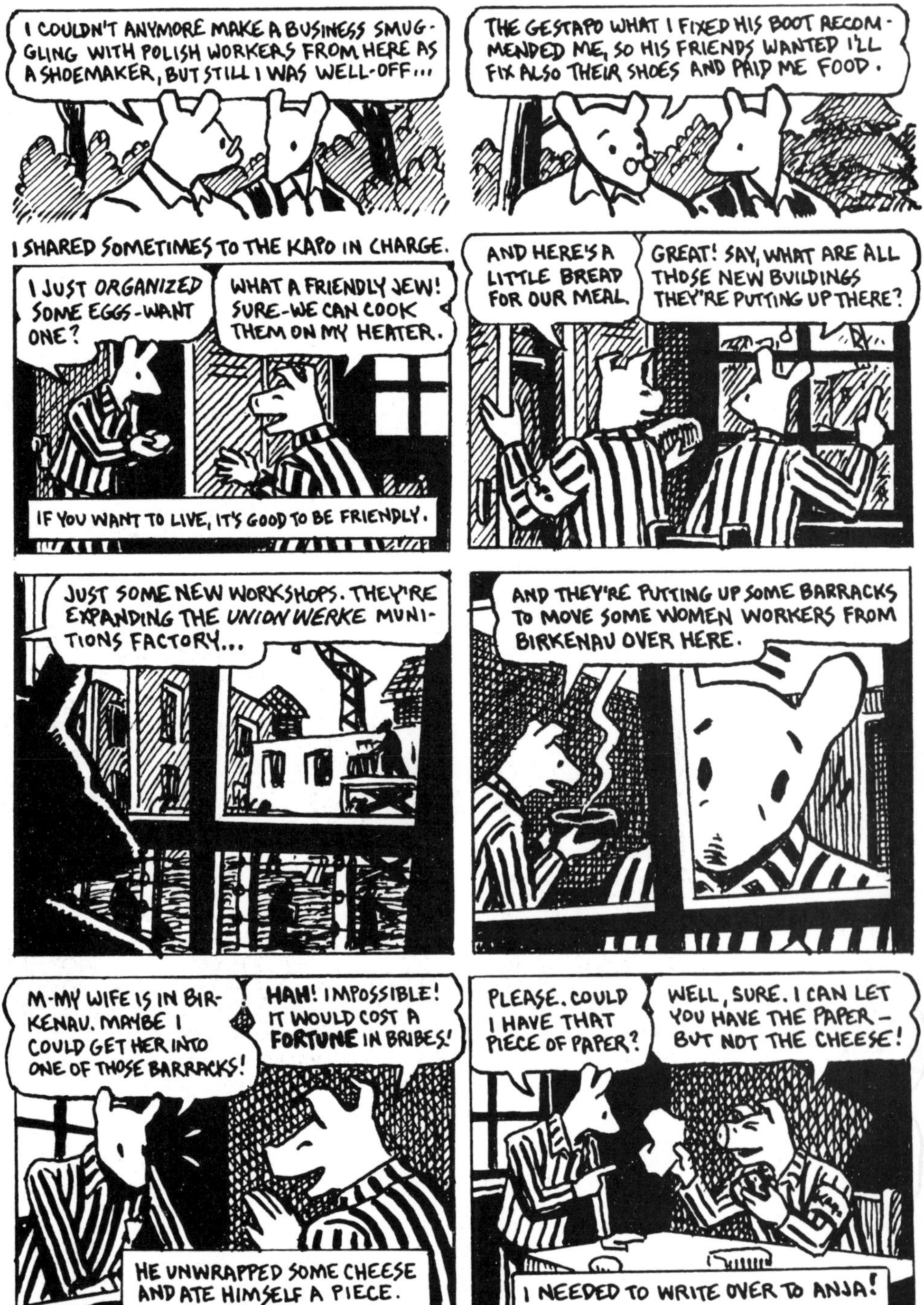
I COULDN'T ANYMORE MAKE A BUSINESS SMUGGLING WITH POLISH WORKERS FROM HERE AS A SHOEMAKER, BUT STILL I WAS WELL-OFF...
THE GESTAPO WHAT I FIXED HIS BOOT RECOMMENDED ME, SO HIS FRIENDS WANTED I'LL FIX ALSO THEIR SHOES AND PAID ME FOOD.
I SHARED SOMETIMES TO THE KAPO IN CHARGE.
I JUST ORGANIZED SOME EGGS-WANT ONE?
WHAT A FRIENDLY JEW! SURE-WE CAN COOK THEM ON MY HEATER.
IF YOU WANT TO LIVE, IT'S GOOD TO BE FRIENDLY.
AND HERE'S A LITTLE BREAD FOR OUR MEAL.
GREAT! SAY, WHAT ARE ALL THOSE NEW BUILDINGS THEY'RE PUTTING UP THERE?
JUST SOME NEW WORKSHOPS. THEY'RE EXPANDING THE UNION WERKE MUNITIONS FACTORY...
AND THEY'RE PUTTING UP SOME BARRACKS TO MOVE SOME WOMEN WORKERS FROM BIRKENAU OVER HERE.
M-MY WIFE IS IN BIRKENAU. MAYBE I COULD GET HER INTO ONE OF THOSE BARRACKS!
HAH! IMPOSSIBLE! IT WOULD COST A FORTUNE IN BRIBES!
HE UNWRAPPED SOME CHEESE AND ATE HIMSELF A PIECE.
PLEASE. COULD I HAVE THAT PIECE OF PAPER?
WELL, SURE. I CAN LET YOU HAVE THE PAPER - BUT NOT THE CHEESE!
I NEEDED TO WRITE OVER TO ANJA!

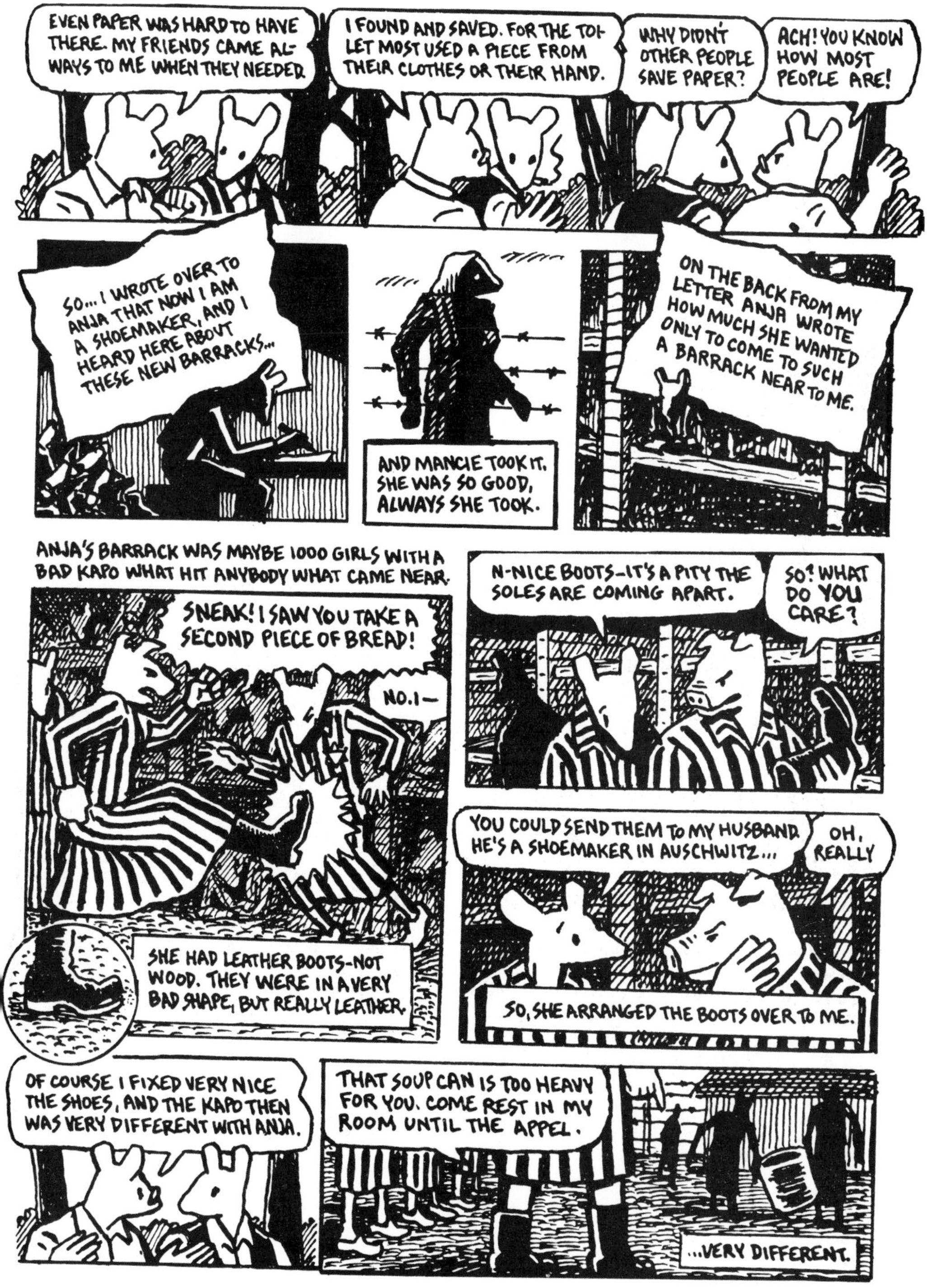
EVEN PAPER WAS HARD TO HAVE THERE. MY FRIENDS CAME ALWAYS TO ME WHEN THEY NEEDED
I FOUND AND SAVED. FOR THE TOILET MOST USED A PIECE FROM THEIR CLOTHES OR THEIR HAND.
WHY DIDN'T OTHER PEOPLE SAVE PAPER?
ACH! YOU KNOW HOW MOST PEOPLE ARE!
SO... I WROTE OVER TO ANJA THAT NOW I AM A SHOEMAKER, AND I HEARD HERE ABOUT THESE NEW BARRACKS...
AND MANCIE TOOK IT. SHE WAS SO GOOD, ALWAYS SHE TOOK.
ON THE BACK FROM MY LETTER ANJA WROTE HOW MUCH SHE WANTED ONLY TO COME TO SUCH A BARRACK NEAR TO ME.
ANJA'S BARRACK WAS MAYBE 1000 GIRLS WITH A BAD KAPO WHAT HIT ANYBODY WHAT CAME NEAR.
SNEAK! I SAW YOU TAKE A SECOND PIECE OF BREAD!
NO. I—
SHE HAD LEATHER BOOTS-NOT WOOD. THEY WERE IN A VERY BAD SHAPE, BUT REALLY LEATHER.
N-NICE BOOTS-IT'S A PITY THE SOLES ARE COMING APART.
SO? WHAT DO YOU CARE?
YOU COULD SEND THEM TO MY HUSBAND. HE'S A SHOEMAKER IN AUSCHWITZ...
OH, REALLY
SO, SHE ARRANGED THE BOOTS OVER TO ME.
OF COURSE I FIXED VERY NICE THE SHOES, AND THE KAPO THEN WAS VERY DIFFERENT WITH ANJA.
THAT SOUP CAN IS TOO HEAVY FOR YOU. COME REST IN MY ROOM UNTIL THE APPEL.
...VERY DIFFERENT.

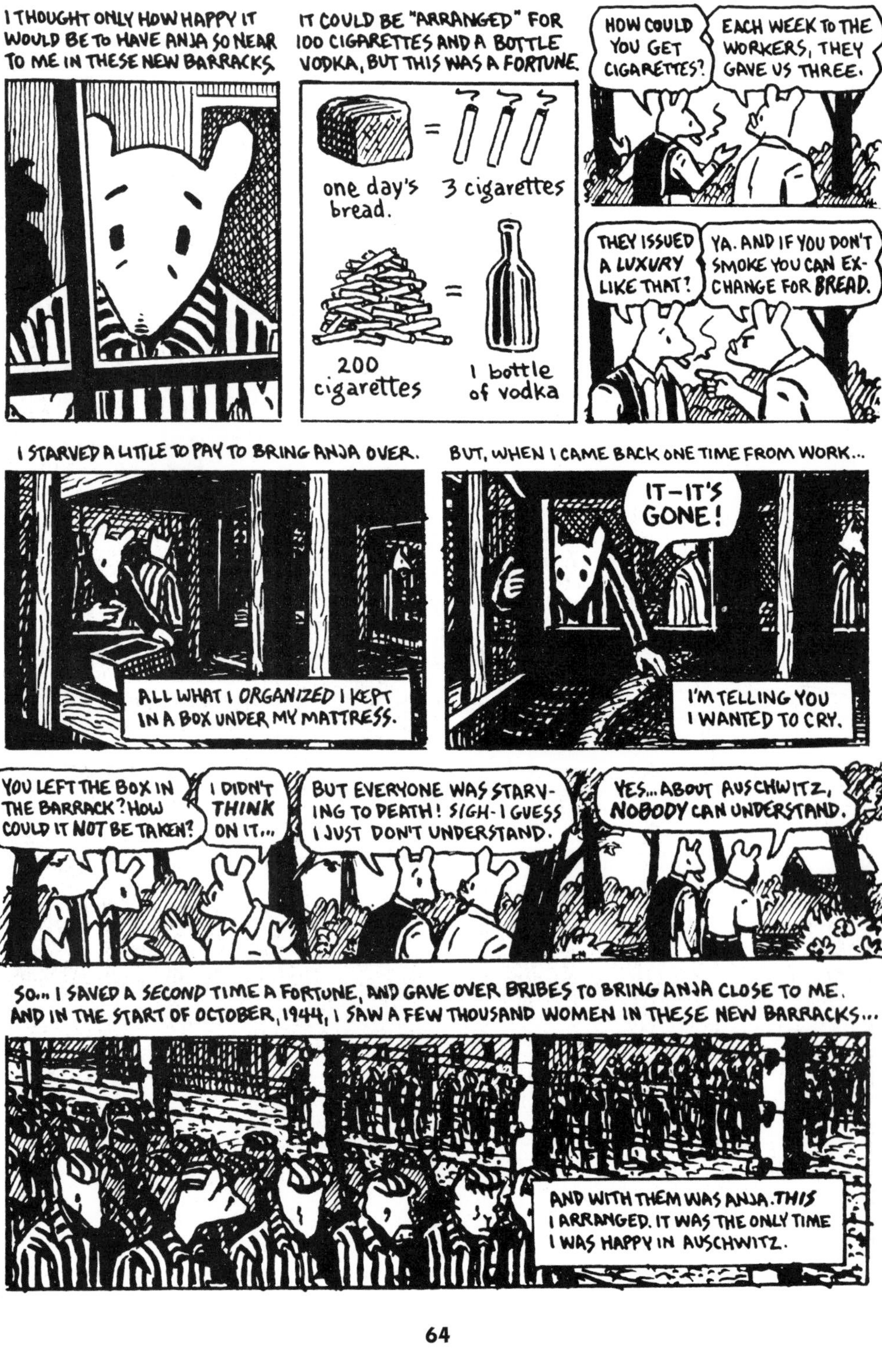

I THOUGHT ONLY HOW HAPPY IT WOULD BE TO HAVE ANJA SO NEAR TO ME IN THESE NEW BARRACKS.
IT COULD BE "ARRANGED" FOR 100 CIGARETTES AND A BOTTLE VODKA, BUT THIS WAS A FORTUNE.
one day's bread.
=
3 cigarettes
200 cigarettes
=
1 bottle of vodka
HOW COULD YOU GET CIGARETTES?
EACH WEEK TO THE WORKERS, THEY GAVE US THREE.
THEY ISSUED A LUXURY LIKE THAT?
YA. AND IF YOU DON'T SMOKE YOU CAN EXCHANGE FOR BREAD.
I STARVED A LITTLE TO PAY TO BRING ANJA OVER.
ALL WHAT I ORGANIZED I KEPT IN A BOX UNDER MY MATTRESS.
BUT, WHEN I CAME BACK ONE TIME FROM WORK...
IT–IT'S GONE!
I'M TELLING YOU I WANTED TO CRY.
YOU LEFT THE BOX IN THE BARRACK? HOW COULD IT NOT BE TAKEN?
I DIDN'T THINK ON IT...
BUT EVERYONE WAS STARVING TO DEATH! SIGH- I GUESS I JUST DON'T UNDERSTAND.
YES... ABOUT AUSCHWITZ, NOBODY CAN UNDERSTAND.
SO... I SAVED A SECOND TIME A FORTUNE, AND GAVE OVER BRIBES TO BRING ANJA CLOSE TO ME.
AND IN THE START OF OCTOBER, 1944, I SAW A FEW THOUSAND WOMEN IN THESE NEW BARRACKS...
AND WITH THEM WAS ANJA. THIS I ARRANGED. IT WAS THE ONLY TIME I WAS HAPPY IN AUSCHWITZ.

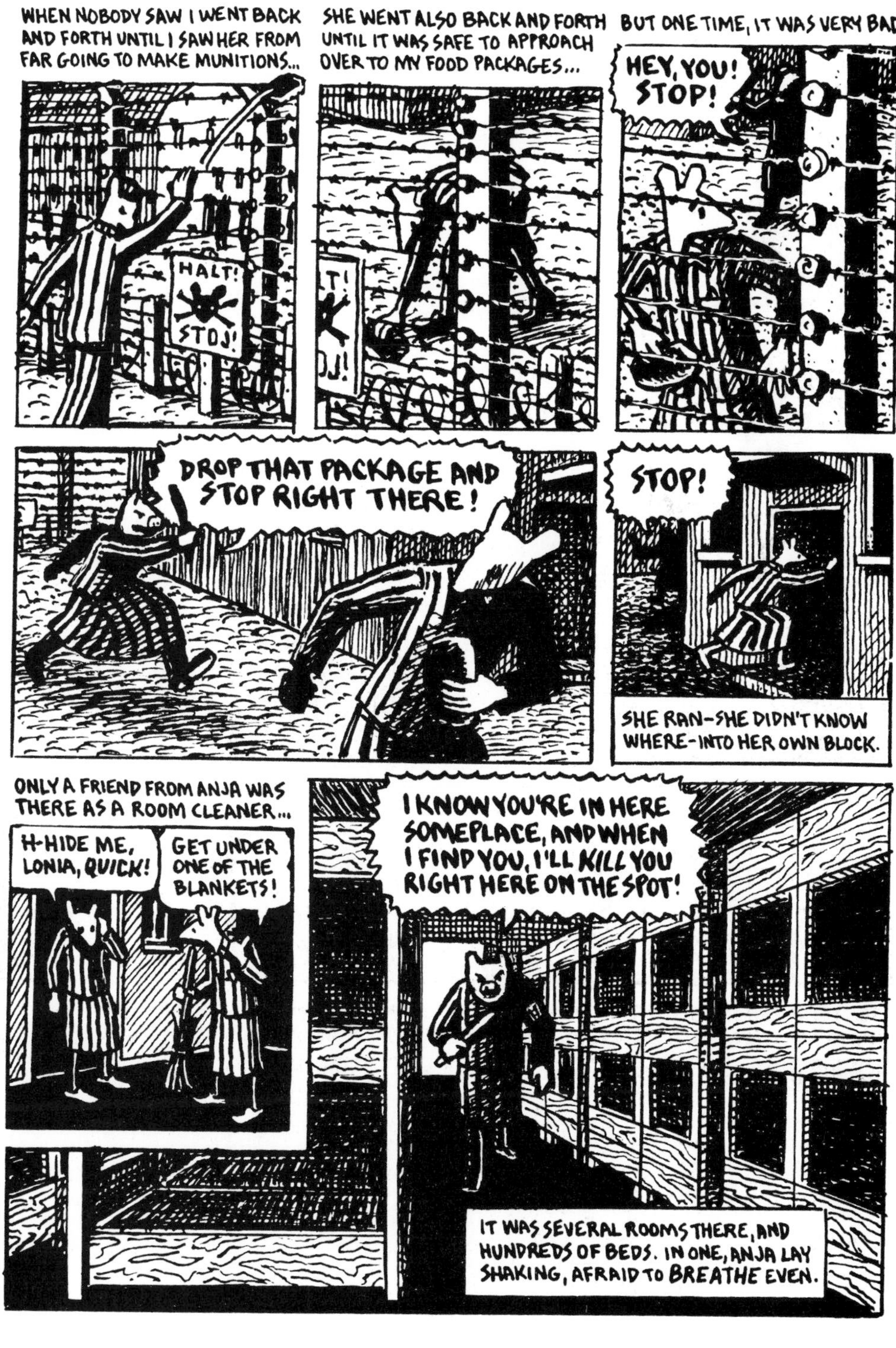
WHEN NOBODY SAW I WENT BACK AND FORTH UNTIL I SAW HER FROM FAR GOING TO MAKE MUNITIONS...
HALT! STOJ!
SHE WENT ALSO BACK AND FORTH UNTIL IT WAS SAFE TO APPROACH OVER TO MY FOOD PACKAGES...
BUT ONE TIME, IT WAS VERY BAD.
HEY, YOU! STOP!
DROP THAT PACKAGE AND STOP RIGHT THERE!
STOP!
SHE RAN–SHE DIDN'T KNOW WHERE–INTO HER OWN BLOCK.
ONLY A FRIEND FROM ANJA WAS THERE AS A ROOM CLEANER...
H-HIDE ME, LONIA, QUICK!
GET UNDER ONE OF THE BLANKETS!
I KNOW YOU'RE IN HERE SOMEPLACE, AND WHEN I FIND YOU, I'LL KILL YOU RIGHT HERE ON THE SPOT!
IT WAS SEVERAL ROOMS THERE, AND HUNDREDS OF BEDS. IN ONE, ANJA LAY SHAKING, AFRAID TO BREATHE EVEN.

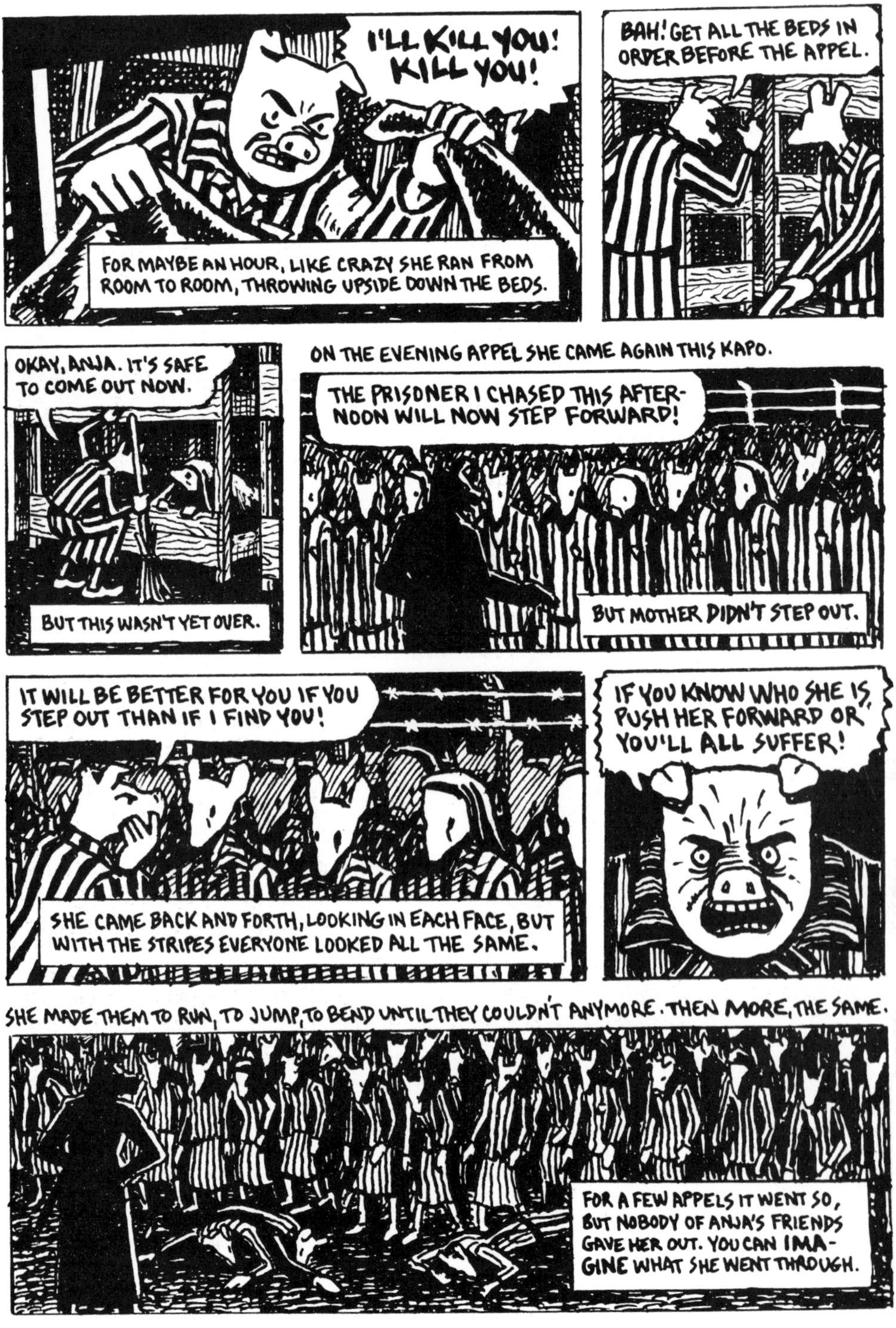
I'LL KILL YOU! KILL YOU!
FOR MAYBE AN HOUR, LIKE CRAZY SHE RAN FROM ROOM TO ROOM, THROWING UPSIDE DOWN THE BEDS.
BAH! GET ALL THE BEDS IN ORDER BEFORE THE APPEL.
OKAY, ANJA. IT'S SAFE TO COME OUT NOW.
BUT THIS WASN'T YET OVER.
ON THE EVENING APPEL SHE CAME AGAIN THIS KAPO.
THE PRISONER I CHASED THIS AFTERNOON WILL NOW STEP FORWARD!
BUT MOTHER DIDN'T STEP OUT.
IT WILL BE BETTER FOR YOU IF YOU STEP OUT THAN IF I FIND YOU!
SHE CAME BACK AND FORTH, LOOKING IN EACH FACE, BUT WITH THE STRIPES EVERYONE LOOKED ALL THE SAME.
IF YOU KNOW WHO SHE IS, PUSH HER FORWARD OR YOU'LL ALL SUFFER!
SHE MADE THEM TO RUN, TO JUMP, TO BEND UNTIL THEY COULDN'T ANYMORE. THEN MORE, THE SAME.
FOR A FEW APPELS IT WENT SO, BUT NOBODY OF ANJA'S FRIENDS GAVE HER OUT. YOU CAN IMAGINE WHAT SHE WENT THROUGH.

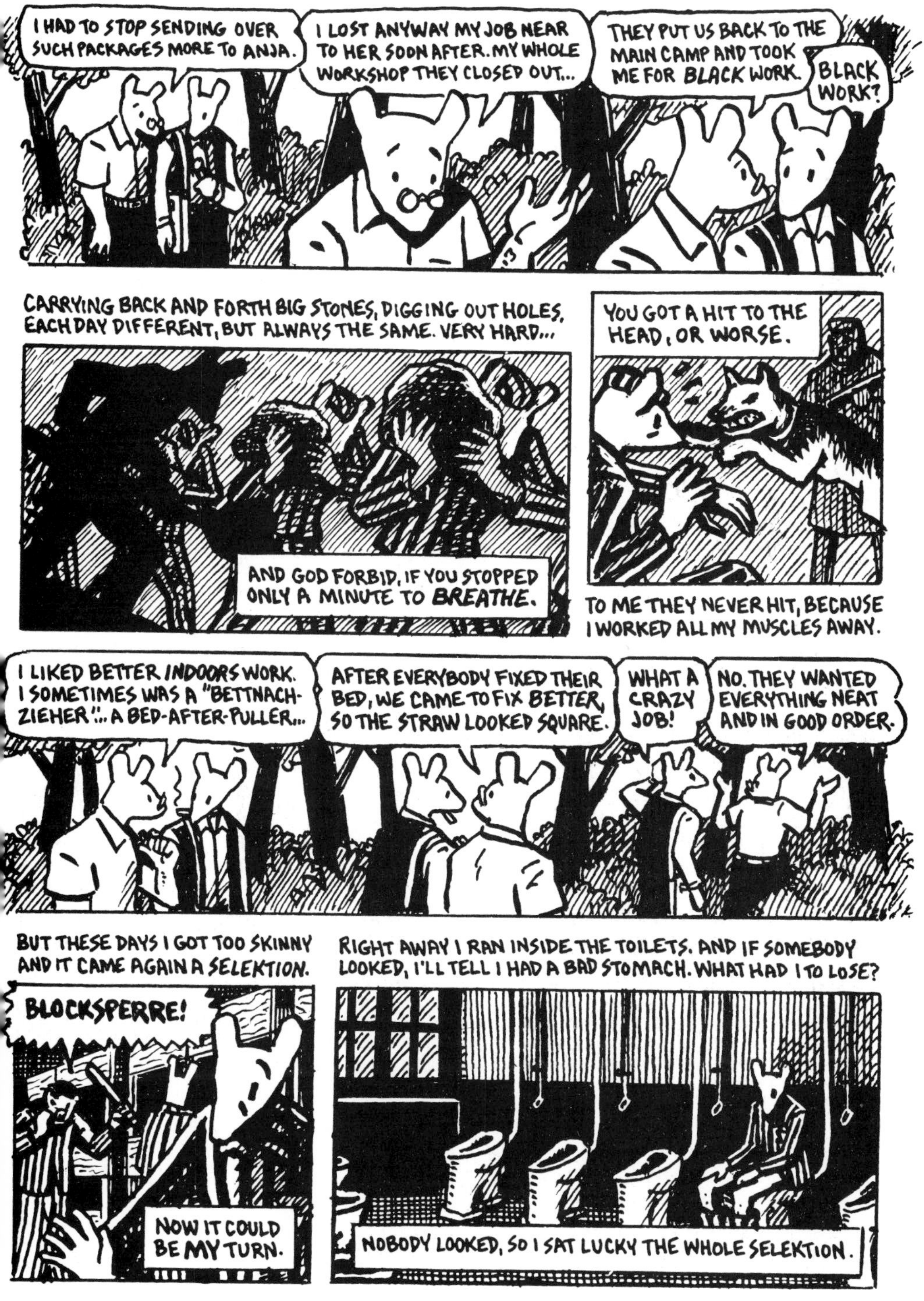
I HAD TO STOP SENDING OVER SUCH PACKAGES MORE TO ANJA.
I LOST ANYWAY MY JOB NEAR TO HER SOON AFTER. MY WHOLE WORKSHOP THEY CLOSED OUT...
THEY PUT US BACK TO THE MAIN CAMP AND TOOK ME FOR BLACK WORK.
BLACK WORK?
CARRYING BACK AND FORTH BIG STONES, DIGGING OUT HOLES. EACH DAY DIFFERENT, BUT ALWAYS THE SAME. VERY HARD...
AND GOD FORBID, IF YOU STOPPED ONLY A MINUTE TO BREATHE.
YOU GOT A HIT TO THE HEAD, OR WORSE.
TO ME THEY NEVER HIT, BECAUSE I WORKED ALL MY MUSCLES AWAY.
I LIKED BETTER INDOORS WORK. I SOMETIMES WAS A "BETTNACHZIEHER"... A BED-AFTER-PULLER...
AFTER EVERYBODY FIXED THEIR BED, WE CAME TO FIX BETTER, SO THE STRAW LOOKED SQUARE.
WHAT A CRAZY JOB!
NO. THEY WANTED EVERYTHING NEAT AND IN GOOD ORDER.
BUT THESE DAYS I GOT TOO SKINNY AND IT CAME AGAIN A SELEKTION.
BLOCKSPERRE!
NOW IT COULD BE MY TURN.
RIGHT AWAY I RAN INSIDE THE TOILETS. AND IF SOMEBODY LOOKED, I'LL TELL I HAD A BAD STOMACH. WHAT HAD I TO LOSE?
NOBODY LOOKED, SO I SAT LUCKY THE WHOLE SELEKTION.

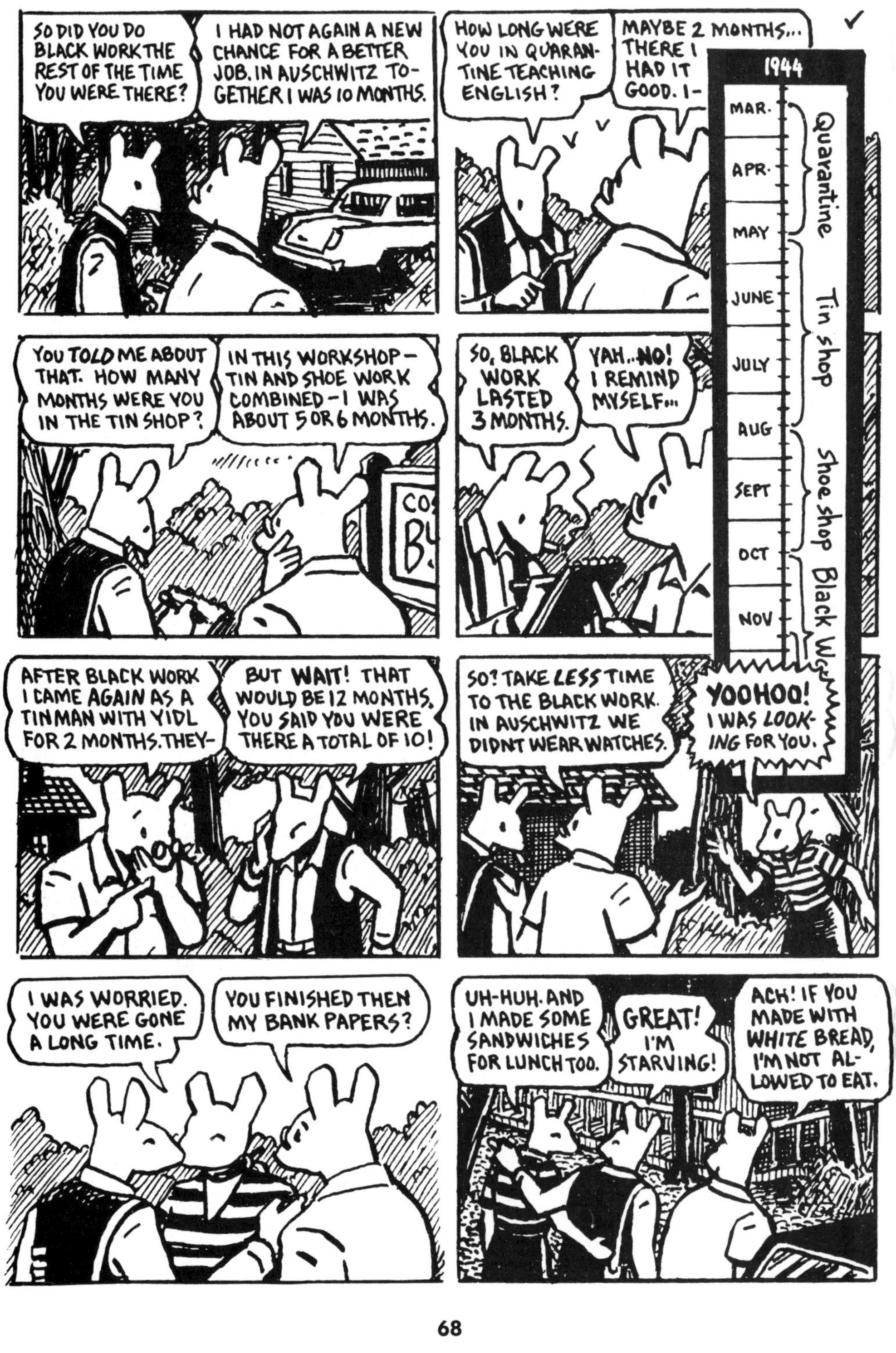
SO DID YOU DO BLACK WORK THE REST OF THE TIME YOU WERE THERE?
I HAD NOT AGAIN A NEW CHANCE FOR A BETTER JOB. IN AUSCHWITZ TOGETHER I WAS 10 MONTHS.
HOW LONG WERE YOU IN QUARANTINE TEACHING ENGLISH?
MAYBE 2 MONTHS... THERE I HAD IT GOOD. I-
1944
MAR.
APR.
MAY
JUNE
JULY
AUG
SEPT
OCT
NOV
Quarantine
Tin shop
Shoe shop
Black Wo
YOU TOLD ME ABOUT THAT. HOW MANY MONTHS WERE YOU IN THE TIN SHOP?
IN THIS WORKSHOP—TIN AND SHOE WORK COMBINED—I WAS ABOUT 5 OR 6 MONTHS.
SO, BLACK WORK LASTED 3 MONTHS.
YAH...NO! I REMIND MYSELF...
AFTER BLACK WORK I CAME AGAIN AS A TINMAN WITH YIDL FOR 2 MONTHS. THEY-
BUT WAIT! THAT WOULD BE 12 MONTHS. YOU SAID YOU WERE THERE A TOTAL OF 10!
SO? TAKE LESS TIME TO THE BLACK WORK. IN AUSCHWITZ WE DIDN'T WEAR WATCHES.
YOOHOO! I WAS LOOKING FOR YOU.
I WAS WORRIED. YOU WERE GONE A LONG TIME.
YOU FINISHED THEN MY BANK PAPERS?
UH-HUH. AND I MADE SOME SANDWICHES FOR LUNCH TOO.
GREAT! I'M STARVING!
ACH! IF YOU MADE WITH WHITE BREAD, I'M NOT ALLOWED TO EAT.

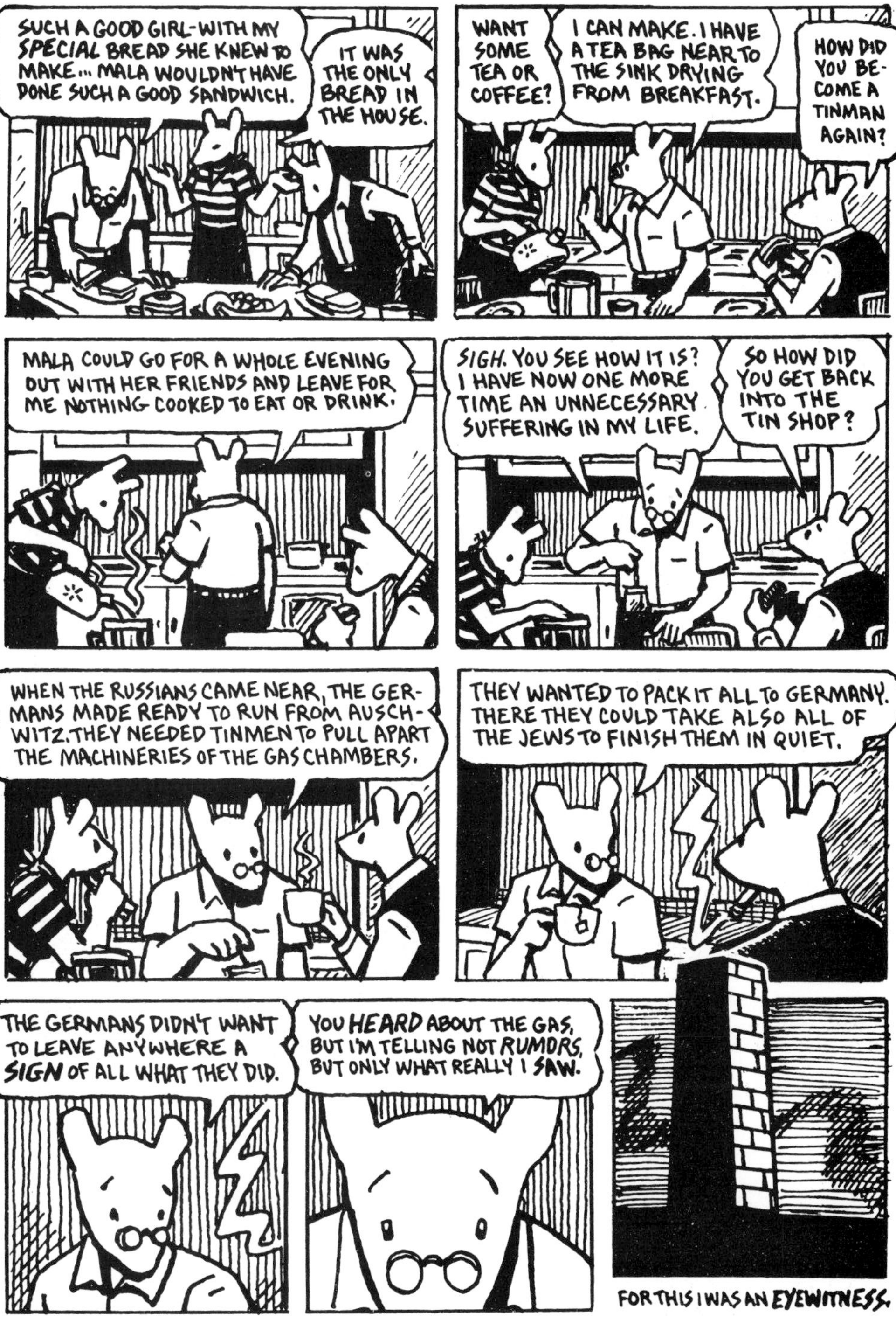
SUCH A GOOD GIRL-WITH MY SPECIAL BREAD SHE KNEW TO MAKE... MALA WOULDN'T HAVE DONE SUCH A GOOD SANDWICH.
IT WAS THE ONLY BREAD IN THE HOUSE.
WANT SOME TEA OR COFFEE?
I CAN MAKE. I HAVE A TEA BAG NEAR TO THE SINK DRYING FROM BREAKFAST.
HOW DID YOU BECOME A TINMAN AGAIN?
MALA COULD GO FOR A WHOLE EVENING OUT WITH HER FRIENDS AND LEAVE FOR ME NOTHING COOKED TO EAT OR DRINK.
SIGH. YOU SEE HOW IT IS? I HAVE NOW ONE MORE TIME AN UNNECESSARY SUFFERING IN MY LIFE.
SO HOW DID YOU GET BACK INTO THE TIN SHOP?
WHEN THE RUSSIANS CAME NEAR, THE GERMANS MADE READY TO RUN FROM AUSCHWITZ. THEY NEEDED TINMEN TO PULL APART THE MACHINERIES OF THE GAS CHAMBERS.
THEY WANTED TO PACK IT ALL TO GERMANY. THERE THEY COULD TAKE ALSO ALL OF THE JEWS TO FINISH THEM IN QUIET.
THE GERMANS DIDN'T WANT TO LEAVE ANYWHERE A SIGN OF ALL WHAT THEY DID.
YOU HEARD ABOUT THE GAS, BUT I'M TELLING NOT RUMORS, BUT ONLY WHAT REALLY I SAW.
FOR THIS I WAS AN EYEWITNESS.

I CAME TO ONE OF THE FOUR CREMO BUILDINGS. IT LOOKED SO LIKE A BIG BAKERY...

EXE-CUTION ROOM

UNDRESS-ING ROOM

RM. FOR MELTING GOLD FILLINGS

GAS CHAMBER

INCINERATION RM. W. OVENS

CORPSE LIFT

TOILET

CHIMNEY

COAL STORAGE

CREMATORIUM II.

FROM BELOW GROUND, IN THE GAS ROOM, WE TINMEN HAD TO TAKE OUT THE PIPES AND FANS FOR VENTILATING.

THIS WAS A FACTORY TO MAKE —ONE, TWO, THREE— ASHES AND SMOKE FROM ALL WHAT CAME HERE.

underground undressing room

underground gas chamber

ovens

SPECIAL PRISONERS WORKED HERE SEPARATE. THEY GOT BETTER BREAD, BUT EACH FEW MONTHS THEY ALSO WERE SENT UP THE CHIMNEY. ONE FROM THEM SHOWED ME EVERYTHING HOW IT WAS.

DISINFEKTION DEZYNFEKCIE DISINFECTION

PEOPLE BELIEVED *REALLY* IT WAS HERE A PLACE FOR SHOWERS. SO THEY WERE TOLD.

THEY CAME TO A BIG ROOM TO UNDRESS THEIR CLOTHES WHAT LOOKS SO, YES—HERE IS A PLACE SO LIKE THEY SAY.

Sauber ein Ges eit

IMPORTANT REMEMBER YOUR HOOK NUMBER

PLEASE TIE YOUR SHOES TO-GETH-ER

IF I SAW A COUPLE MONTHS BEFORE HOW IT WAS ALL ARRANGED HERE, ONLY *ONE* TIME I COULD SEE IT!

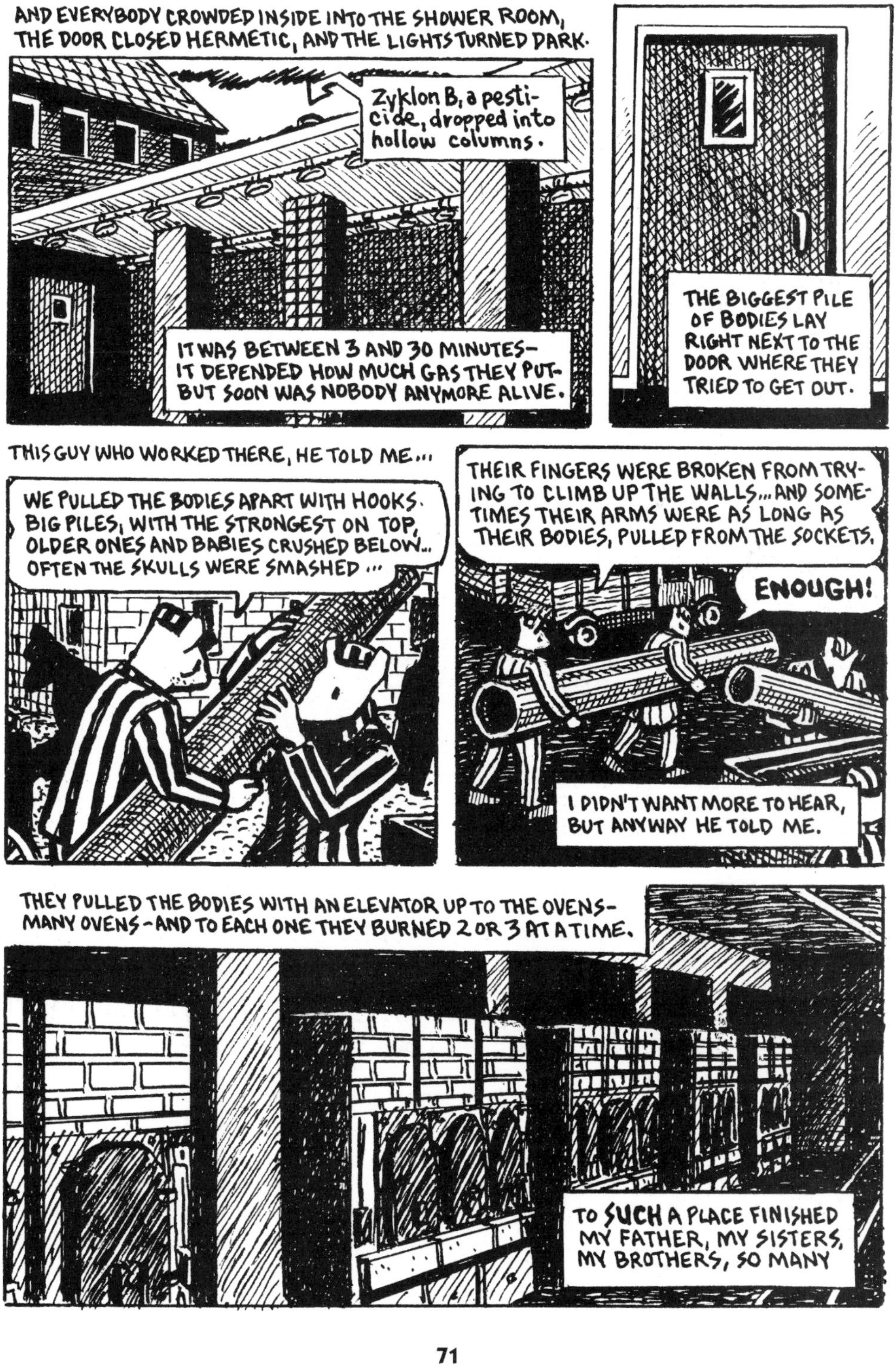
AND EVERYBODY CROWDED INSIDE INTO THE SHOWER ROOM, THE DOOR CLOSED HERMETIC, AND THE LIGHTS TURNED DARK.
Zyklon B, a pesticide, dropped into hollow columns.
IT WAS BETWEEN 3 AND 30 MINUTES- IT DEPENDED HOW MUCH GAS THEY PUT- BUT SOON WAS NOBODY ANYMORE ALIVE.
THE BIGGEST PILE OF BODIES LAY RIGHT NEXT TO THE DOOR WHERE THEY TRIED TO GET OUT.
THIS GUY WHO WORKED THERE, HE TOLD ME...
WE PULLED THE BODIES APART WITH HOOKS. BIG PILES, WITH THE STRONGEST ON TOP, OLDER ONES AND BABIES CRUSHED BELOW... OFTEN THE SKULLS WERE SMASHED ...
THEIR FINGERS WERE BROKEN FROM TRYING TO CLIMB UP THE WALLS... AND SOMETIMES THEIR ARMS WERE AS LONG AS THEIR BODIES, PULLED FROM THE SOCKETS.
ENOUGH!
I DIDN'T WANT MORE TO HEAR, BUT ANYWAY HE TOLD ME.
THEY PULLED THE BODIES WITH AN ELEVATOR UP TO THE OVENS- MANY OVENS - AND TO EACH ONE THEY BURNED 2 OR 3 AT A TIME.
TO SUCH A PLACE FINISHED MY FATHER, MY SISTERS, MY BROTHERS, SO MANY

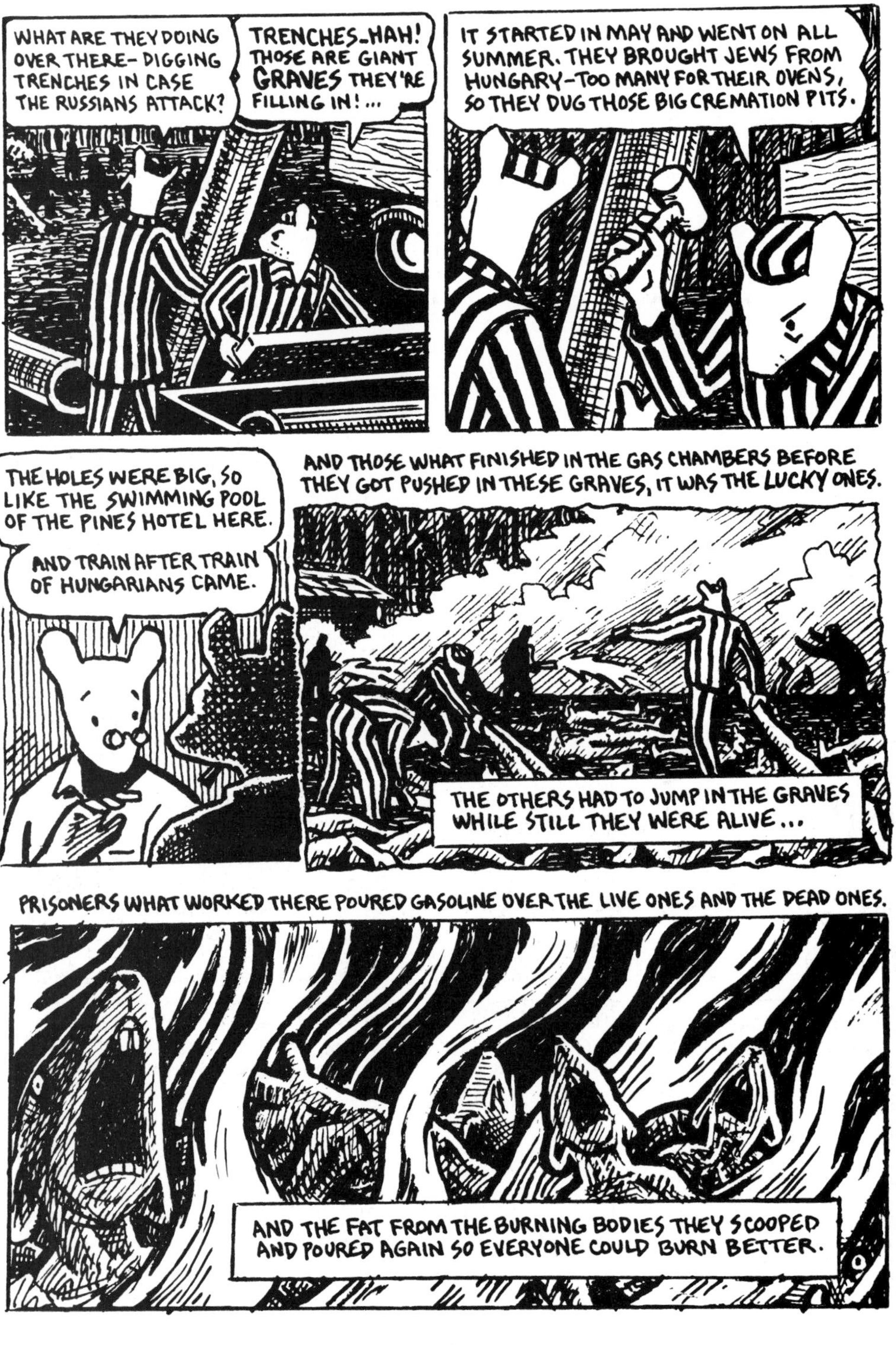
WHAT ARE THEY DOING OVER THERE- DIGGING TRENCHES IN CASE THE RUSSIANS ATTACK?
TRENCHES-HAH! THOSE ARE GIANT GRAVES THEY'RE FILLING IN! ...
IT STARTED IN MAY AND WENT ON ALL SUMMER. THEY BROUGHT JEWS FROM HUNGARY-TOO MANY FOR THEIR OVENS, SO THEY DUG THOSE BIG CREMATION PITS.
THE HOLES WERE BIG, SO LIKE THE SWIMMING POOL OF THE PINES HOTEL HERE.
AND TRAIN AFTER TRAIN OF HUNGARIANS CAME.
AND THOSE WHAT FINISHED IN THE GAS CHAMBERS BEFORE THEY GOT PUSHED IN THESE GRAVES, IT WAS THE LUCKY ONES.
THE OTHERS HAD TO JUMP IN THE GRAVES WHILE STILL THEY WERE ALIVE...
PRISONERS WHAT WORKED THERE POURED GASOLINE OVER THE LIVE ONES AND THE DEAD ONES.
AND THE FAT FROM THE BURNING BODIES THEY SCOOPED AND POURED AGAIN SO EVERYONE COULD BURN BETTER.

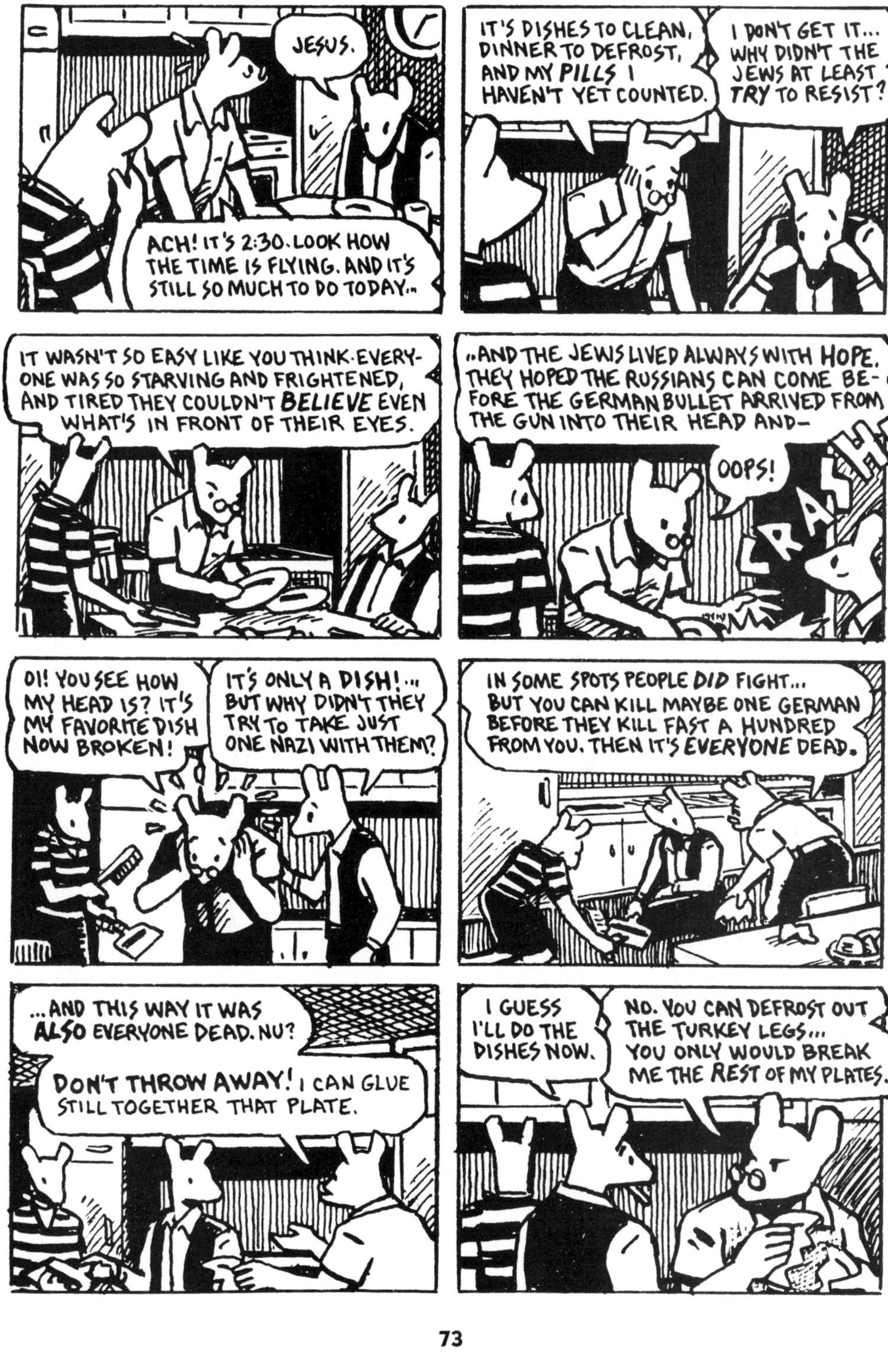
JESUS.
ACH! IT'S 2:30. LOOK HOW THE TIME IS FLYING. AND IT'S STILL SO MUCH TO DO TODAY..
IT'S DISHES TO CLEAN, DINNER TO DEFROST, AND MY PILLS I HAVEN'T YET COUNTED.
I DON'T GET IT... WHY DIDN'T THE JEWS AT LEAST TRY TO RESIST?
IT WASN'T SO EASY LIKE YOU THINK. EVERYONE WAS SO STARVING AND FRIGHTENED, AND TIRED THEY COULDN'T BELIEVE EVEN WHAT'S IN FRONT OF THEIR EYES.
..AND THE JEWS LIVED ALWAYS WITH HOPE. THEY HOPED THE RUSSIANS CAN COME BEFORE THE GERMAN BULLET ARRIVED FROM THE GUN INTO THEIR HEAD AND—
OOPS!
CRASH!
OI! YOU SEE HOW MY HEAD IS? IT'S MY FAVORITE DISH NOW BROKEN!
IT'S ONLY A DISH!... BUT WHY DIDN'T THEY TRY TO TAKE JUST ONE NAZI WITH THEM?
IN SOME SPOTS PEOPLE DID FIGHT... BUT YOU CAN KILL MAYBE ONE GERMAN BEFORE THEY KILL FAST A HUNDRED FROM YOU. THEN IT'S EVERYONE DEAD.
...AND THIS WAY IT WAS ALSO EVERYONE DEAD. NU?
DON'T THROW AWAY! I CAN GLUE STILL TOGETHER THAT PLATE.
I GUESS I'LL DO THE DISHES NOW.
NO. YOU CAN DEFROST OUT THE TURKEY LEGS... YOU ONLY WOULD BREAK ME THE REST OF MY PLATES.

That night...

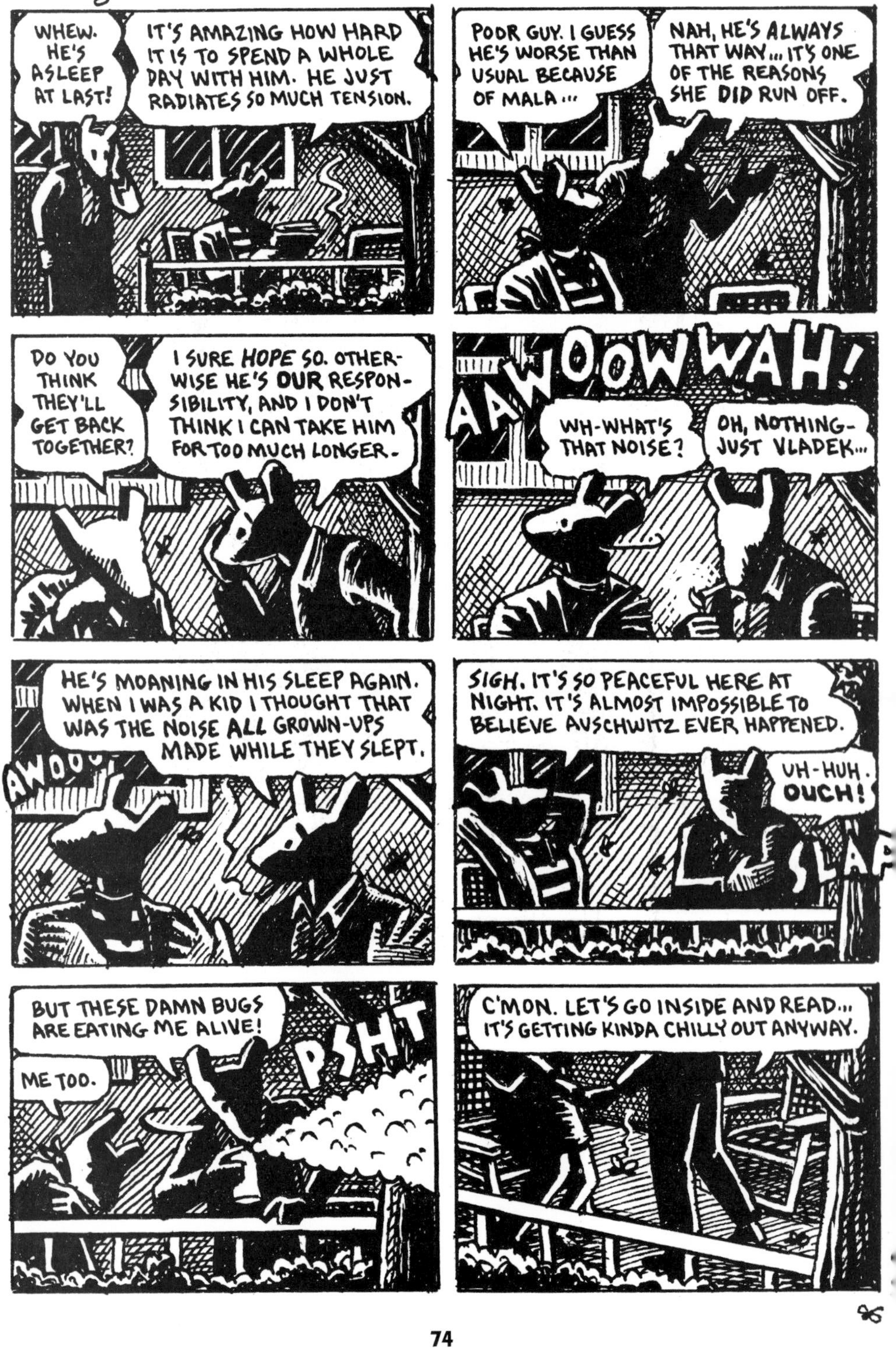
WHEW. HE'S ASLEEP AT LAST!
IT'S AMAZING HOW HARD IT IS TO SPEND A WHOLE DAY WITH HIM. HE JUST RADIATES SO MUCH TENSION.
POOR GUY. I GUESS HE'S WORSE THAN USUAL BECAUSE OF MALA...
NAH, HE'S ALWAYS THAT WAY... IT'S ONE OF THE REASONS SHE DID RUN OFF.
DO YOU THINK THEY'LL GET BACK TOGETHER?
I SURE HOPE SO. OTHERWISE HE'S OUR RESPONSIBILITY, AND I DON'T THINK I CAN TAKE HIM FOR TOO MUCH LONGER.
AAWOOOWWAH!
WH-WHAT'S THAT NOISE?
OH, NOTHING- JUST VLADEK...
HE'S MOANING IN HIS SLEEP AGAIN. WHEN I WAS A KID I THOUGHT THAT WAS THE NOISE ALL GROWN-UPS MADE WHILE THEY SLEPT.
AWOOO-
SIGH. IT'S SO PEACEFUL HERE AT NIGHT. IT'S ALMOST IMPOSSIBLE TO BELIEVE AUSCHWITZ EVER HAPPENED.
UH-HUH. OUCH!
SLAP
BUT THESE DAMN BUGS ARE EATING ME ALIVE!
ME TOO.
PSHT
C'MON. LET'S GO INSIDE AND READ... IT'S GETTING KINDA CHILLY OUT ANYWAY.

CHAPTER THREE

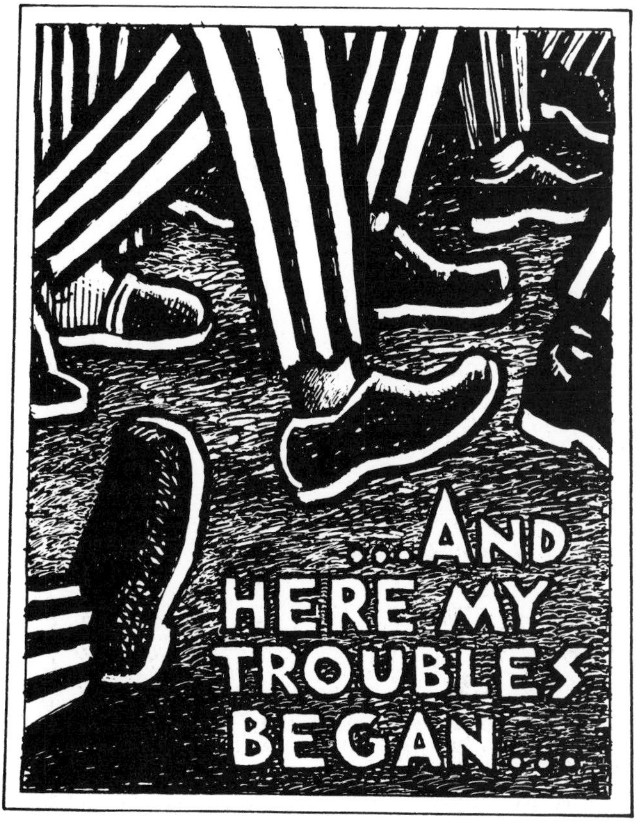
...AND HERE MY TROUBLES BEGAN...

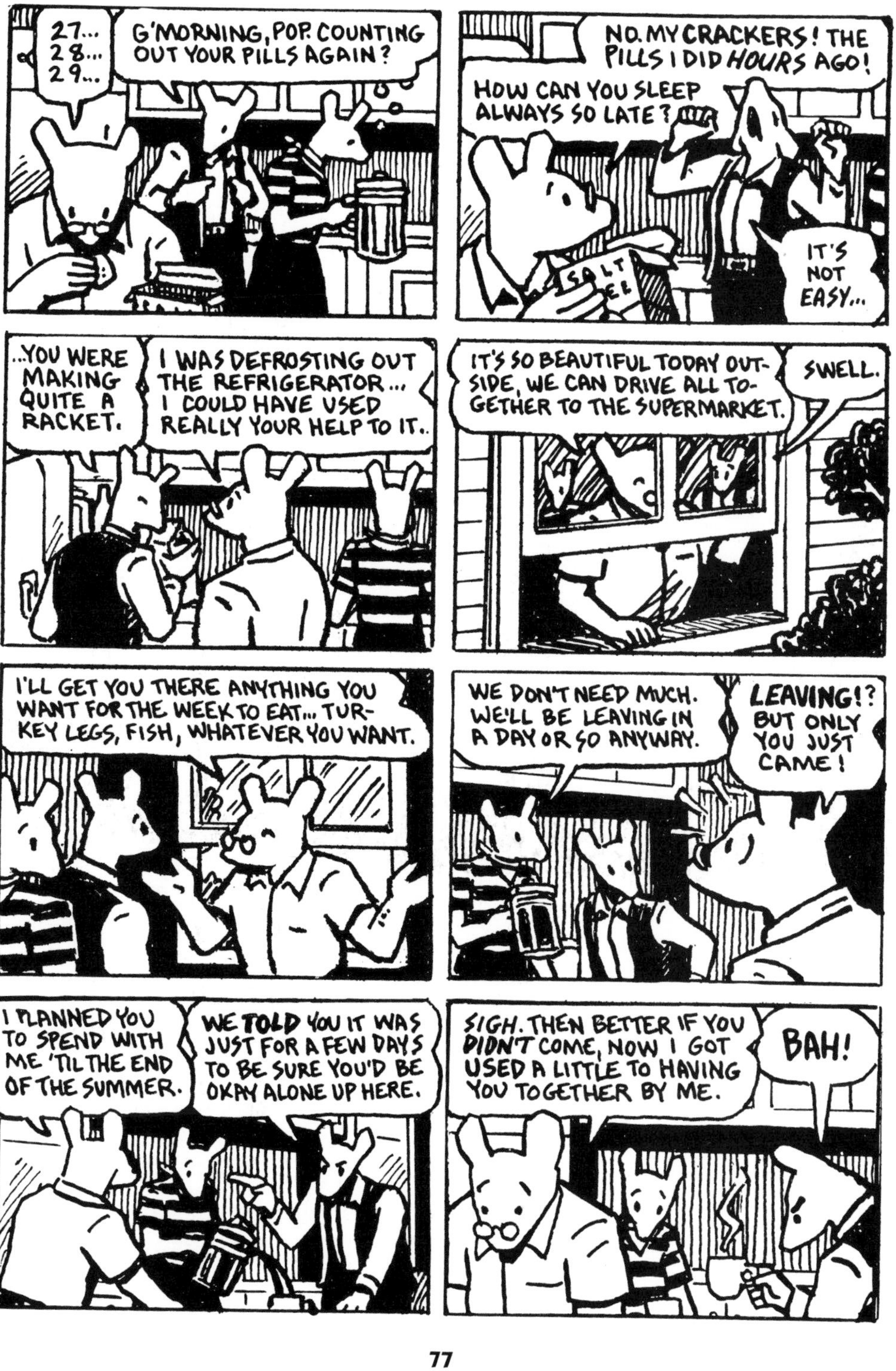
27... 28... 29...
G'MORNING, POP. COUNTING OUT YOUR PILLS AGAIN?
NO. MY CRACKERS! THE PILLS I DID HOURS AGO!
HOW CAN YOU SLEEP ALWAYS SO LATE?
IT'S NOT EASY...
SALT
...YOU WERE MAKING QUITE A RACKET.
I WAS DEFROSTING OUT THE REFRIGERATOR... I COULD HAVE USED REALLY YOUR HELP TO IT..
IT'S SO BEAUTIFUL TODAY OUTSIDE, WE CAN DRIVE ALL TOGETHER TO THE SUPERMARKET.
SWELL.
I'LL GET YOU THERE ANYTHING YOU WANT FOR THE WEEK TO EAT... TURKEY LEGS, FISH, WHATEVER YOU WANT.
WE DON'T NEED MUCH. WE'LL BE LEAVING IN A DAY OR SO ANYWAY.
LEAVING!? BUT ONLY YOU JUST CAME!
I PLANNED YOU TO SPEND WITH ME 'TIL THE END OF THE SUMMER.
WE TOLD YOU IT WAS JUST FOR A FEW DAYS TO BE SURE YOU'D BE OKAY ALONE UP HERE.
SIGH. THEN BETTER IF YOU DIDN'T COME, NOW I GOT USED A LITTLE TO HAVING YOU TOGETHER BY ME.
BAH!

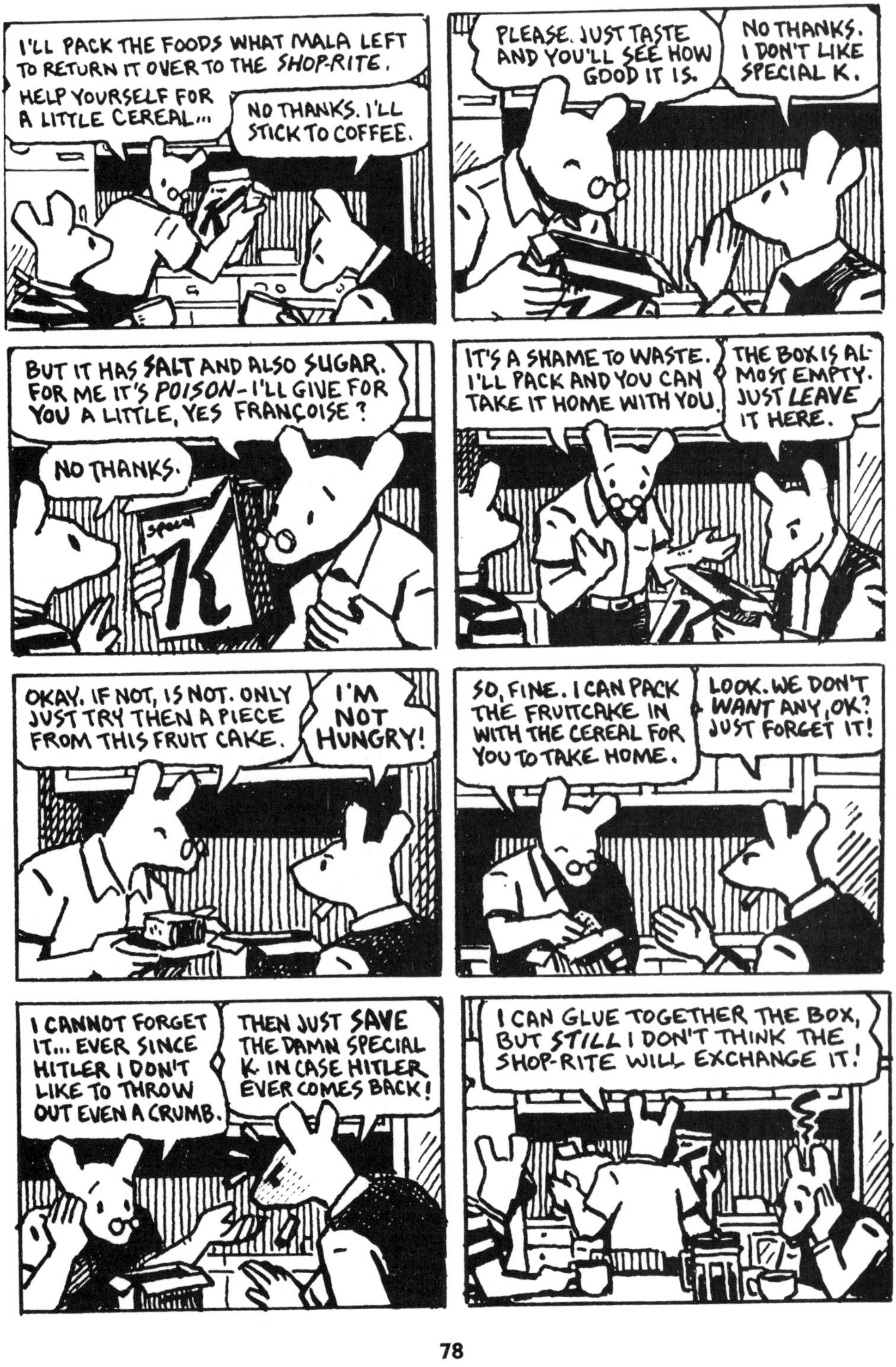
I'LL PACK THE FOODS WHAT MALA LEFT TO RETURN IT OVER TO THE SHOP-RITE.
HELP YOURSELF FOR A LITTLE CEREAL...
NO THANKS. I'LL STICK TO COFFEE.
PLEASE. JUST TASTE AND YOU'LL SEE HOW GOOD IT IS.
NO THANKS. I DON'T LIKE SPECIAL K.
BUT IT HAS SALT AND ALSO SUGAR. FOR ME IT'S POISON - I'LL GIVE FOR YOU A LITTLE, YES FRANÇOISE?
NO THANKS.
IT'S A SHAME TO WASTE. I'LL PACK AND YOU CAN TAKE IT HOME WITH YOU.
THE BOX IS ALMOST EMPTY. JUST LEAVE IT HERE.
OKAY. IF NOT, IS NOT. ONLY JUST TRY THEN A PIECE FROM THIS FRUIT CAKE.
I'M NOT HUNGRY!
SO, FINE. I CAN PACK THE FRUITCAKE IN WITH THE CEREAL FOR YOU TO TAKE HOME.
LOOK. WE DON'T WANT ANY, OK? JUST FORGET IT!
I CANNOT FORGET IT... EVER SINCE HITLER I DON'T LIKE TO THROW OUT EVEN A CRUMB.
THEN JUST SAVE THE DAMN SPECIAL K IN CASE HITLER EVER COMES BACK!
I CAN GLUE TOGETHER THE BOX, BUT STILL I DON'T THINK THE SHOP-RITE WILL EXCHANGE IT!

And so...

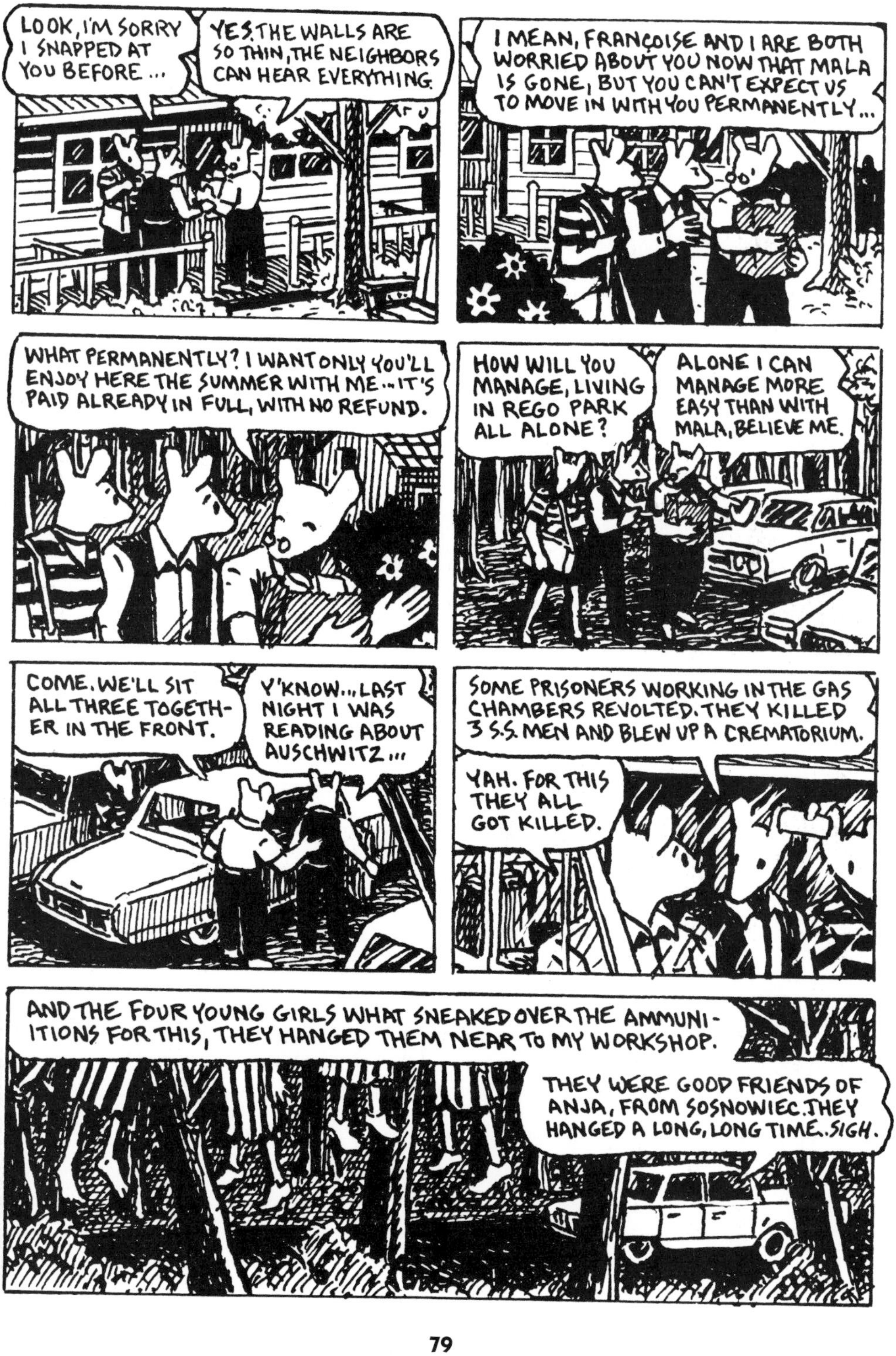
LOOK, I'M SORRY I SNAPPED AT YOU BEFORE...
YES. THE WALLS ARE SO THIN, THE NEIGHBORS CAN HEAR EVERYTHING.
I MEAN, FRANÇOISE AND I ARE BOTH WORRIED ABOUT YOU NOW THAT MALA IS GONE, BUT YOU CAN'T EXPECT US TO MOVE IN WITH YOU PERMANENTLY...
WHAT PERMANENTLY? I WANT ONLY YOU'LL ENJOY HERE THE SUMMER WITH ME.. IT'S PAID ALREADY IN FULL, WITH NO REFUND.
HOW WILL YOU MANAGE, LIVING IN REGO PARK ALL ALONE?
ALONE I CAN MANAGE MORE EASY THAN WITH MALA, BELIEVE ME.
COME. WE'LL SIT ALL THREE TOGETHER IN THE FRONT.
Y'KNOW... LAST NIGHT I WAS READING ABOUT AUSCHWITZ...
SOME PRISONERS WORKING IN THE GAS CHAMBERS REVOLTED. THEY KILLED 3 S.S. MEN AND BLEW UP A CREMATORIUM.
YAH. FOR THIS THEY ALL GOT KILLED.
AND THE FOUR YOUNG GIRLS WHAT SNEAKED OVER THE AMMUNITIONS FOR THIS, THEY HANGED THEM NEAR TO MY WORKSHOP.
THEY WERE GOOD FRIENDS OF ANJA, FROM SOSNOWIEC. THEY HANGED A LONG, LONG TIME.. SIGH.

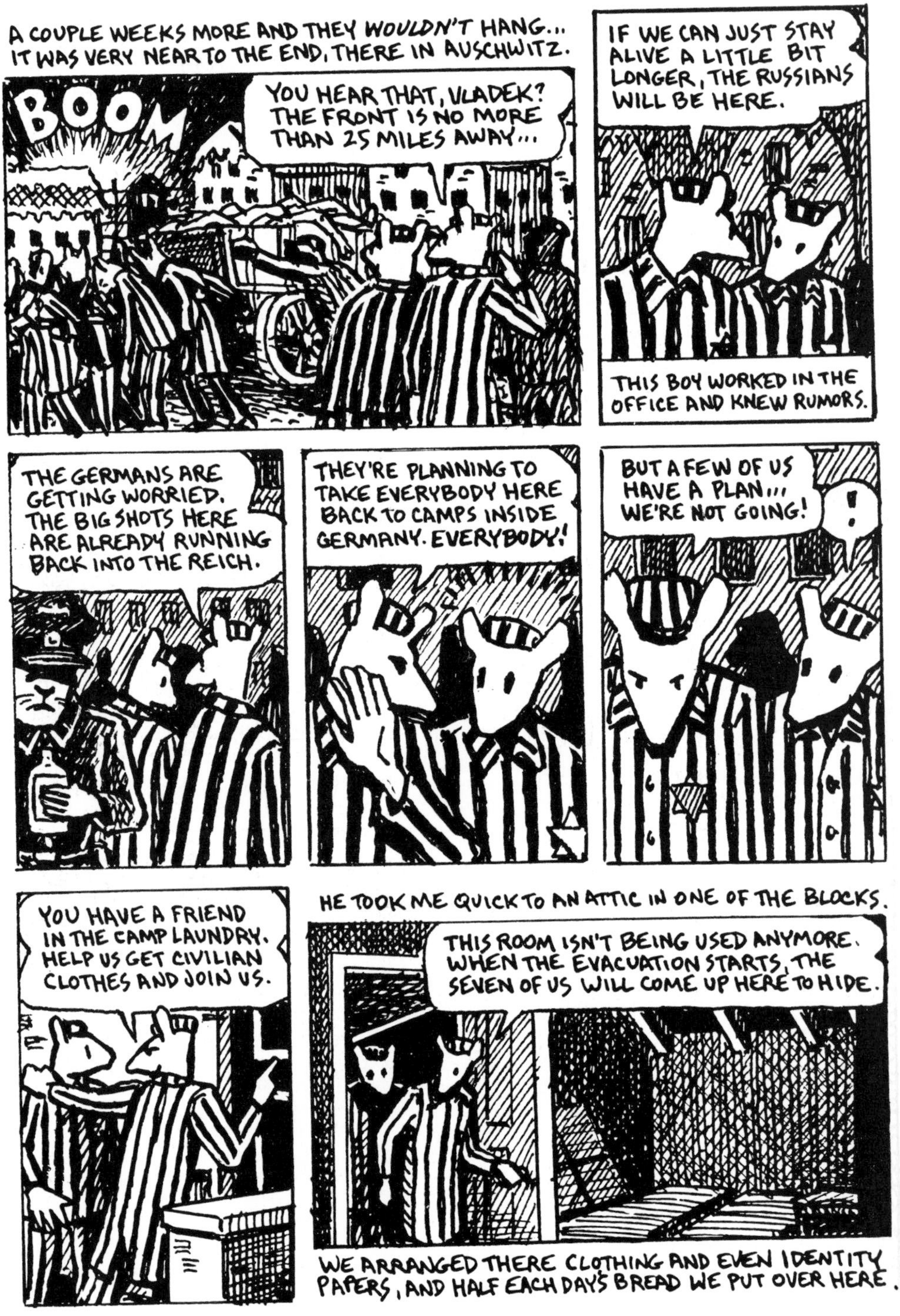
A COUPLE WEEKS MORE AND THEY WOULDN'T HANG... IT WAS VERY NEAR TO THE END, THERE IN AUSCHWITZ.
BOOM
YOU HEAR THAT, VLADEK? THE FRONT IS NO MORE THAN 25 MILES AWAY...
IF WE CAN JUST STAY ALIVE A LITTLE BIT LONGER, THE RUSSIANS WILL BE HERE.
THIS BOY WORKED IN THE OFFICE AND KNEW RUMORS.
THE GERMANS ARE GETTING WORRIED. THE BIG SHOTS HERE ARE ALREADY RUNNING BACK INTO THE REICH.
THEY'RE PLANNING TO TAKE EVERYBODY HERE BACK TO CAMPS INSIDE GERMANY. EVERYBODY!
BUT A FEW OF US HAVE A PLAN... WE'RE NOT GOING!
!
YOU HAVE A FRIEND IN THE CAMP LAUNDRY. HELP US GET CIVILIAN CLOTHES AND JOIN US.
HE TOOK ME QUICK TO AN ATTIC IN ONE OF THE BLOCKS.
THIS ROOM ISN'T BEING USED ANYMORE. WHEN THE EVACUATION STARTS, THE SEVEN OF US WILL COME UP HERE TO HIDE.
WE ARRANGED THERE CLOTHING AND EVEN IDENTITY PAPERS, AND HALF EACH DAY'S BREAD WE PUT OVER HERE.

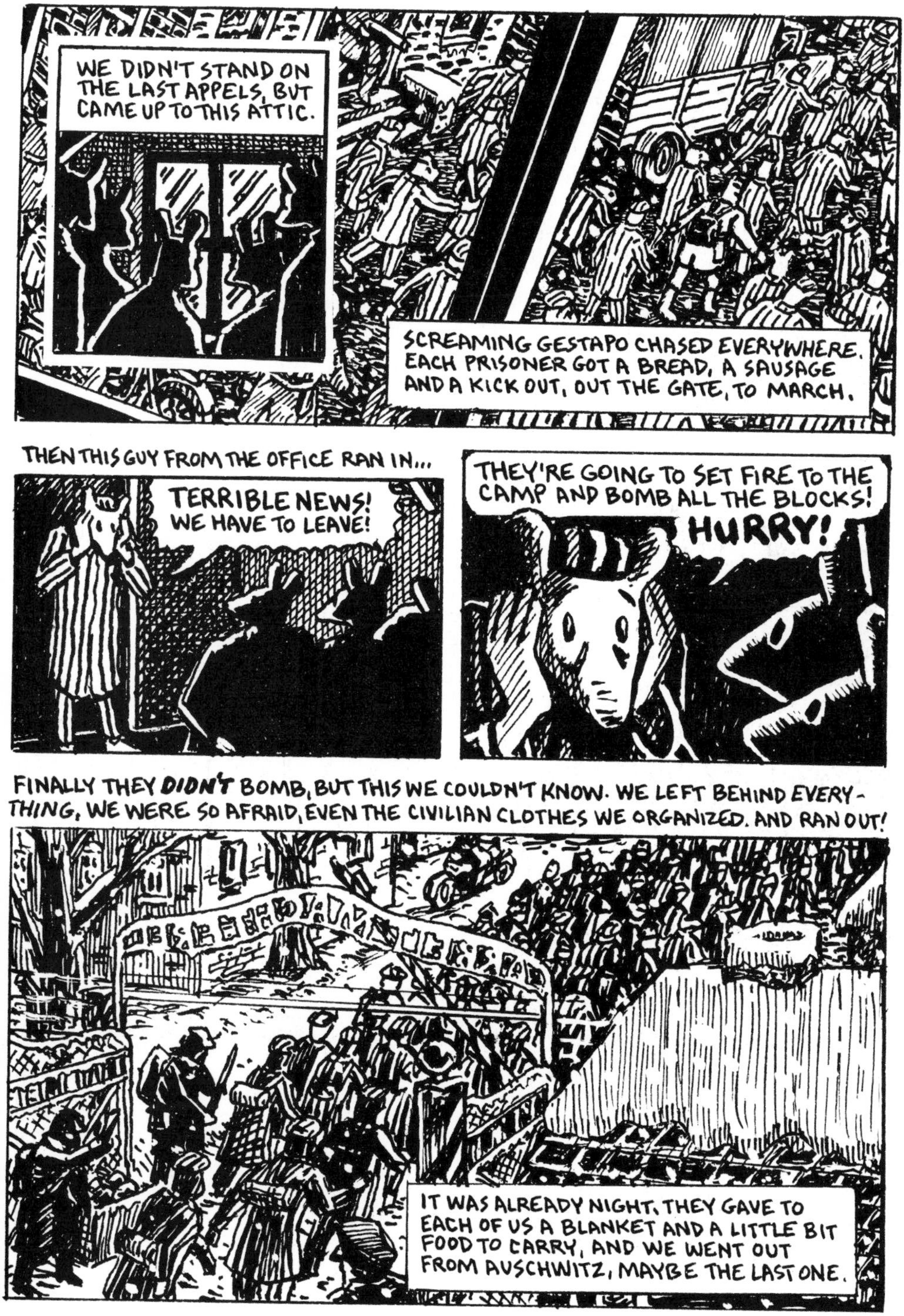
WE DIDN'T STAND ON THE LAST APPELS, BUT CAME UP TO THIS ATTIC.
SCREAMING GESTAPO CHASED EVERYWHERE. EACH PRISONER GOT A BREAD, A SAUSAGE AND A KICK OUT, OUT THE GATE, TO MARCH.
THEN THIS GUY FROM THE OFFICE RAN IN...
TERRIBLE NEWS! WE HAVE TO LEAVE!
THEY'RE GOING TO SET FIRE TO THE CAMP AND BOMB ALL THE BLOCKS!
HURRY!
FINALLY THEY *DIDN'T* BOMB, BUT THIS WE COULDN'T KNOW. WE LEFT BEHIND EVERY-THING, WE WERE SO AFRAID, EVEN THE CIVILIAN CLOTHES WE ORGANIZED. AND RAN OUT!
IT WAS ALREADY NIGHT. THEY GAVE TO EACH OF US A BLANKET AND A LITTLE BIT FOOD TO CARRY, AND WE WENT OUT FROM AUSCHWITZ, MAYBE THE LAST ONE.

ALL NIGHT I HEARD SHOOTING. HE WHO GOT TIRED, WHO CAN'T WALK SO FAST, THEY SHOT.

THE MORE WE WALKED, THE MORE I HEARD SHOOTING...

AND IN THE DAYLIGHT, FAR AHEAD, I SAW IT.

SOMEBODY IS JUMPING, TURNING, ROLLING 25 OR 35 TIMES AROUND. AND STOPS.

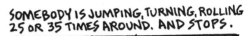

"OH," I SAID. "THEY MAYBE KILLED THERE A DOG."

WHEN I WAS A BOY OUR NEIGHBOR HAD A DOG WHAT GOT MAD AND WAS BITING.

THE NEIGHBOR CAME OUT WITH A RIFLE AND SHOT.

THE DOG WAS ROLLING SO, AROUND AND AROUND, KICKING, BEFORE HE LAY QUIET.

AND NOW I THOUGHT: "HOW AMAZING IT IS THAT A HUMAN BEING REACTS THE SAME LIKE THIS NEIGHBOR'S DOG."

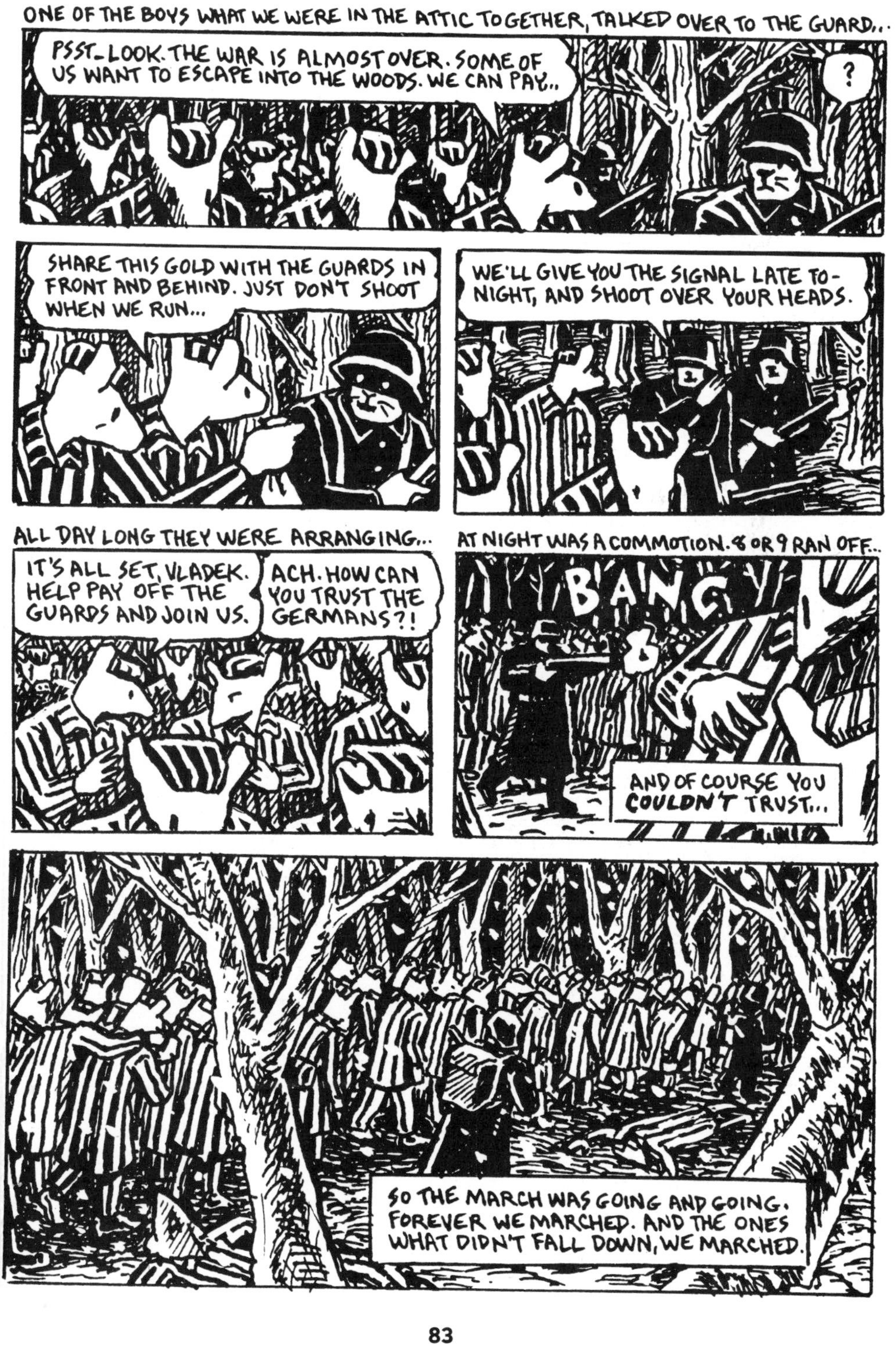

ONE OF THE BOYS WHAT WE WERE IN THE ATTIC TOGETHER, TALKED OVER TO THE GUARD...
PSST_LOOK. THE WAR IS ALMOST OVER. SOME OF US WANT TO ESCAPE INTO THE WOODS. WE CAN PAY..
?
SHARE THIS GOLD WITH THE GUARDS IN FRONT AND BEHIND. JUST DON'T SHOOT WHEN WE RUN...
WE'LL GIVE YOU THE SIGNAL LATE TO-NIGHT, AND SHOOT OVER YOUR HEADS.
ALL DAY LONG THEY WERE ARRANGING...
IT'S ALL SET, VLADEK. HELP PAY OFF THE GUARDS AND JOIN US.
ACH. HOW CAN YOU TRUST THE GERMANS?!
AT NIGHT WAS A COMMOTION. 8 OR 9 RAN OFF...
BANG
AND OF COURSE YOU COULDN'T TRUST...
SO THE MARCH WAS GOING AND GOING. FOREVER WE MARCHED. AND THE ONES WHAT DIDN'T FALL DOWN, WE MARCHED.

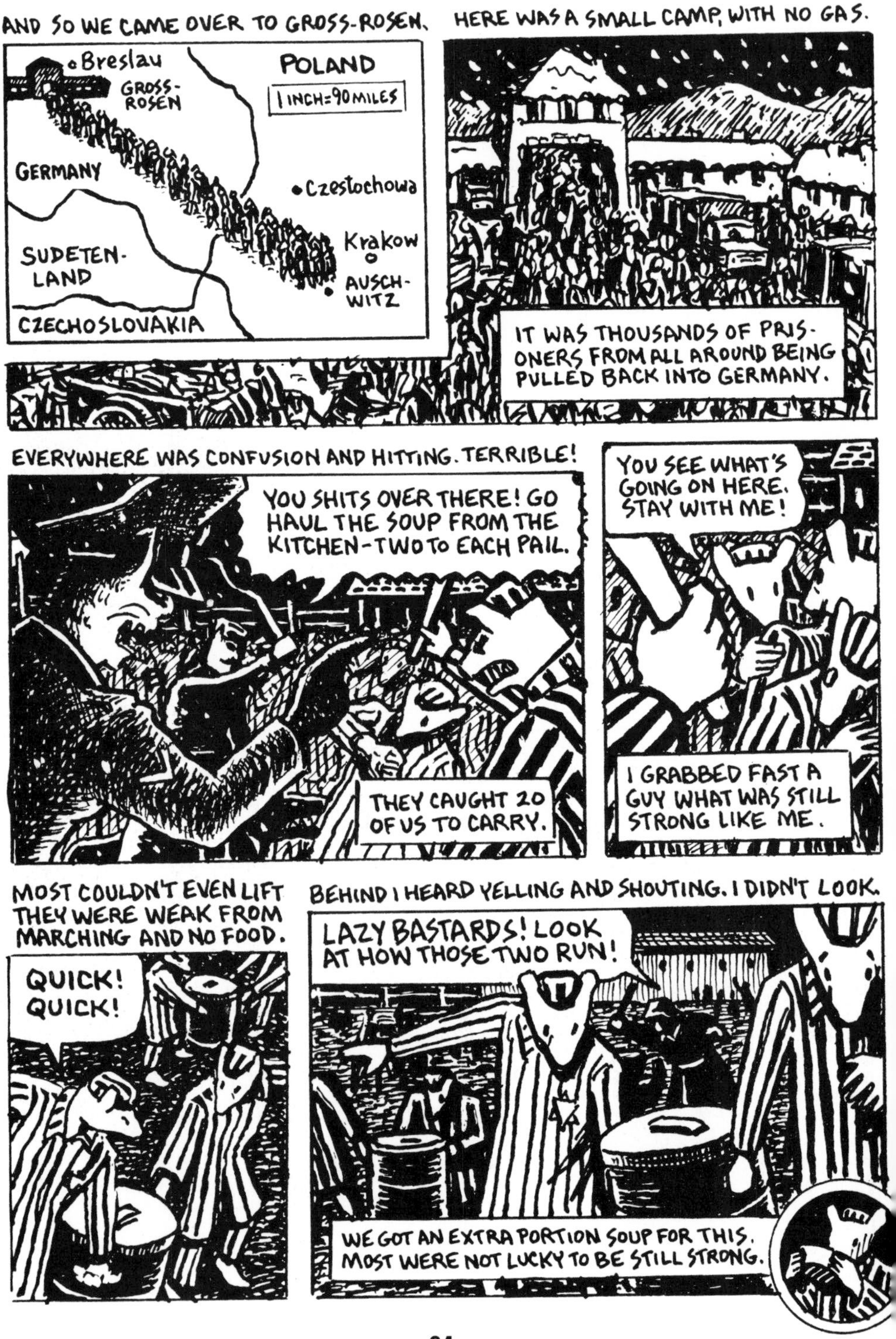
AND SO WE CAME OVER TO GROSS-ROSEN.
Breslau
GROSS-ROSEN
POLAND
1 INCH=90 MILES
GERMANY
Czestochowa
SUDETEN-LAND
Krakow
AUSCH-WITZ
CZECHOSLOVAKIA
HERE WAS A SMALL CAMP, WITH NO GAS.
IT WAS THOUSANDS OF PRISONERS FROM ALL AROUND BEING PULLED BACK INTO GERMANY.
EVERYWHERE WAS CONFUSION AND HITTING. TERRIBLE!
YOU SHITS OVER THERE! GO HAUL THE SOUP FROM THE KITCHEN-TWO TO EACH PAIL.
THEY CAUGHT 20 OF US TO CARRY.
YOU SEE WHAT'S GOING ON HERE. STAY WITH ME!
I GRABBED FAST A GUY WHAT WAS STILL STRONG LIKE ME.
MOST COULDN'T EVEN LIFT THEY WERE WEAK FROM MARCHING AND NO FOOD.
QUICK! QUICK!
BEHIND I HEARD YELLING AND SHOUTING. I DIDN'T LOOK.
LAZY BASTARDS! LOOK AT HOW THOSE TWO RUN!
WE GOT AN EXTRA PORTION SOUP FOR THIS. MOST WERE NOT LUCKY TO BE STILL STRONG.

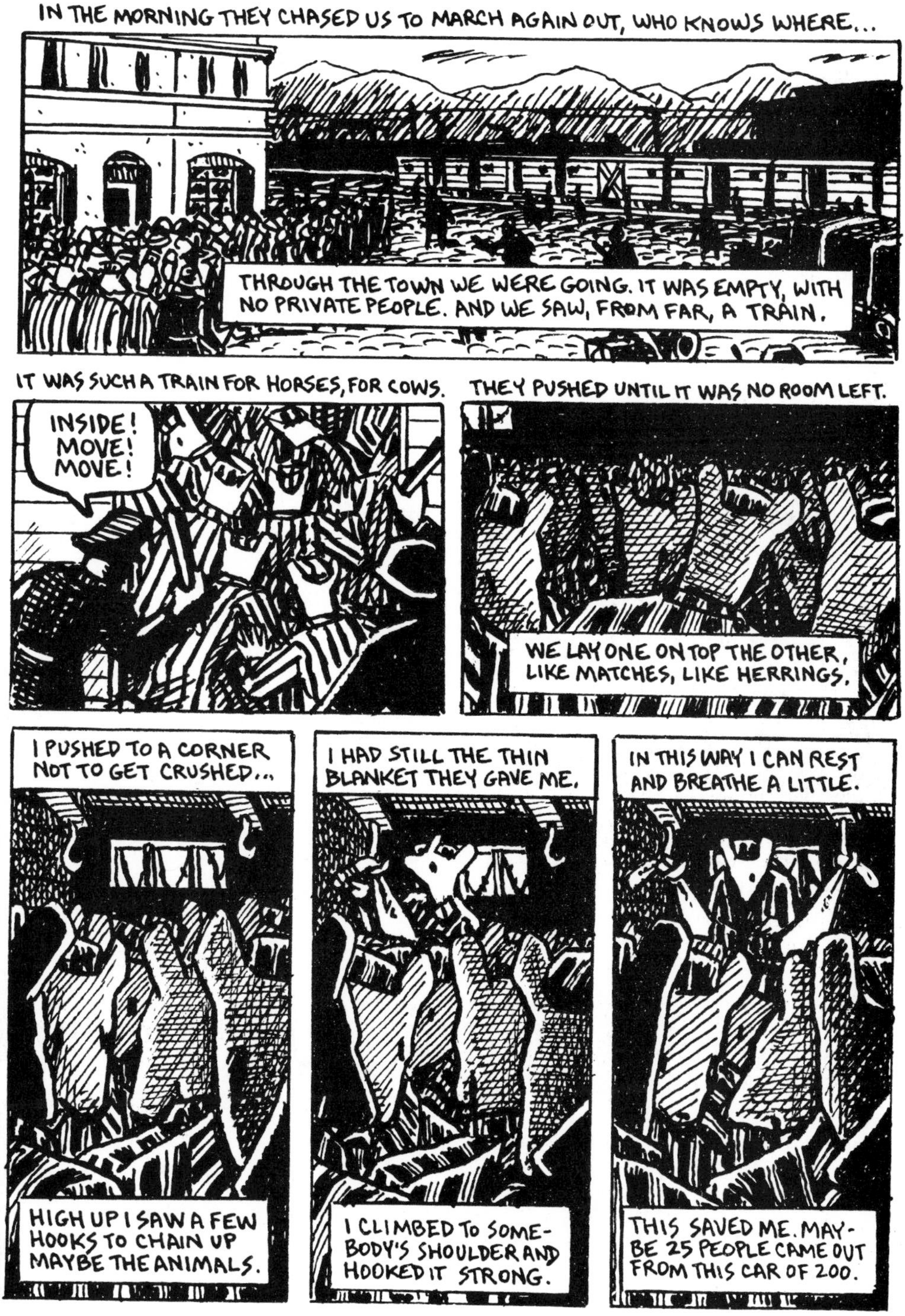
IN THE MORNING THEY CHASED US TO MARCH AGAIN OUT, WHO KNOWS WHERE...
THROUGH THE TOWN WE WERE GOING. IT WAS EMPTY, WITH NO PRIVATE PEOPLE. AND WE SAW, FROM FAR, A TRAIN.
IT WAS SUCH A TRAIN FOR HORSES, FOR COWS.
INSIDE! MOVE! MOVE!
THEY PUSHED UNTIL IT WAS NO ROOM LEFT.
WE LAY ONE ON TOP THE OTHER, LIKE MATCHES, LIKE HERRINGS.
I PUSHED TO A CORNER NOT TO GET CRUSHED...
HIGH UP I SAW A FEW HOOKS TO CHAIN UP MAYBE THE ANIMALS.
I HAD STILL THE THIN BLANKET THEY GAVE ME.
I CLIMBED TO SOMEBODY'S SHOULDER AND HOOKED IT STRONG.
IN THIS WAY I CAN REST AND BREATHE A LITTLE.
THIS SAVED ME. MAYBE 25 PEOPLE CAME OUT FROM THIS CAR OF 200.

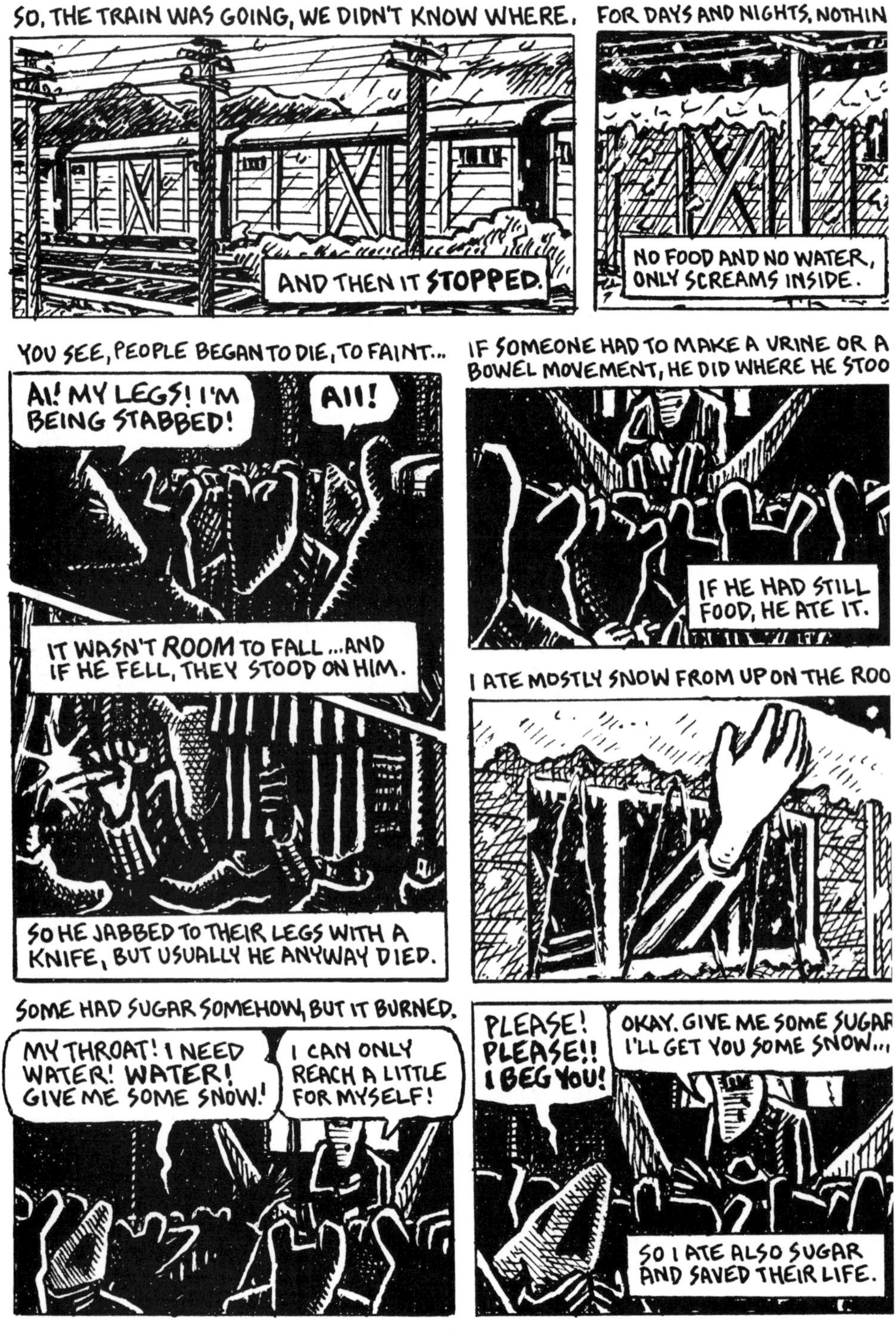
SO, THE TRAIN WAS GOING, WE DIDN'T KNOW WHERE.
AND THEN IT STOPPED.
FOR DAYS AND NIGHTS, NOTHIN
NO FOOD AND NO WATER, ONLY SCREAMS INSIDE.
YOU SEE, PEOPLE BEGAN TO DIE, TO FAINT...
AI! MY LEGS! I'M BEING STABBED!
AII!
IT WASN'T ROOM TO FALL ...AND IF HE FELL, THEY STOOD ON HIM.
SO HE JABBED TO THEIR LEGS WITH A KNIFE, BUT USUALLY HE ANYWAY DIED.
IF SOMEONE HAD TO MAKE A URINE OR A BOWEL MOVEMENT, HE DID WHERE HE STOO
IF HE HAD STILL FOOD, HE ATE IT.
I ATE MOSTLY SNOW FROM UP ON THE ROO
SOME HAD SUGAR SOMEHOW, BUT IT BURNED.
MY THROAT! I NEED WATER! WATER! GIVE ME SOME SNOW!
I CAN ONLY REACH A LITTLE FOR MYSELF!
PLEASE! PLEASE!! I BEG YOU!
OKAY. GIVE ME SOME SUGAR I'LL GET YOU SOME SNOW...
SO I ATE ALSO SUGAR AND SAVED THEIR LIFE.

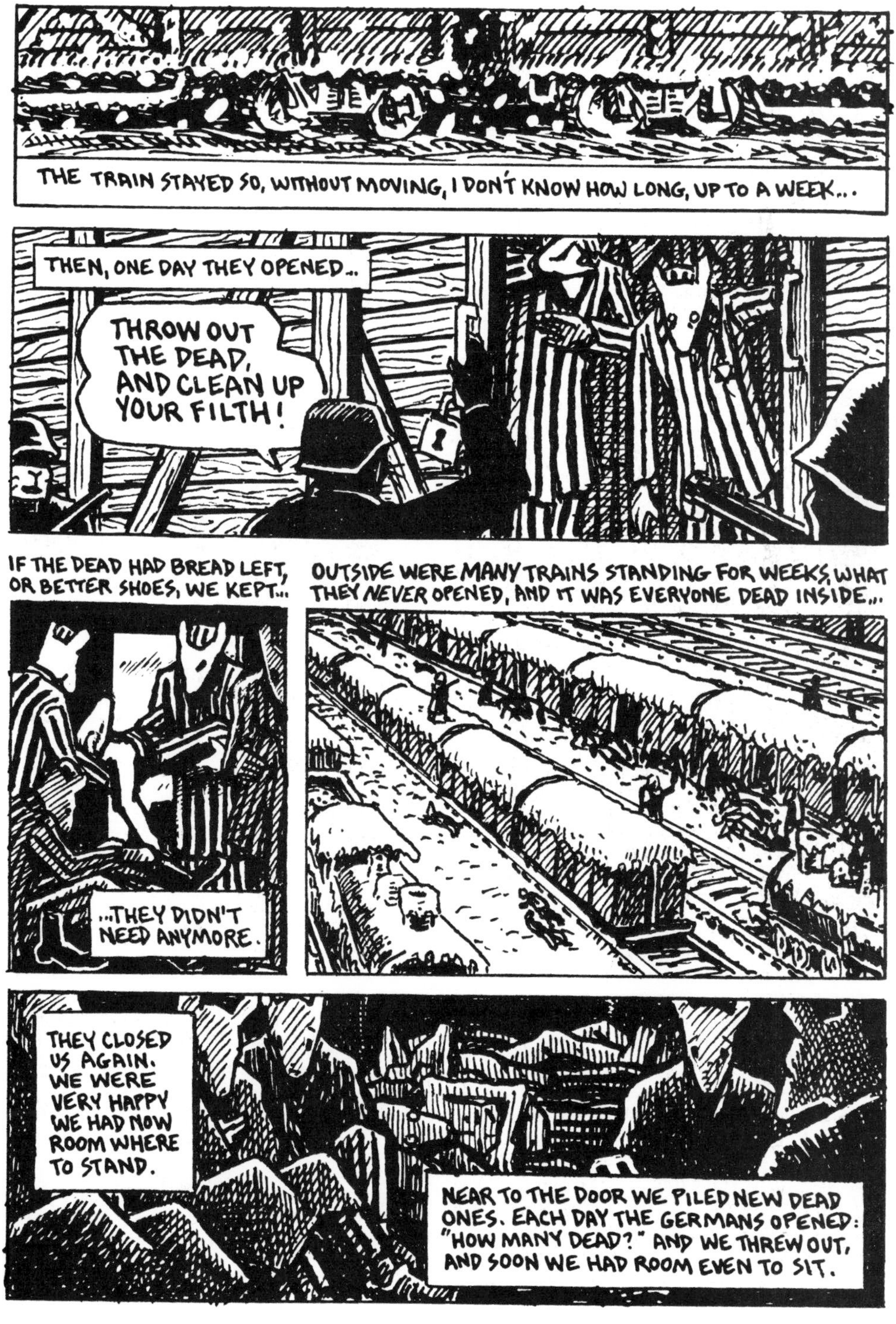
THE TRAIN STAYED SO, WITHOUT MOVING, I DON'T KNOW HOW LONG, UP TO A WEEK...
THEN, ONE DAY THEY OPENED...
THROW OUT THE DEAD, AND CLEAN UP YOUR FILTH!
IF THE DEAD HAD BREAD LEFT, OR BETTER SHOES, WE KEPT...
...THEY DIDN'T NEED ANYMORE.
OUTSIDE WERE MANY TRAINS STANDING FOR WEEKS, WHAT THEY NEVER OPENED, AND IT WAS EVERYONE DEAD INSIDE...
THEY CLOSED US AGAIN. WE WERE VERY HAPPY WE HAD NOW ROOM WHERE TO STAND.
NEAR TO THE DOOR WE PILED NEW DEAD ONES. EACH DAY THE GERMANS OPENED: "HOW MANY DEAD?" AND WE THREW OUT, AND SOON WE HAD ROOM EVEN TO SIT.

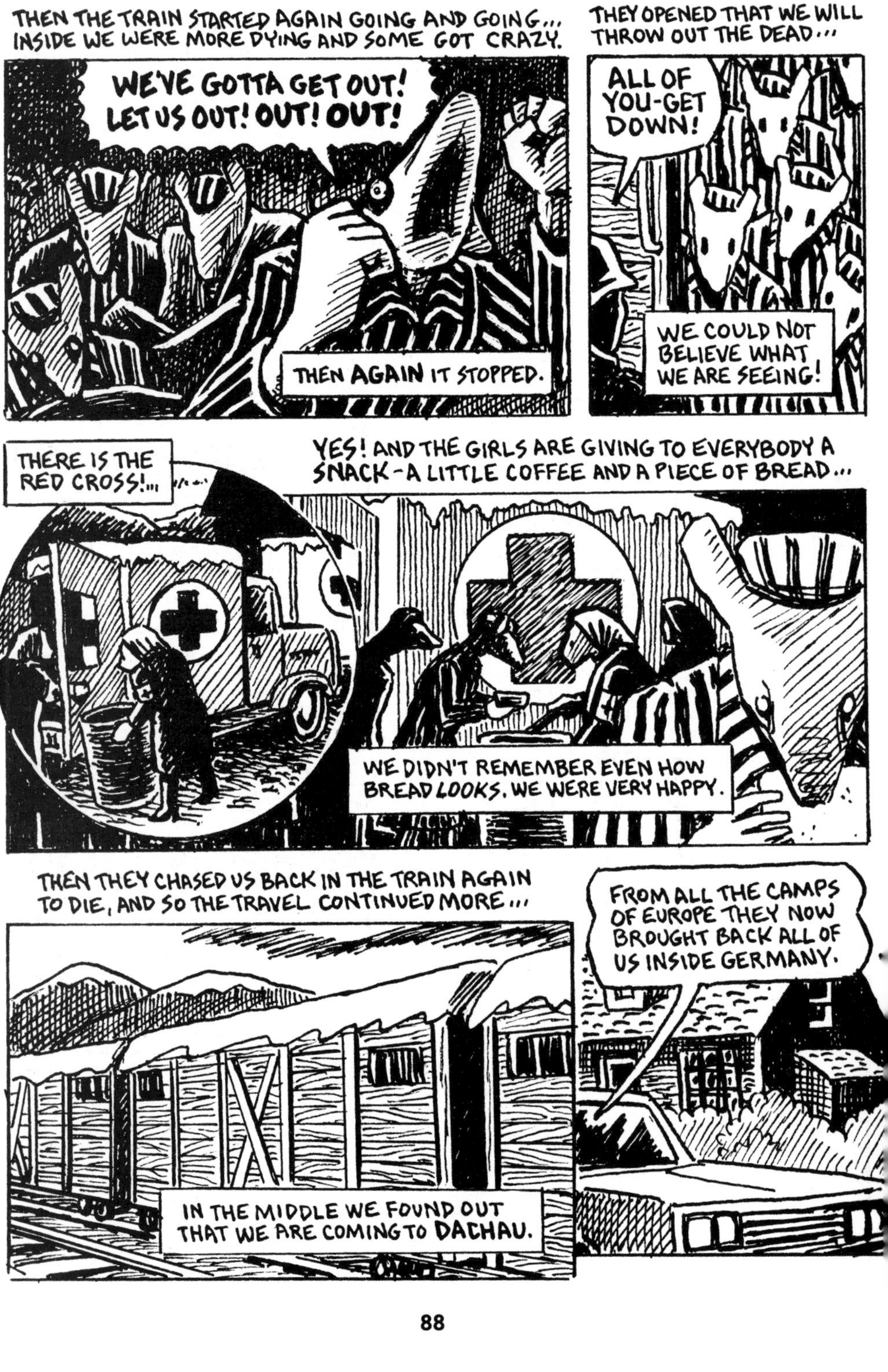
THEN THE TRAIN STARTED AGAIN GOING AND GOING... INSIDE WE WERE MORE DYING AND SOME GOT CRAZY.
WE'VE GOTTA GET OUT! LET US OUT! OUT! OUT!
THEN AGAIN IT STOPPED.
THEY OPENED THAT WE WILL THROW OUT THE DEAD...
ALL OF YOU-GET DOWN!
WE COULD NOT BELIEVE WHAT WE ARE SEEING!
THERE IS THE RED CROSS!...
YES! AND THE GIRLS ARE GIVING TO EVERYBODY A SNACK-A LITTLE COFFEE AND A PIECE OF BREAD...
WE DIDN'T REMEMBER EVEN HOW BREAD LOOKS. WE WERE VERY HAPPY.
THEN THEY CHASED US BACK IN THE TRAIN AGAIN TO DIE, AND SO THE TRAVEL CONTINUED MORE...
IN THE MIDDLE WE FOUND OUT THAT WE ARE COMING TO DACHAU.
FROM ALL THE CAMPS OF EUROPE THEY NOW BROUGHT BACK ALL OF US INSIDE GERMANY.

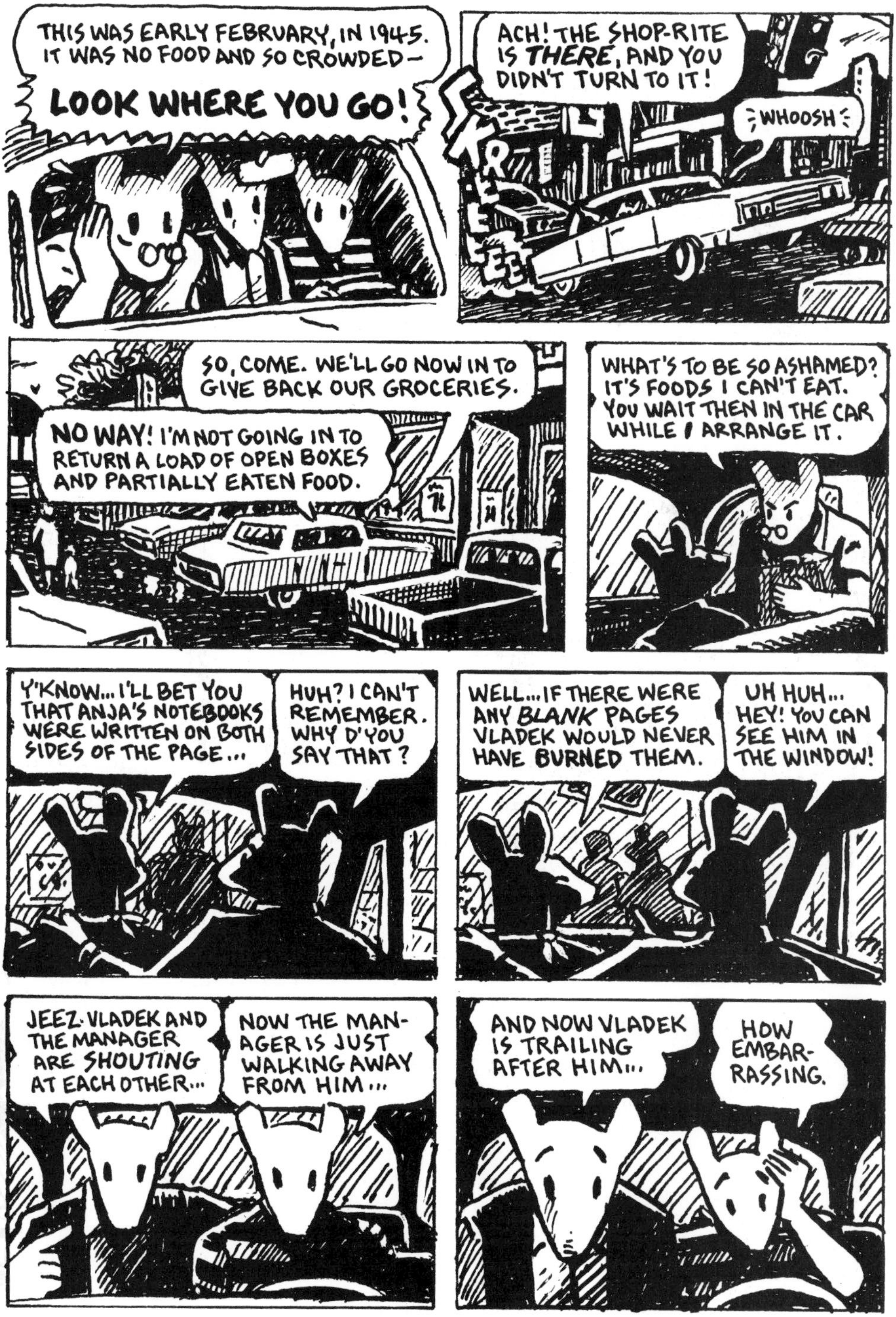
THIS WAS EARLY FEBRUARY, IN 1945. IT WAS NO FOOD AND SO CROWDED—
LOOK WHERE YOU GO!
ACH! THE SHOP-RITE IS THERE, AND YOU DIDN'T TURN TO IT!
WHOOSH
SO, COME. WE'LL GO NOW IN TO GIVE BACK OUR GROCERIES.
NO WAY! I'M NOT GOING IN TO RETURN A LOAD OF OPEN BOXES AND PARTIALLY EATEN FOOD.
WHAT'S TO BE SO ASHAMED? IT'S FOODS I CAN'T EAT. YOU WAIT THEN IN THE CAR WHILE I ARRANGE IT.
Y'KNOW... I'LL BET YOU THAT ANJA'S NOTEBOOKS WERE WRITTEN ON BOTH SIDES OF THE PAGE...
HUH? I CAN'T REMEMBER. WHY D'YOU SAY THAT?
WELL... IF THERE WERE ANY BLANK PAGES VLADEK WOULD NEVER HAVE BURNED THEM.
UH HUH... HEY! YOU CAN SEE HIM IN THE WINDOW!
JEEZ. VLADEK AND THE MANAGER ARE SHOUTING AT EACH OTHER...
NOW THE MANAGER IS JUST WALKING AWAY FROM HIM...
AND NOW VLADEK IS TRAILING AFTER HIM...
HOW EMBARRASSING.

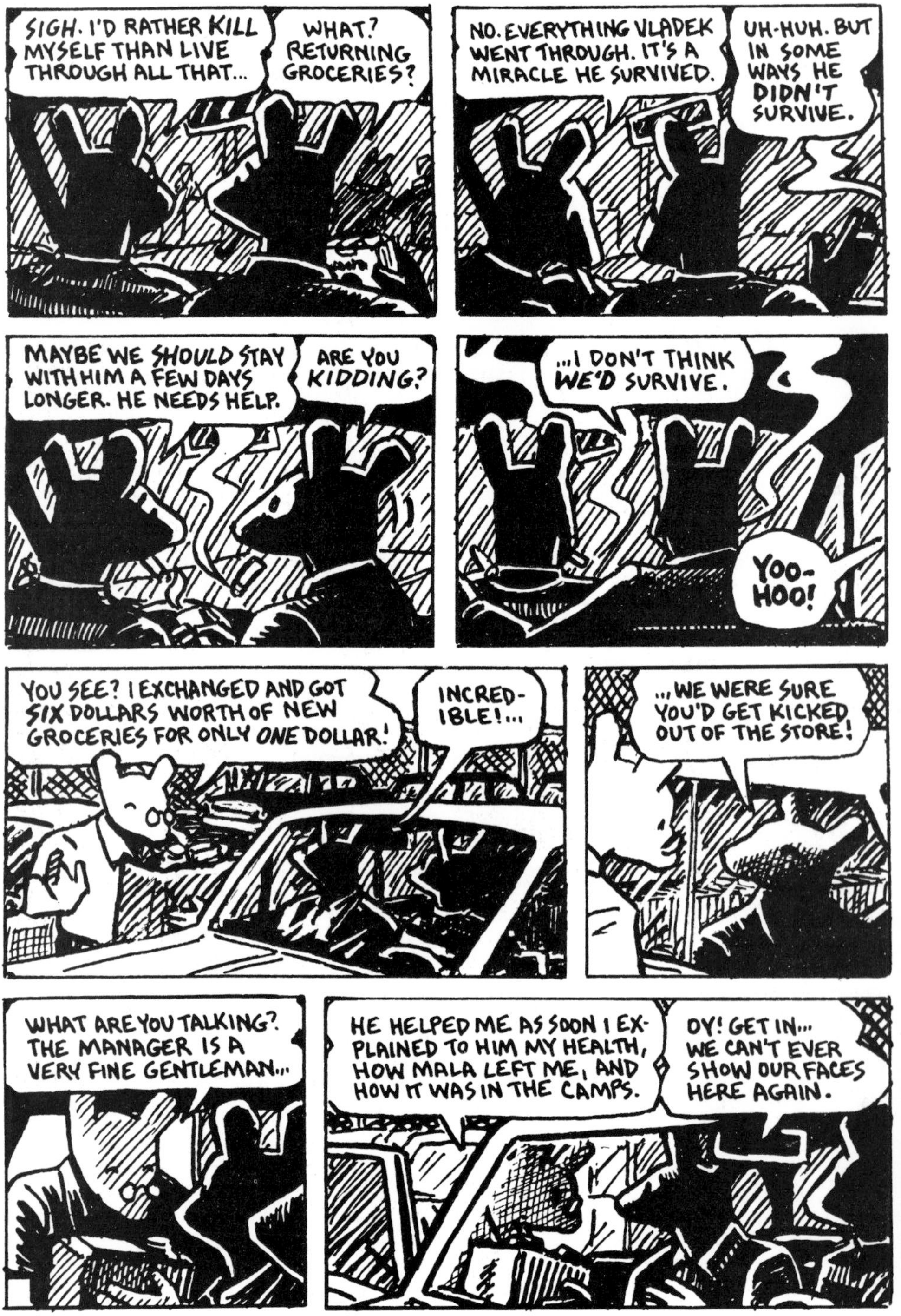

SIGH. I'D RATHER KILL MYSELF THAN LIVE THROUGH ALL THAT...
WHAT? RETURNING GROCERIES?
NO. EVERYTHING VLADEK WENT THROUGH. IT'S A MIRACLE HE SURVIVED.
UH-HUH. BUT IN SOME WAYS HE DIDN'T SURVIVE.
MAYBE WE SHOULD STAY WITH HIM A FEW DAYS LONGER. HE NEEDS HELP.
ARE YOU KIDDING?
...I DON'T THINK WE'D SURVIVE.
YOO-HOO!
YOU SEE? I EXCHANGED AND GOT SIX DOLLARS WORTH OF NEW GROCERIES FOR ONLY ONE DOLLAR!
INCRED-IBLE!...
...WE WERE SURE YOU'D GET KICKED OUT OF THE STORE!
WHAT ARE YOU TALKING? THE MANAGER IS A VERY FINE GENTLEMAN...
HE HELPED ME AS SOON I EX-PLAINED TO HIM MY HEALTH, HOW MALA LEFT ME, AND HOW IT WAS IN THE CAMPS.
OY! GET IN... WE CAN'T EVER SHOW OUR FACES HERE AGAIN.

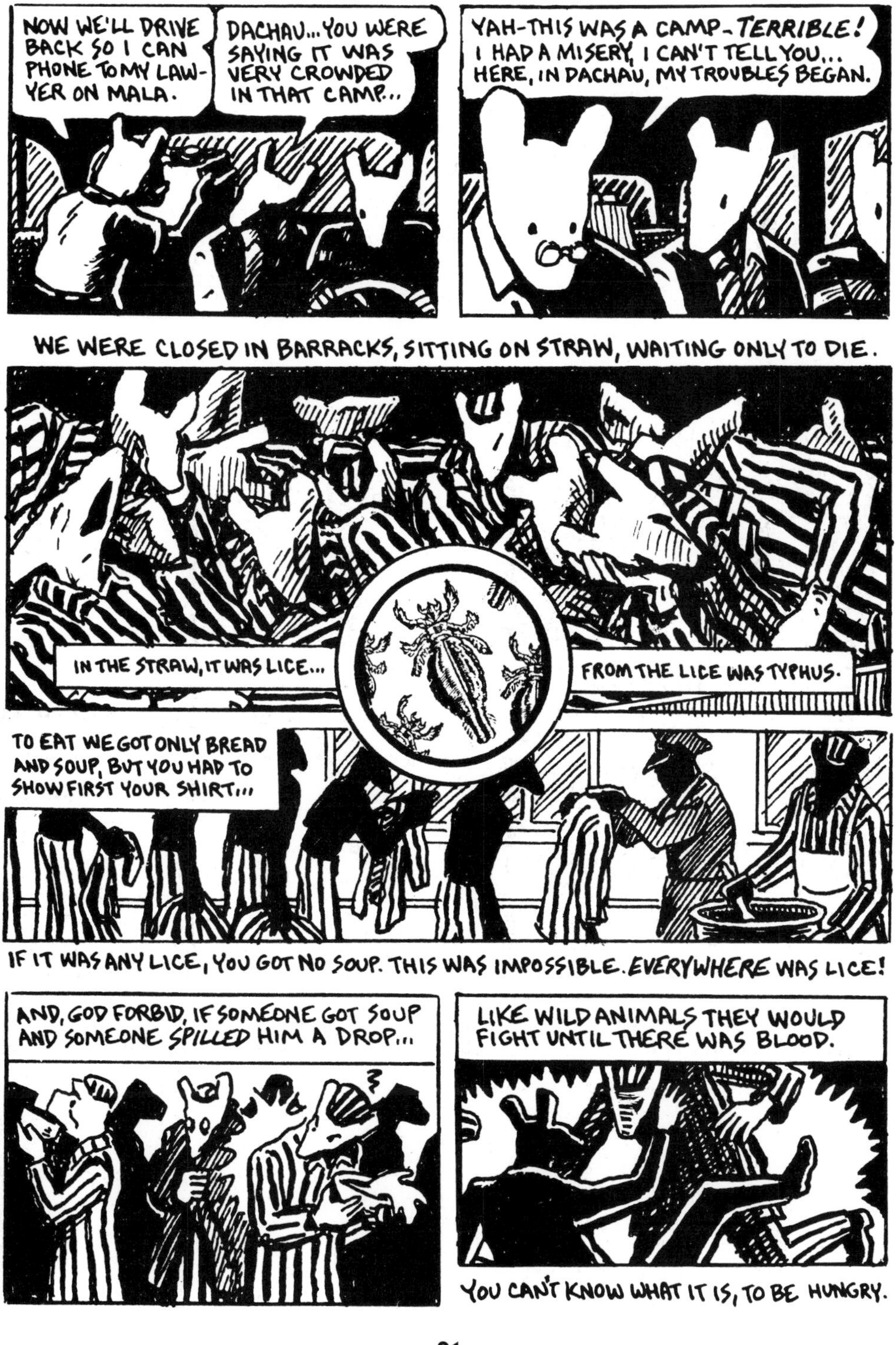
NOW WE'LL DRIVE BACK SO I CAN PHONE TO MY LAWYER ON MALA.
DACHAU... YOU WERE SAYING IT WAS VERY CROWDED IN THAT CAMP...
YAH-THIS WAS A CAMP-TERRIBLE! I HAD A MISERY, I CAN'T TELL YOU... HERE, IN DACHAU, MY TROUBLES BEGAN.
WE WERE CLOSED IN BARRACKS, SITTING ON STRAW, WAITING ONLY TO DIE.
IN THE STRAW, IT WAS LICE...
FROM THE LICE WAS TYPHUS.
TO EAT WE GOT ONLY BREAD AND SOUP, BUT YOU HAD TO SHOW FIRST YOUR SHIRT...
IF IT WAS ANY LICE, YOU GOT NO SOUP. THIS WAS IMPOSSIBLE. EVERYWHERE WAS LICE!
AND, GOD FORBID, IF SOMEONE GOT SOUP AND SOMEONE SPILLED HIM A DROP...
LIKE WILD ANIMALS THEY WOULD FIGHT UNTIL THERE WAS BLOOD.
YOU CAN'T KNOW WHAT IT IS, TO BE HUNGRY.

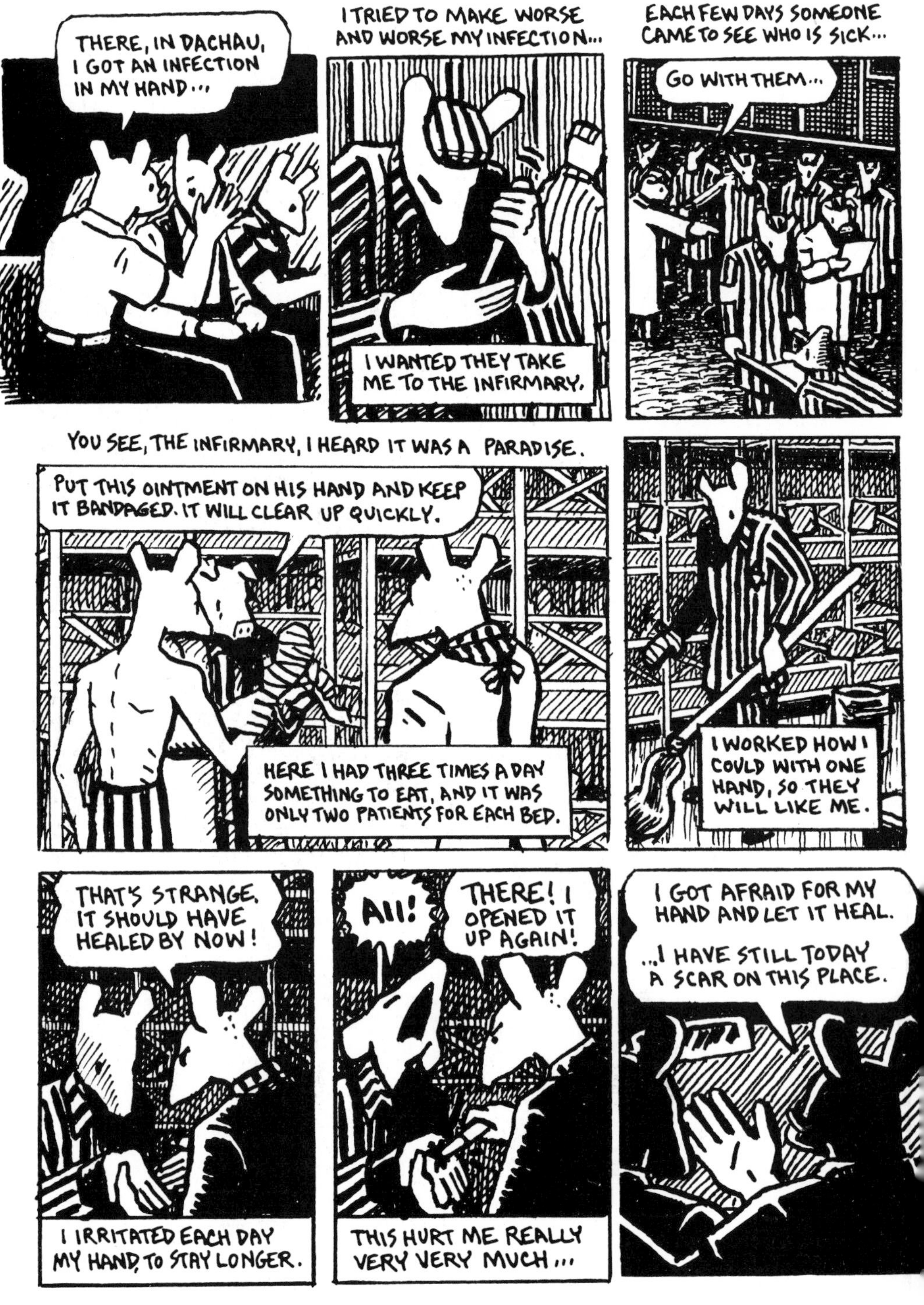
THERE, IN DACHAU, I GOT AN INFECTION IN MY HAND...
I TRIED TO MAKE WORSE AND WORSE MY INFECTION...
I WANTED THEY TAKE ME TO THE INFIRMARY.
EACH FEW DAYS SOMEONE CAME TO SEE WHO IS SICK...
GO WITH THEM...
YOU SEE, THE INFIRMARY, I HEARD IT WAS A PARADISE.
PUT THIS OINTMENT ON HIS HAND AND KEEP IT BANDAGED. IT WILL CLEAR UP QUICKLY.
HERE I HAD THREE TIMES A DAY SOMETHING TO EAT, AND IT WAS ONLY TWO PATIENTS FOR EACH BED.
I WORKED HOW I COULD WITH ONE HAND, SO THEY WILL LIKE ME.
THAT'S STRANGE. IT SHOULD HAVE HEALED BY NOW!
I IRRITATED EACH DAY MY HAND, TO STAY LONGER.
AII!
THERE! I OPENED IT UP AGAIN!
THIS HURT ME REALLY VERY VERY MUCH...
I GOT AFRAID FOR MY HAND AND LET IT HEAL.
...I HAVE STILL TODAY A SCAR ON THIS PLACE.

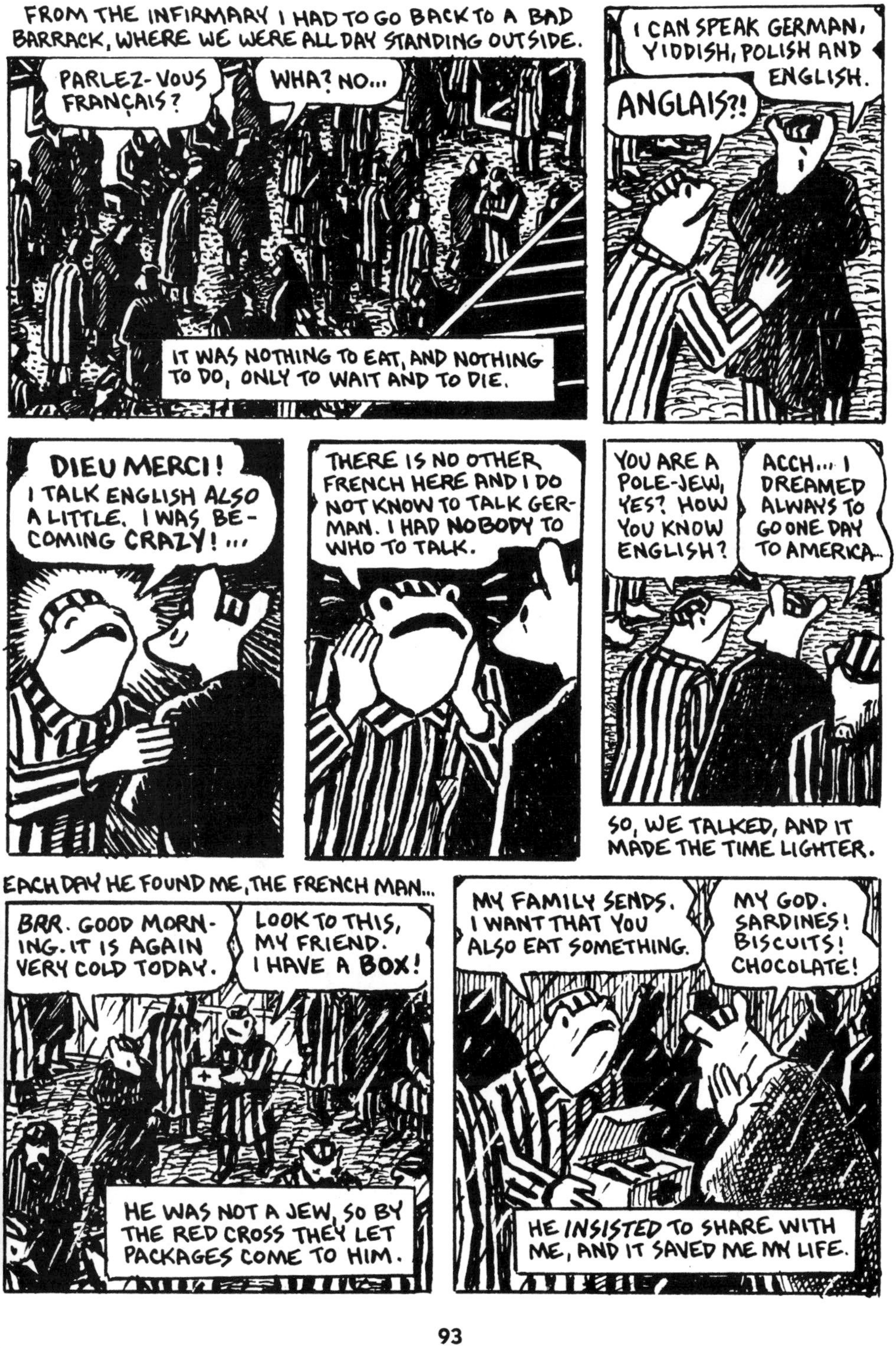
FROM THE INFIRMARY I HAD TO GO BACK TO A BAD BARRACK, WHERE WE WERE ALL DAY STANDING OUTSIDE.
PARLEZ-VOUS FRANÇAIS?
WHA? NO...
IT WAS NOTHING TO EAT, AND NOTHING TO DO, ONLY TO WAIT AND TO DIE.
I CAN SPEAK GERMAN, YIDDISH, POLISH AND ENGLISH.
ANGLAIS?!
DIEU MERCI! I TALK ENGLISH ALSO A LITTLE. I WAS BECOMING CRAZY!...
THERE IS NO OTHER FRENCH HERE AND I DO NOT KNOW TO TALK GERMAN. I HAD NOBODY TO WHO TO TALK.
YOU ARE A POLE-JEW, YES? HOW YOU KNOW ENGLISH?
ACCH... I DREAMED ALWAYS TO GO ONE DAY TO AMERICA...
SO, WE TALKED, AND IT MADE THE TIME LIGHTER.
EACH DAY HE FOUND ME, THE FRENCH MAN...
BRR. GOOD MORNING. IT IS AGAIN VERY COLD TODAY.
LOOK TO THIS, MY FRIEND. I HAVE A BOX!
HE WAS NOT A JEW, SO BY THE RED CROSS THEY LET PACKAGES COME TO HIM.
MY FAMILY SENDS. I WANT THAT YOU ALSO EAT SOMETHING.
MY GOD. SARDINES! BISCUITS! CHOCOLATE!
HE INSISTED TO SHARE WITH ME, AND IT SAVED ME MY LIFE.

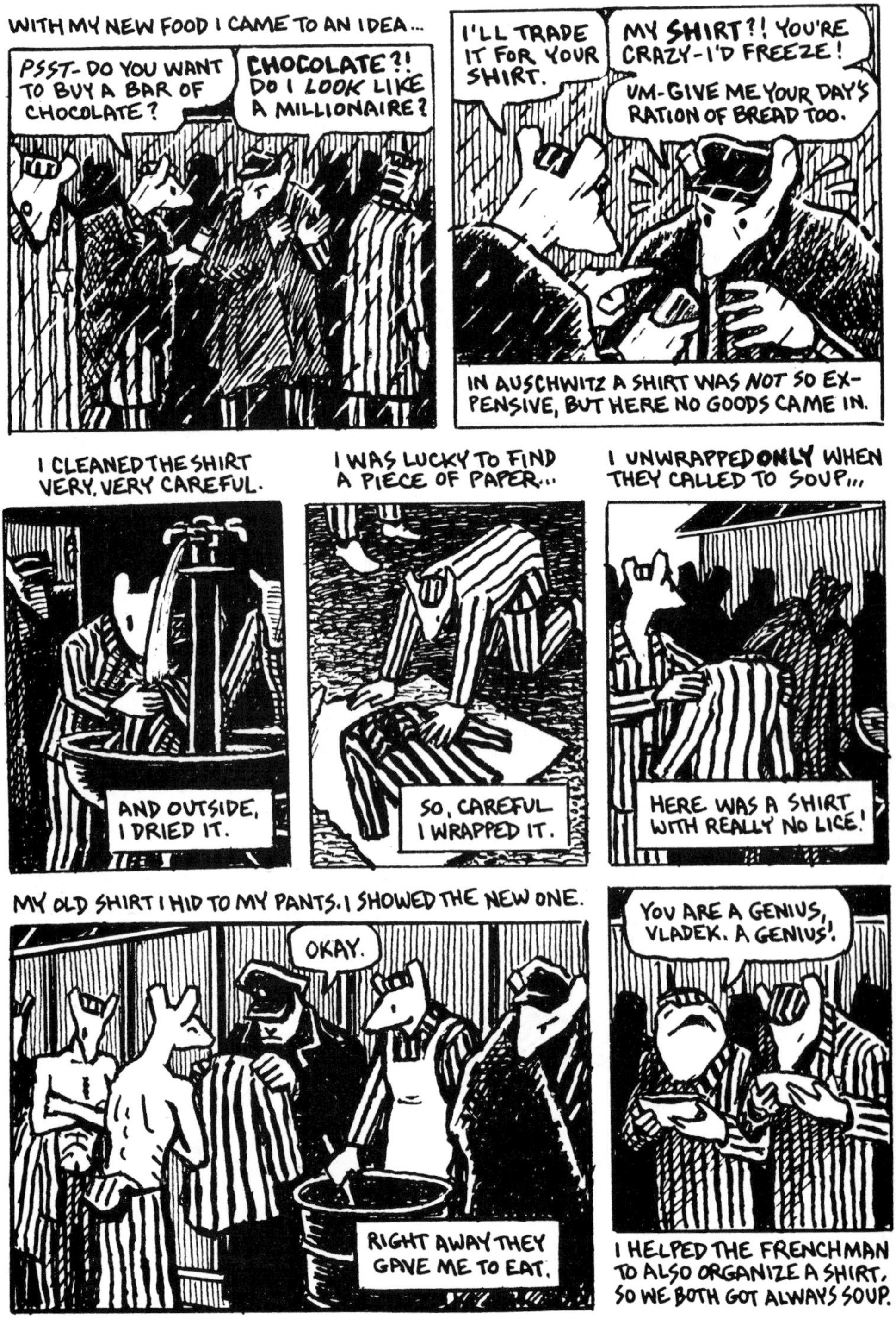
WITH MY NEW FOOD I CAME TO AN IDEA...
PSST- DO YOU WANT TO BUY A BAR OF CHOCOLATE?
CHOCOLATE?! DO I LOOK LIKE A MILLIONAIRE?
I'LL TRADE IT FOR YOUR SHIRT.
MY SHIRT?! YOU'RE CRAZY-I'D FREEZE!
UM-GIVE ME YOUR DAY'S RATION OF BREAD TOO.
IN AUSCHWITZ A SHIRT WAS NOT SO EXPENSIVE, BUT HERE NO GOODS CAME IN.
I CLEANED THE SHIRT VERY, VERY CAREFUL.
AND OUTSIDE, I DRIED IT.
I WAS LUCKY TO FIND A PIECE OF PAPER...
SO, CAREFUL I WRAPPED IT.
I UNWRAPPED ONLY WHEN THEY CALLED TO SOUP...
HERE WAS A SHIRT WITH REALLY NO LICE!
MY OLD SHIRT I HID TO MY PANTS. I SHOWED THE NEW ONE.
OKAY.
RIGHT AWAY THEY GAVE ME TO EAT.
YOU ARE A GENIUS, VLADEK. A GENIUS!
I HELPED THE FRENCHMAN TO ALSO ORGANIZE A SHIRT, SO WE BOTH GOT ALWAYS SOUP.

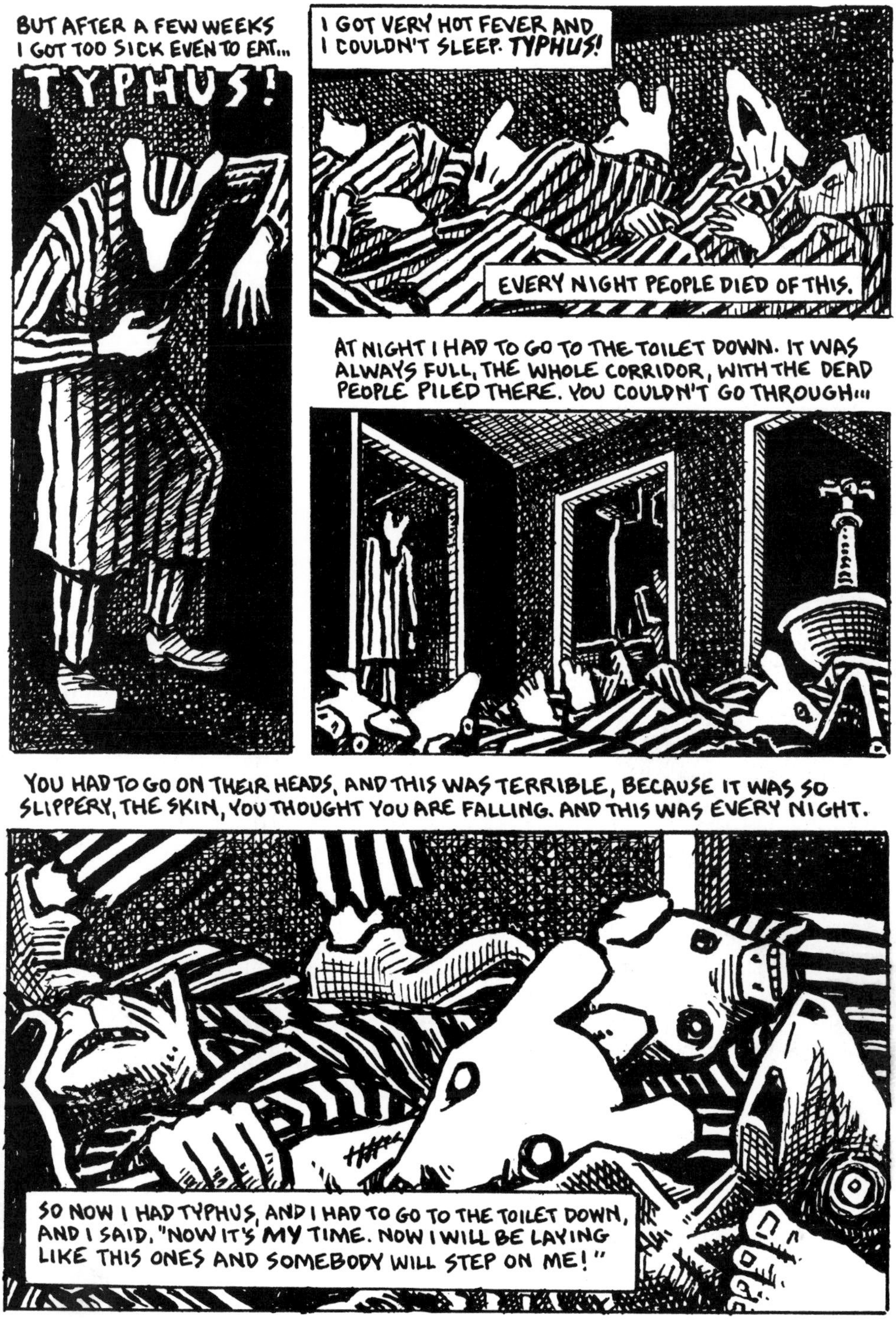
BUT AFTER A FEW WEEKS I GOT TOO SICK EVEN TO EAT...
TYPHUS!
I GOT VERY HOT FEVER AND I COULDN'T SLEEP. TYPHUS!
EVERY NIGHT PEOPLE DIED OF THIS.
AT NIGHT I HAD TO GO TO THE TOILET DOWN. IT WAS ALWAYS FULL, THE WHOLE CORRIDOR, WITH THE DEAD PEOPLE PILED THERE. YOU COULDN'T GO THROUGH...
YOU HAD TO GO ON THEIR HEADS, AND THIS WAS TERRIBLE, BECAUSE IT WAS SO SLIPPERY, THE SKIN, YOU THOUGHT YOU ARE FALLING. AND THIS WAS EVERY NIGHT.
SO NOW I HAD TYPHUS, AND I HAD TO GO TO THE TOILET DOWN, AND I SAID, "NOW IT'S MY TIME. NOW I WILL BE LAYING LIKE THIS ONES AND SOMEBODY WILL STEP ON ME!"

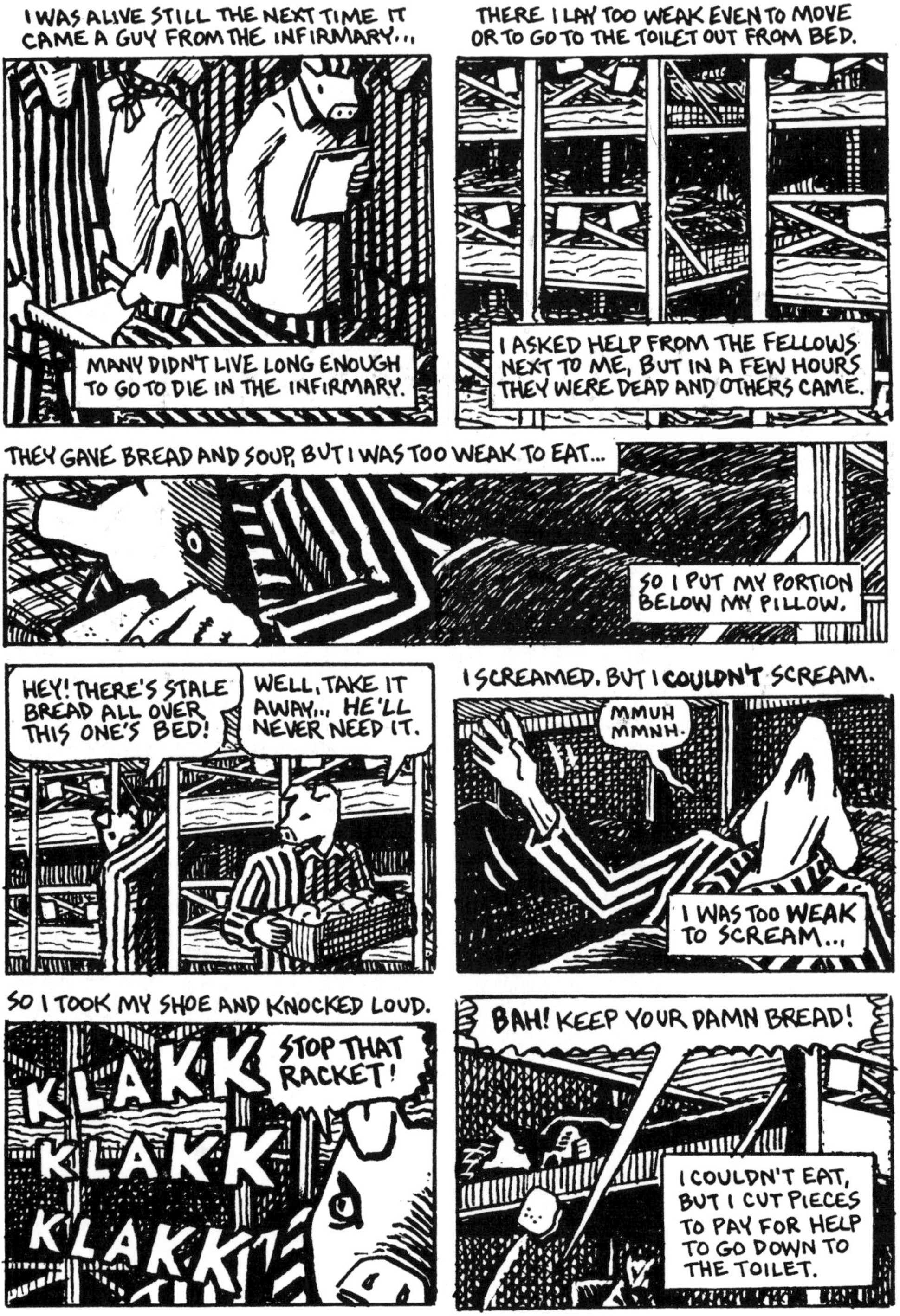
I WAS ALIVE STILL THE NEXT TIME IT CAME A GUY FROM THE INFIRMARY...
MANY DIDN'T LIVE LONG ENOUGH TO GO TO DIE IN THE INFIRMARY.
THERE I LAY TOO WEAK EVEN TO MOVE OR TO GO TO THE TOILET OUT FROM BED.
I ASKED HELP FROM THE FELLOWS NEXT TO ME, BUT IN A FEW HOURS THEY WERE DEAD AND OTHERS CAME.
THEY GAVE BREAD AND SOUP, BUT I WAS TOO WEAK TO EAT...
SO I PUT MY PORTION BELOW MY PILLOW.
HEY! THERE'S STALE BREAD ALL OVER THIS ONE'S BED!
WELL, TAKE IT AWAY... HE'LL NEVER NEED IT.
I SCREAMED. BUT I COULDN'T SCREAM.
MMUH MMNH.
I WAS TOO WEAK TO SCREAM...
SO I TOOK MY SHOE AND KNOCKED LOUD.
KLAKK
STOP THAT RACKET!
KLAKK
KLAKK
BAH! KEEP YOUR DAMN BREAD!
I COULDN'T EAT, BUT I CUT PIECES TO PAY FOR HELP TO GO DOWN TO THE TOILET.

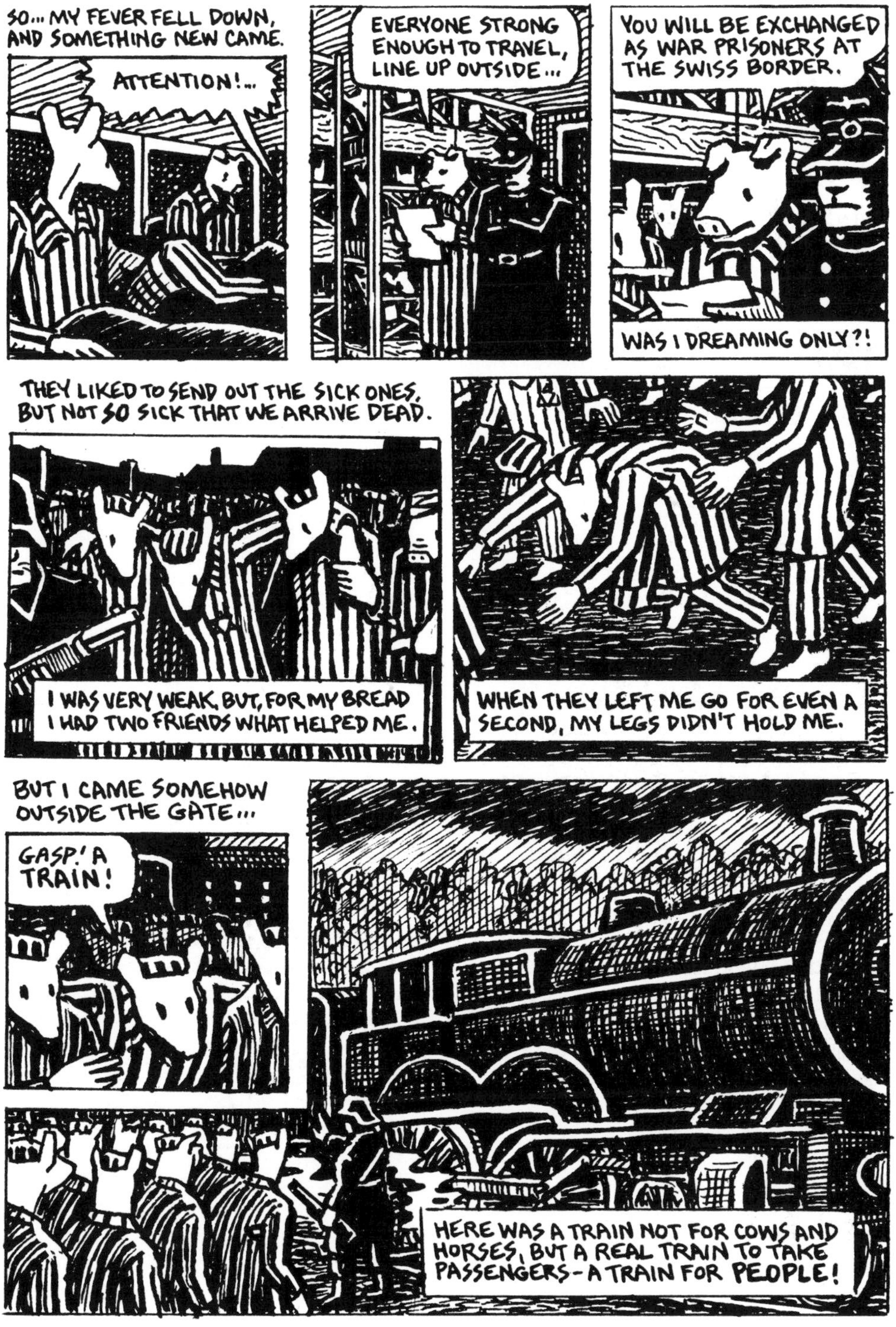
SO... MY FEVER FELL DOWN, AND SOMETHING NEW CAME.
ATTENTION!...
EVERYONE STRONG ENOUGH TO TRAVEL, LINE UP OUTSIDE...
YOU WILL BE EXCHANGED AS WAR PRISONERS AT THE SWISS BORDER.
WAS I DREAMING ONLY?!
THEY LIKED TO SEND OUT THE SICK ONES. BUT NOT SO SICK THAT WE ARRIVE DEAD.
I WAS VERY WEAK, BUT, FOR MY BREAD I HAD TWO FRIENDS WHAT HELPED ME.
WHEN THEY LEFT ME GO FOR EVEN A SECOND, MY LEGS DIDN'T HOLD ME.
BUT I CAME SOMEHOW OUTSIDE THE GATE...
GASP! A TRAIN!
HERE WAS A TRAIN NOT FOR COWS AND HORSES, BUT A REAL TRAIN TO TAKE PASSENGERS - A TRAIN FOR PEOPLE!

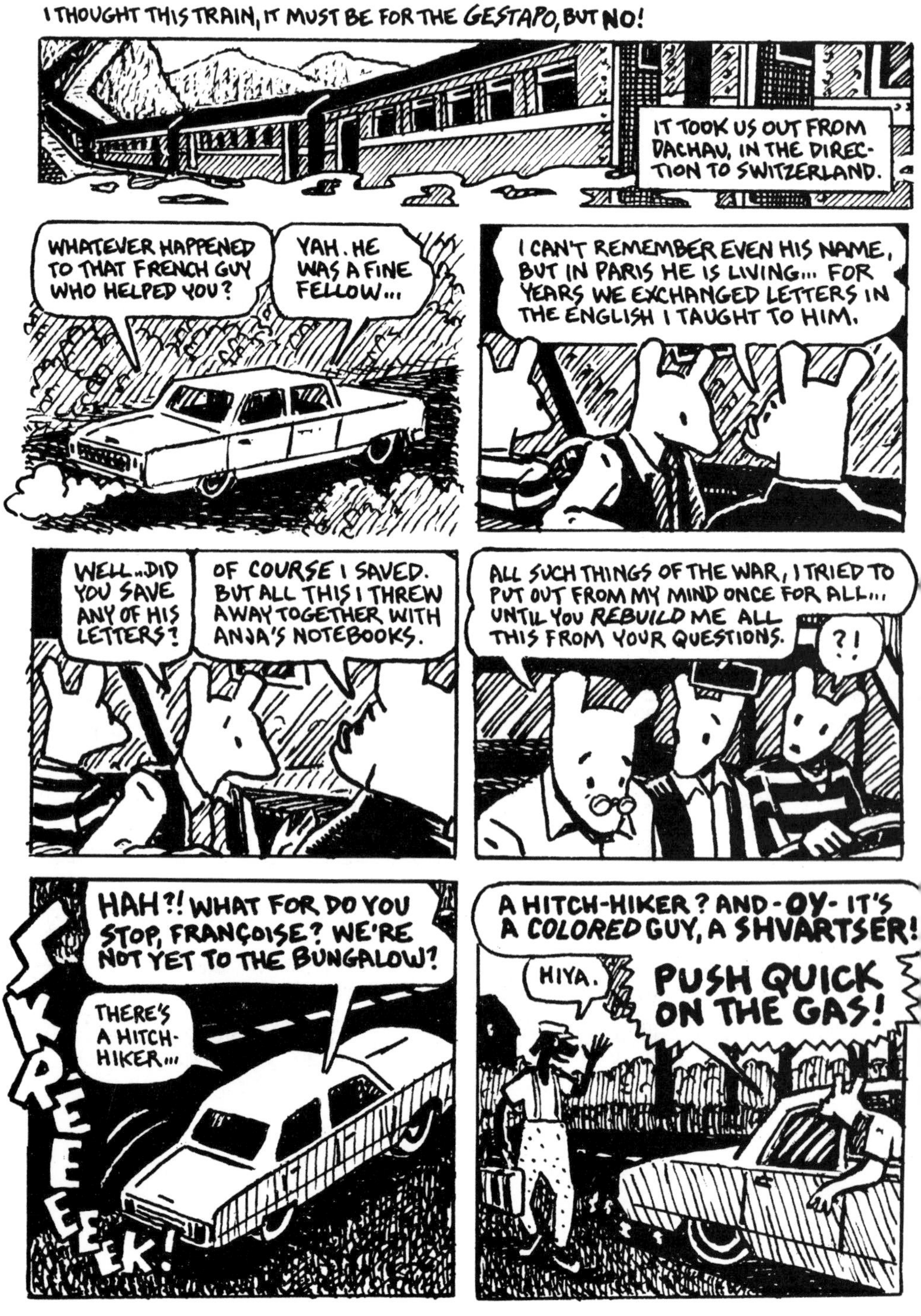
I THOUGHT THIS TRAIN, IT MUST BE FOR THE GESTAPO, BUT NO!
IT TOOK US OUT FROM DACHAU, IN THE DIRECTION TO SWITZERLAND.
WHATEVER HAPPENED TO THAT FRENCH GUY WHO HELPED YOU?
YAH. HE WAS A FINE FELLOW...
I CAN'T REMEMBER EVEN HIS NAME, BUT IN PARIS HE IS LIVING... FOR YEARS WE EXCHANGED LETTERS IN THE ENGLISH I TAUGHT TO HIM.
WELL.. DID YOU SAVE ANY OF HIS LETTERS?
OF COURSE I SAVED. BUT ALL THIS I THREW AWAY TOGETHER WITH ANJA'S NOTEBOOKS.
ALL SUCH THINGS OF THE WAR, I TRIED TO PUT OUT FROM MY MIND ONCE FOR ALL... UNTIL YOU REBUILD ME ALL THIS FROM YOUR QUESTIONS.
?!
HAH?! WHAT FOR DO YOU STOP, FRANÇOISE? WE'RE NOT YET TO THE BUNGALOW?
THERE'S A HITCH-HIKER...
SKREEEEEEK!
A HITCH-HIKER? AND-OY- IT'S A COLORED GUY, A SHVARTSER!
HIYA.
PUSH QUICK ON THE GAS!

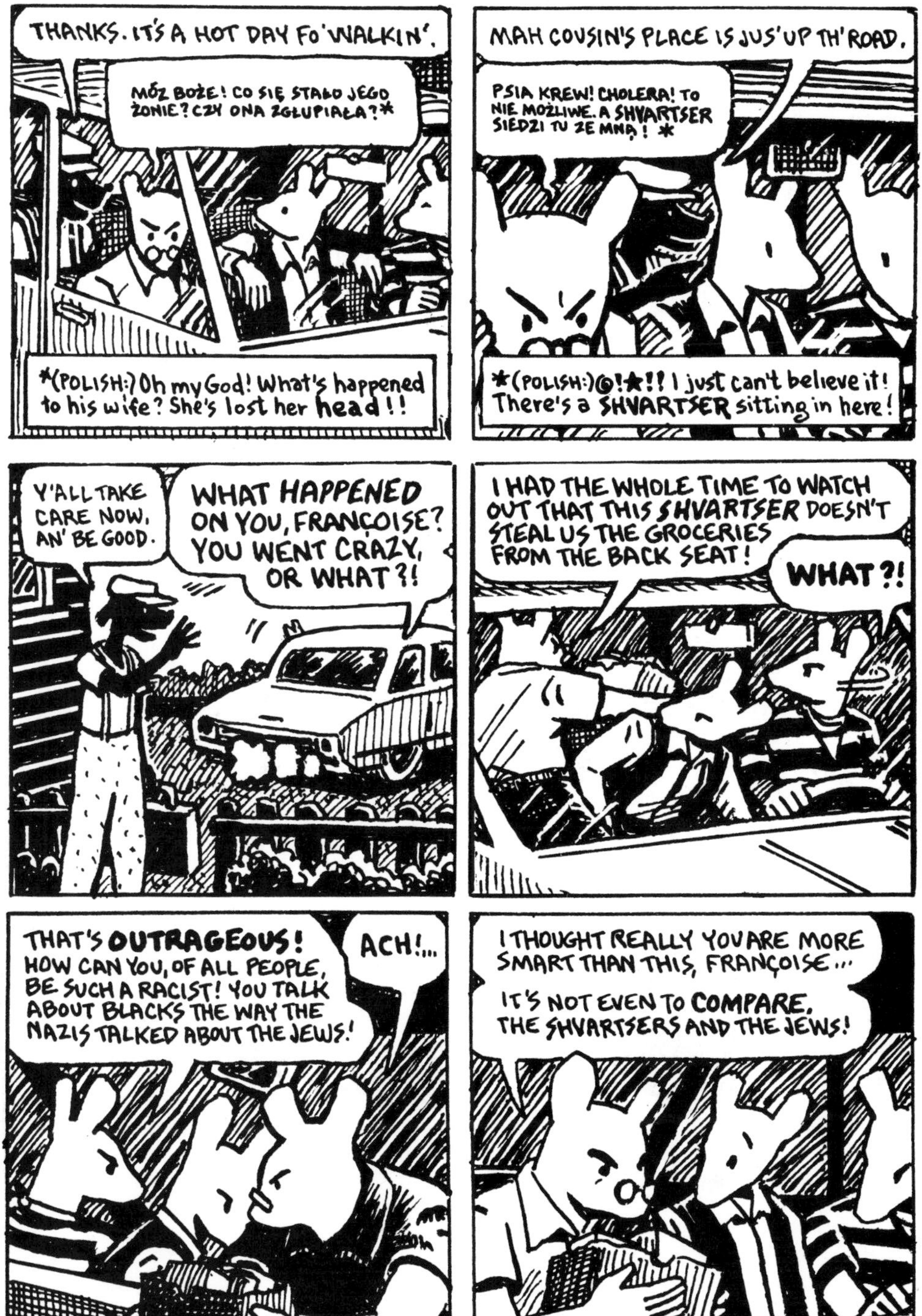

THANKS. IT'S A HOT DAY FO' WALKIN'.
MÓZ BOŻE! CO SIĘ STAŁO JEGO ŻONIE? CZY ONA ZGŁUPIAŁA?*
*(POLISH:) Oh my God! What's happened to his wife? She's lost her head!!
MAH COUSIN'S PLACE IS JUS' UP TH' ROAD.
PSIA KREW! CHOLERA! TO NIE MOŻLIWE. A SHVARTSER SIEDZI TU ZE MNĄ! *
*(POLISH:) @!★!! I just can't believe it! There's a SHVARTSER sitting in here!
Y'ALL TAKE CARE NOW. AN' BE GOOD.
WHAT HAPPENED ON YOU, FRANÇOISE? YOU WENT CRAZY, OR WHAT?!
I HAD THE WHOLE TIME TO WATCH OUT THAT THIS SHVARTSER DOESN'T STEAL US THE GROCERIES FROM THE BACK SEAT!
WHAT?!
THAT'S OUTRAGEOUS! HOW CAN YOU, OF ALL PEOPLE, BE SUCH A RACIST! YOU TALK ABOUT BLACKS THE WAY THE NAZIS TALKED ABOUT THE JEWS!
ACH!...
I THOUGHT REALLY YOU ARE MORE SMART THAN THIS, FRANÇOISE...
IT'S NOT EVEN TO COMPARE, THE SHVARTSERS AND THE JEWS!

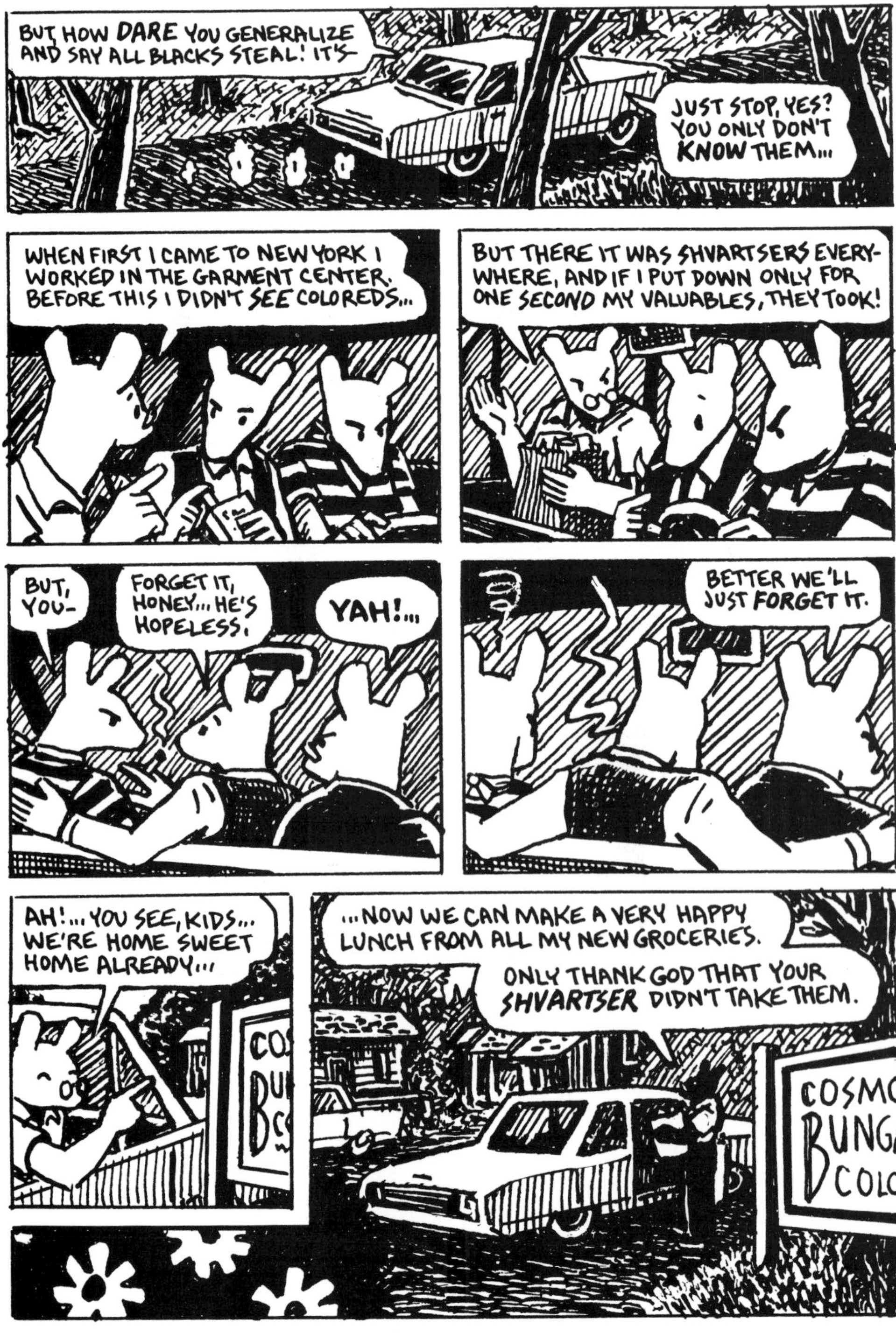
BUT HOW DARE YOU GENERALIZE AND SAY ALL BLACKS STEAL! IT'S-
JUST STOP, YES? YOU ONLY DON'T KNOW THEM...
WHEN FIRST I CAME TO NEW YORK I WORKED IN THE GARMENT CENTER. BEFORE THIS I DIDN'T SEE COLOREDS...
BUT THERE IT WAS SHVARTSERS EVERYWHERE, AND IF I PUT DOWN ONLY FOR ONE SECOND MY VALUABLES, THEY TOOK!
BUT, YOU-
FORGET IT, HONEY... HE'S HOPELESS.
YAH!...
BETTER WE'LL JUST FORGET IT.
AH!... YOU SEE, KIDS... WE'RE HOME SWEET HOME ALREADY...
...NOW WE CAN MAKE A VERY HAPPY LUNCH FROM ALL MY NEW GROCERIES.
ONLY THANK GOD THAT YOUR SHVARTSER DIDN'T TAKE THEM.
COSMO
BUNG
COLO

CHAPTER FOUR

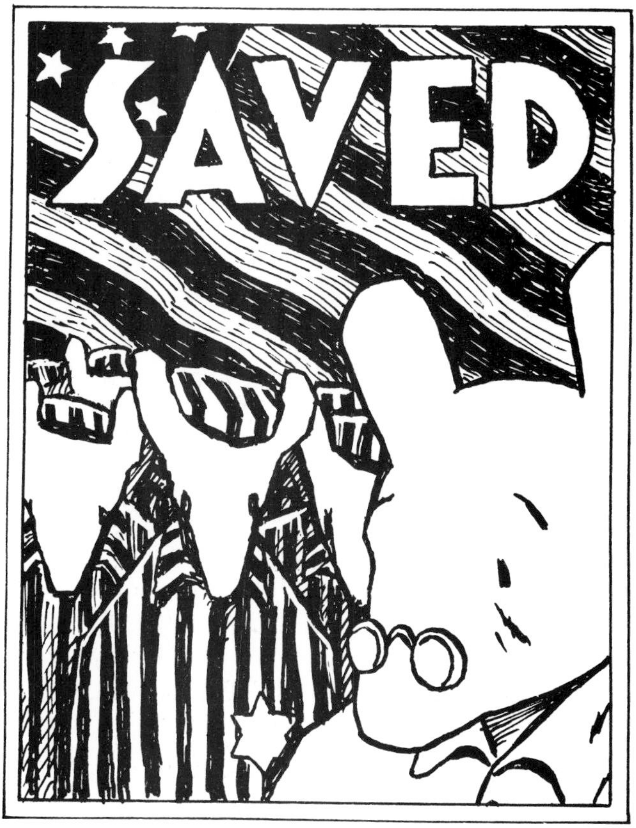
SAVED

Back in Rego Park. Late Autumn...

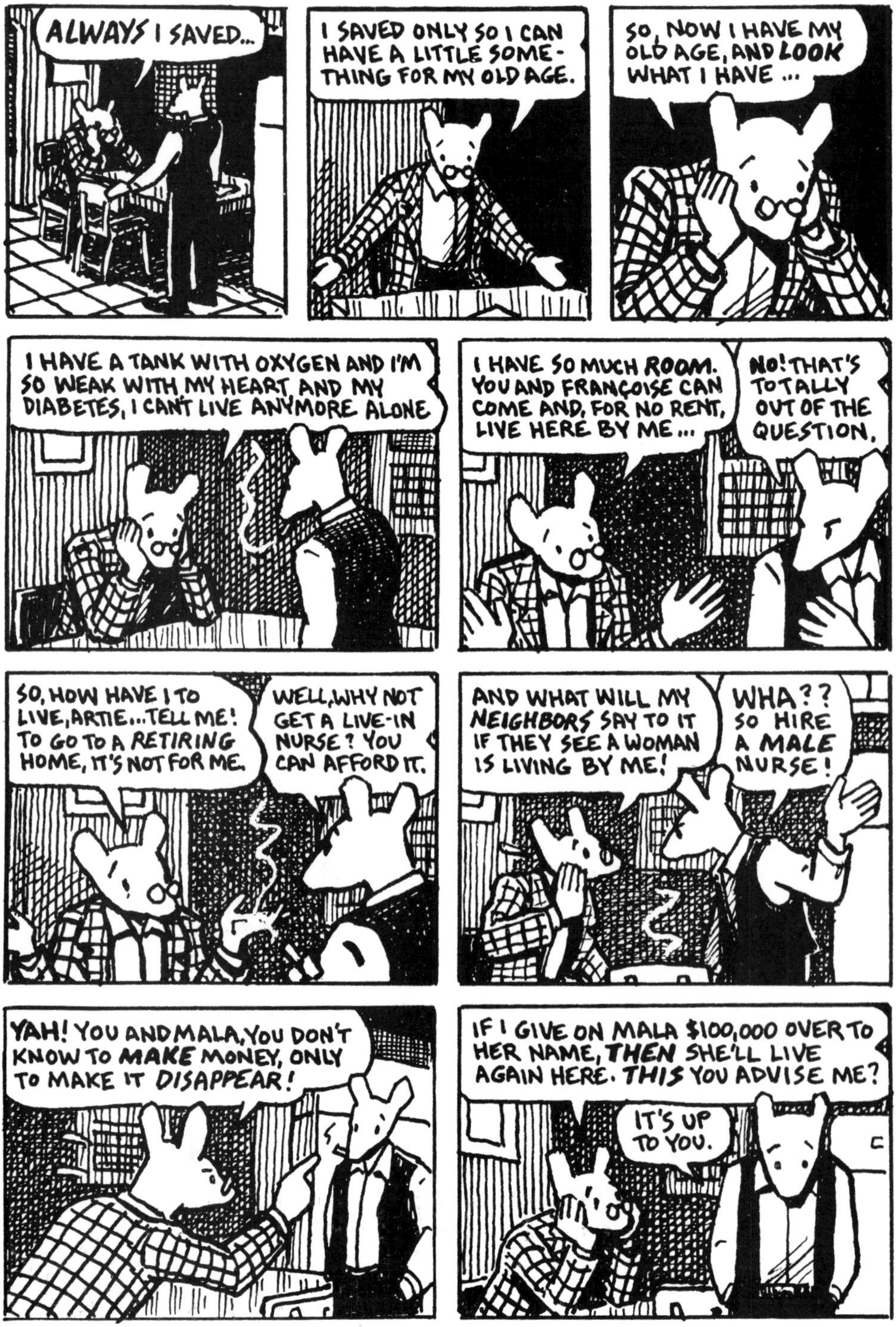
ALWAYS I SAVED...
I SAVED ONLY SO I CAN HAVE A LITTLE SOMETHING FOR MY OLD AGE.
SO, NOW I HAVE MY OLD AGE, AND LOOK WHAT I HAVE ...
I HAVE A TANK WITH OXYGEN AND I'M SO WEAK WITH MY HEART AND MY DIABETES, I CAN'T LIVE ANYMORE ALONE
I HAVE SO MUCH ROOM. YOU AND FRANÇOISE CAN COME AND, FOR NO RENT, LIVE HERE BY ME...
NO! THAT'S TOTALLY OUT OF THE QUESTION.
SO, HOW HAVE I TO LIVE, ARTIE...TELL ME! TO GO TO A RETIRING HOME, IT'S NOT FOR ME.
WELL, WHY NOT GET A LIVE-IN NURSE? YOU CAN AFFORD IT.
AND WHAT WILL MY NEIGHBORS SAY TO IT IF THEY SEE A WOMAN IS LIVING BY ME!
WHA?? SO HIRE A MALE NURSE!
YAH! YOU AND MALA, YOU DON'T KNOW TO MAKE MONEY, ONLY TO MAKE IT DISAPPEAR!
IF I GIVE ON MALA $100,000 OVER TO HER NAME, THEN SHE'LL LIVE AGAIN HERE. THIS YOU ADVISE ME?
IT'S UP TO YOU.

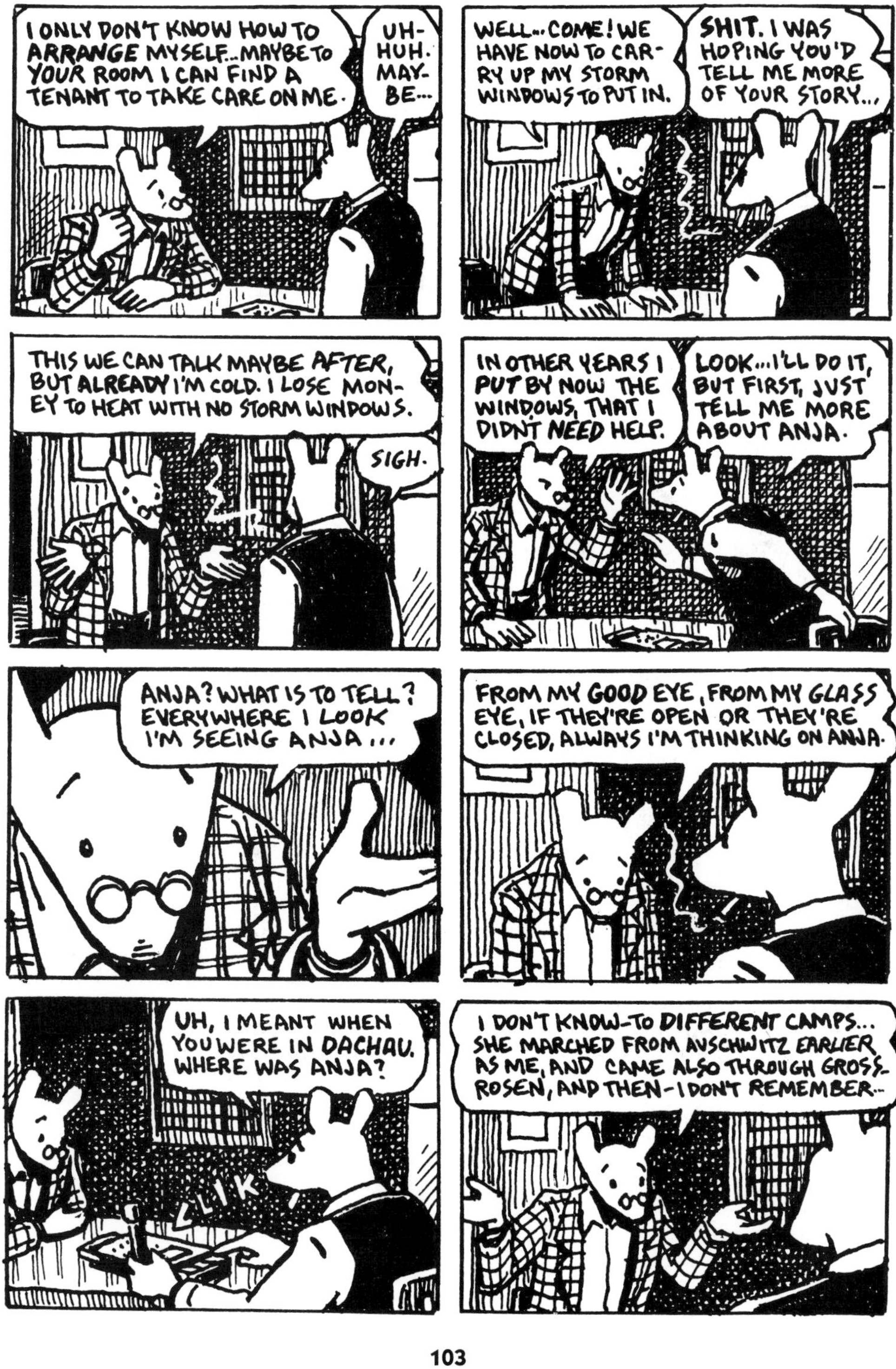
I ONLY DON'T KNOW HOW TO ARRANGE MYSELF...MAYBE TO YOUR ROOM I CAN FIND A TENANT TO TAKE CARE ON ME.
UH-HUH. MAY-BE...
WELL...COME! WE HAVE NOW TO CAR-RY UP MY STORM WINDOWS TO PUT IN.
SHIT. I WAS HOPING YOU'D TELL ME MORE OF YOUR STORY...
THIS WE CAN TALK MAYBE AFTER, BUT ALREADY I'M COLD. I LOSE MON-EY TO HEAT WITH NO STORM WINDOWS.
SIGH.
IN OTHER YEARS I PUT BY NOW THE WINDOWS, THAT I DIDN'T NEED HELP.
LOOK...I'LL DO IT, BUT FIRST, JUST TELL ME MORE ABOUT ANJA.
ANJA? WHAT IS TO TELL? EVERYWHERE I LOOK I'M SEEING ANJA...
FROM MY GOOD EYE, FROM MY GLASS EYE, IF THEY'RE OPEN OR THEY'RE CLOSED, ALWAYS I'M THINKING ON ANJA.
UH, I MEANT WHEN YOU WERE IN DACHAU. WHERE WAS ANJA?
CLIK!
I DON'T KNOW-TO DIFFERENT CAMPS... SHE MARCHED FROM AUSCHWITZ EARLIER AS ME, AND CAME ALSO THROUGH GROSS-ROSEN, AND THEN-I DON'T REMEMBER...

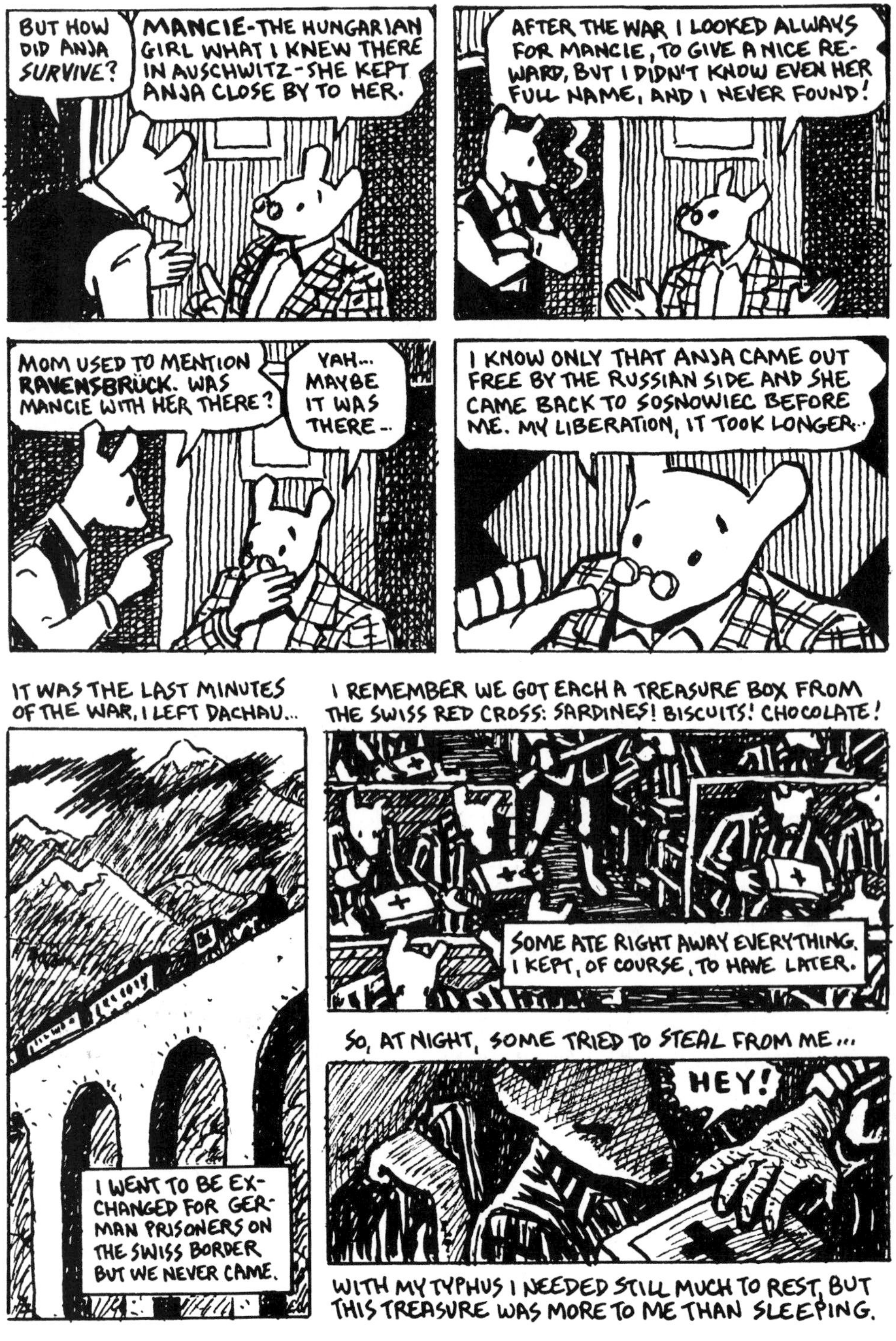
BUT HOW DID ANJA SURVIVE?
MANCIE-THE HUNGARIAN GIRL WHAT I KNEW THERE IN AUSCHWITZ-SHE KEPT ANJA CLOSE BY TO HER.
AFTER THE WAR I LOOKED ALWAYS FOR MANCIE, TO GIVE A NICE REWARD, BUT I DIDN'T KNOW EVEN HER FULL NAME, AND I NEVER FOUND!
MOM USED TO MENTION RAVENSBRÜCK. WAS MANCIE WITH HER THERE?
YAH... MAYBE IT WAS THERE...
I KNOW ONLY THAT ANJA CAME OUT FREE BY THE RUSSIAN SIDE AND SHE CAME BACK TO SOSNOWIEC BEFORE ME. MY LIBERATION, IT TOOK LONGER...
IT WAS THE LAST MINUTES OF THE WAR, I LEFT DACHAU...
I WENT TO BE EXCHANGED FOR GERMAN PRISONERS ON THE SWISS BORDER BUT WE NEVER CAME.
I REMEMBER WE GOT EACH A TREASURE BOX FROM THE SWISS RED CROSS: SARDINES! BISCUITS! CHOCOLATE!
SOME ATE RIGHT AWAY EVERYTHING. I KEPT, OF COURSE, TO HAVE LATER.
SO, AT NIGHT, SOME TRIED TO STEAL FROM ME...
HEY!
WITH MY TYPHUS I NEEDED STILL MUCH TO REST, BUT THIS TREASURE WAS MORE TO ME THAN SLEEPING.

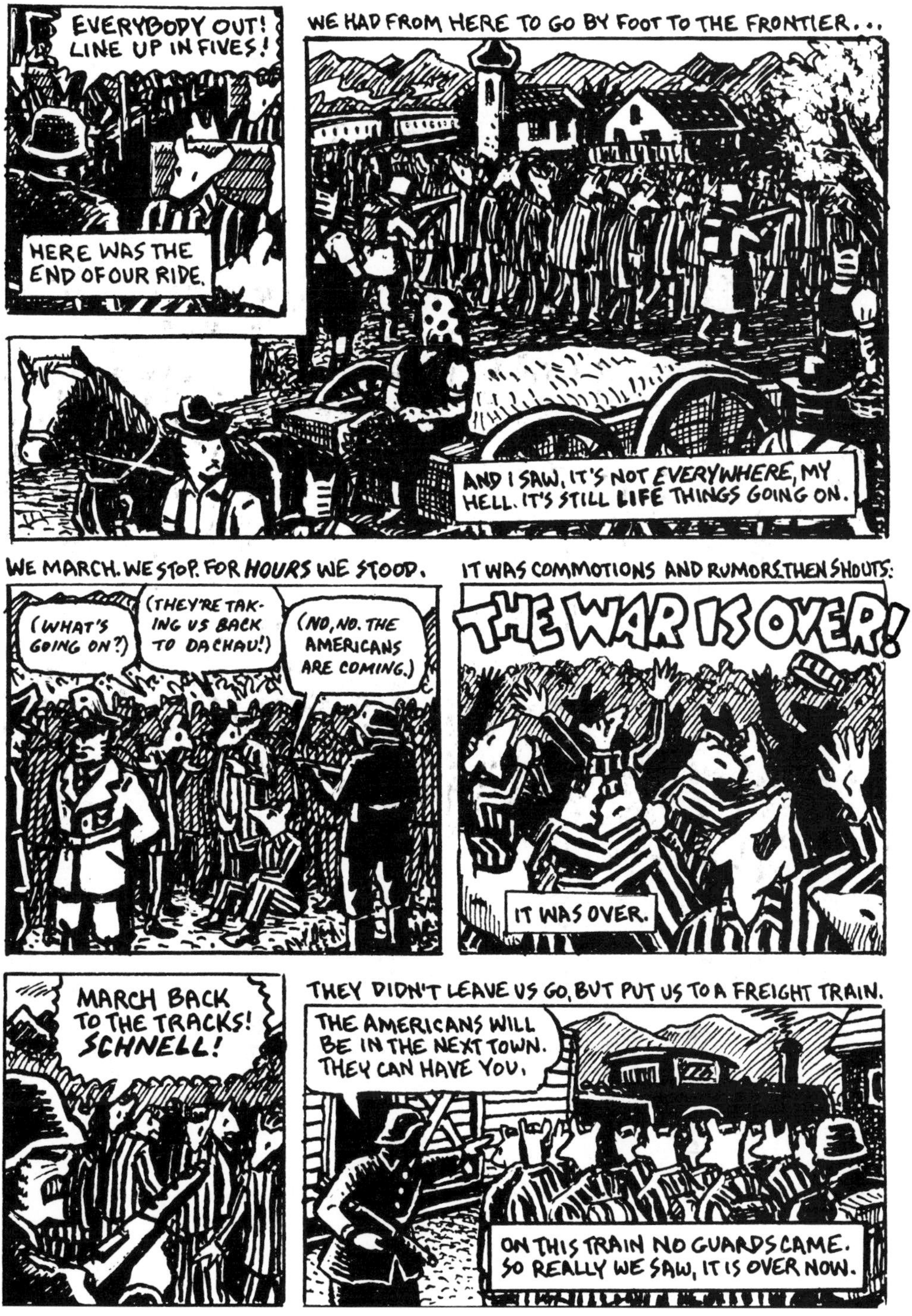
EVERYBODY OUT! LINE UP IN FIVES!
HERE WAS THE END OF OUR RIDE.
WE HAD FROM HERE TO GO BY FOOT TO THE FRONTIER...
AND I SAW, IT'S NOT EVERYWHERE, MY HELL. IT'S STILL LIFE THINGS GOING ON.
WE MARCH. WE STOP. FOR HOURS WE STOOD.
(WHAT'S GOING ON?)
(THEY'RE TAKING US BACK TO DACHAU!)
(NO, NO. THE AMERICANS ARE COMING.)
IT WAS COMMOTIONS AND RUMORS. THEN SHOUTS:
THE WAR IS OVER!
IT WAS OVER.
MARCH BACK TO THE TRACKS! SCHNELL!
THEY DIDN'T LEAVE US GO, BUT PUT US TO A FREIGHT TRAIN.
THE AMERICANS WILL BE IN THE NEXT TOWN. THEY CAN HAVE YOU.
ON THIS TRAIN NO GUARDS CAME. SO REALLY WE SAW, IT IS OVER NOW.

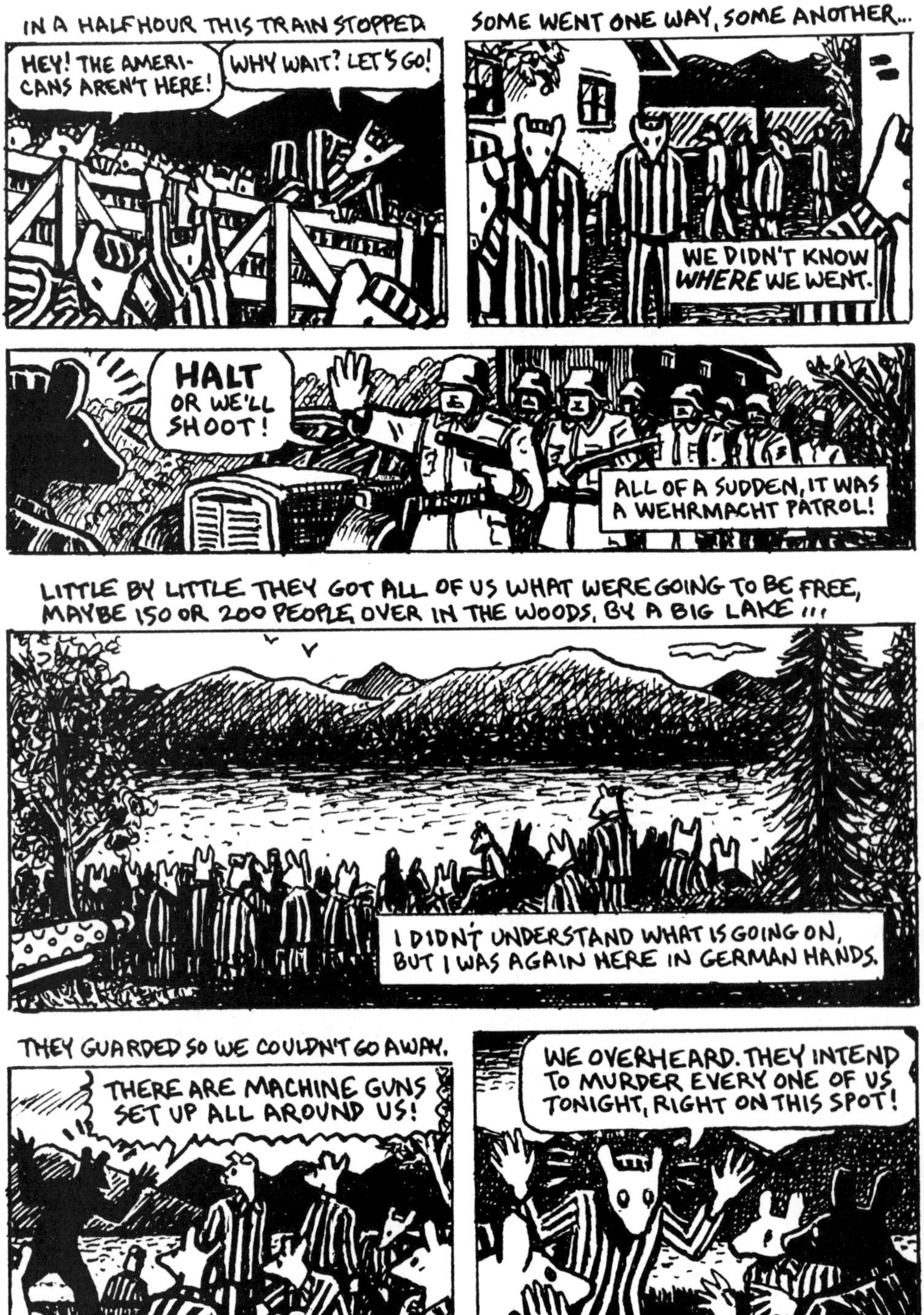

IN A HALFHOUR THIS TRAIN STOPPED.
HEY! THE AMERICANS AREN'T HERE!
WHY WAIT? LET'S GO!
SOME WENT ONE WAY, SOME ANOTHER...
WE DIDN'T KNOW WHERE WE WENT.
HALT OR WE'LL SHOOT!
ALL OF A SUDDEN, IT WAS A WEHRMACHT PATROL!
LITTLE BY LITTLE THEY GOT ALL OF US WHAT WERE GOING TO BE FREE, MAYBE 150 OR 200 PEOPLE, OVER IN THE WOODS, BY A BIG LAKE...
I DIDN'T UNDERSTAND WHAT IS GOING ON, BUT I WAS AGAIN HERE IN GERMAN HANDS.
THEY GUARDED SO WE COULDN'T GO AWAY.
THERE ARE MACHINE GUNS SET UP ALL AROUND US!
WE OVERHEARD. THEY INTEND TO MURDER EVERY ONE OF US TONIGHT, RIGHT ON THIS SPOT!

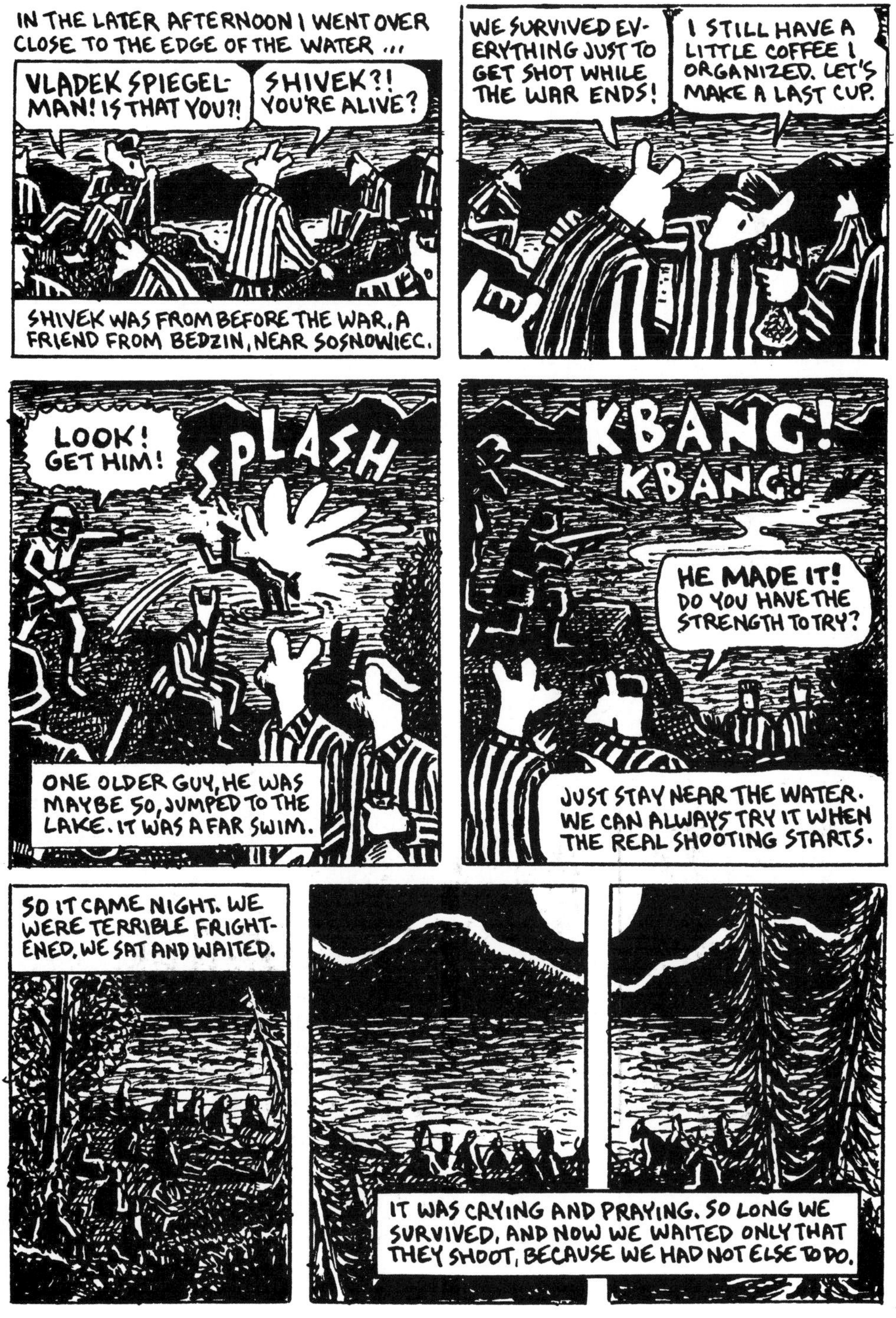
IN THE LATER AFTERNOON I WENT OVER CLOSE TO THE EDGE OF THE WATER ...
VLADEK SPIEGELMAN! IS THAT YOU?!
SHIVEK?! YOU'RE ALIVE?
SHIVEK WAS FROM BEFORE THE WAR. A FRIEND FROM BEDZIN, NEAR SOSNOWIEC.
WE SURVIVED EVERYTHING JUST TO GET SHOT WHILE THE WAR ENDS!
I STILL HAVE A LITTLE COFFEE I ORGANIZED. LET'S MAKE A LAST CUP.
LOOK! GET HIM!
SPLASH
ONE OLDER GUY, HE WAS MAYBE 50, JUMPED TO THE LAKE. IT WAS A FAR SWIM.
KBANG! KBANG!
HE MADE IT! DO YOU HAVE THE STRENGTH TO TRY?
JUST STAY NEAR THE WATER. WE CAN ALWAYS TRY IT WHEN THE REAL SHOOTING STARTS.
SO IT CAME NIGHT. WE WERE TERRIBLE FRIGHTENED. WE SAT AND WAITED.
IT WAS CRYING AND PRAYING. SO LONG WE SURVIVED, AND NOW WE WAITED ONLY THAT THEY SHOOT, BECAUSE WE HAD NOT ELSE TO DO.

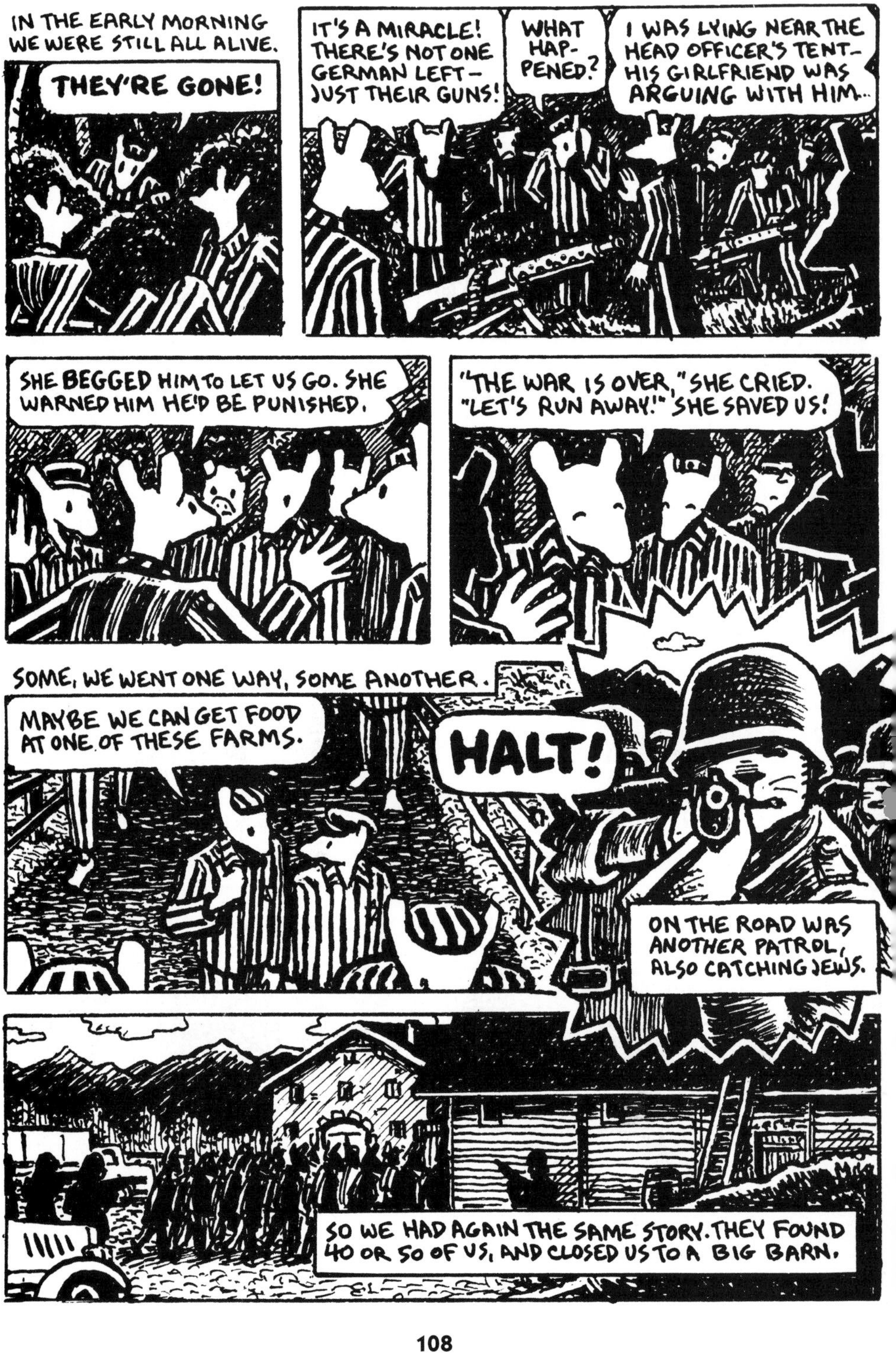
IN THE EARLY MORNING WE WERE STILL ALL ALIVE.
THEY'RE GONE!
IT'S A MIRACLE! THERE'S NOT ONE GERMAN LEFT—JUST THEIR GUNS!
WHAT HAPPENED?
I WAS LYING NEAR THE HEAD OFFICER'S TENT—HIS GIRLFRIEND WAS ARGUING WITH HIM...
SHE BEGGED HIM TO LET US GO. SHE WARNED HIM HE'D BE PUNISHED.
"THE WAR IS OVER," SHE CRIED. "LET'S RUN AWAY!" SHE SAVED US!
SOME, WE WENT ONE WAY, SOME ANOTHER.
MAYBE WE CAN GET FOOD AT ONE OF THESE FARMS.
HALT!
ON THE ROAD WAS ANOTHER PATROL, ALSO CATCHING JEWS.
SO WE HAD AGAIN THE SAME STORY. THEY FOUND 40 OR 50 OF US, AND CLOSED US TO A BIG BARN.

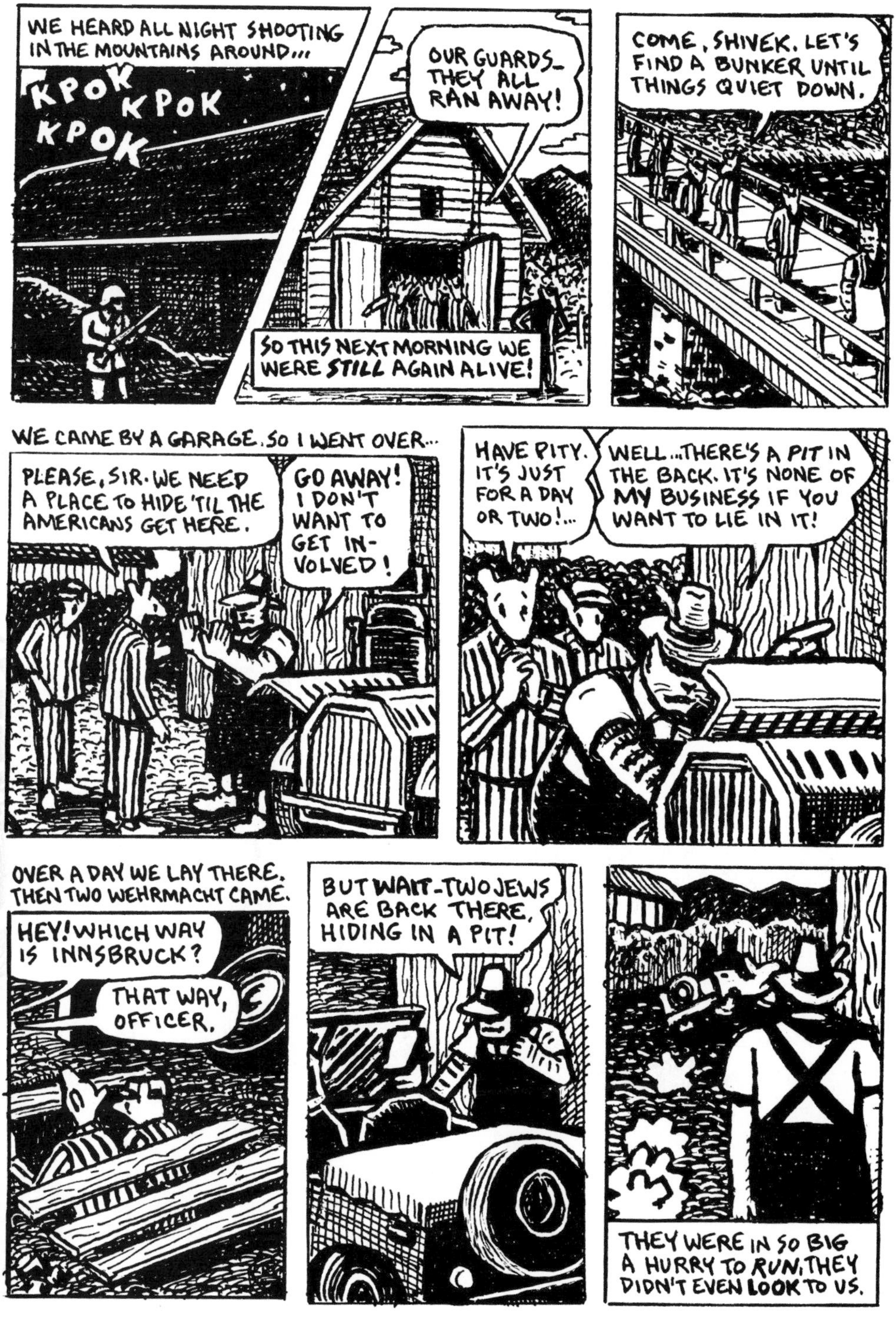

WE HEARD ALL NIGHT SHOOTING IN THE MOUNTAINS AROUND...
KPOK KPOK KPOK
OUR GUARDS- THEY ALL RAN AWAY!
SO THIS NEXT MORNING WE WERE STILL AGAIN ALIVE!
COME, SHIVEK. LET'S FIND A BUNKER UNTIL THINGS QUIET DOWN.
WE CAME BY A GARAGE. SO I WENT OVER...
PLEASE, SIR. WE NEED A PLACE TO HIDE 'TIL THE AMERICANS GET HERE.
GO AWAY! I DON'T WANT TO GET IN-VOLVED!
HAVE PITY. IT'S JUST FOR A DAY OR TWO!...
WELL...THERE'S A PIT IN THE BACK. IT'S NONE OF MY BUSINESS IF YOU WANT TO LIE IN IT!
OVER A DAY WE LAY THERE. THEN TWO WEHRMACHT CAME.
HEY! WHICH WAY IS INNSBRUCK?
THAT WAY, OFFICER.
BUT WAIT-TWO JEWS ARE BACK THERE, HIDING IN A PIT!
THEY WERE IN SO BIG A HURRY TO RUN, THEY DIDN'T EVEN LOOK TO US.

LET'S GO, SHIVEK. WE'LL FIND A SAFER SPOT.

WE PASSED TO A FEW HOUSES AND PEEKED INSIDE...

LOOK. NOBODY SEEMS TO BE HOME HERE.

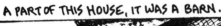

A PART OF THIS HOUSE, IT WAS A BARN.

WE CAN HIDE UP HERE UNDER THE HAY.

FROM THE WALLS WE HEARD SHOUTING:

SCHNELL, ELSA! PACK WHAT YOU CAN.

HURRY! THIS MAY BECOME A BATTLEFIELD ANY MINUTE!

THE VILLAGERS ARE RUNNING AWAY!

FINE. THE FARTHER THE BETTER!

KKABOOMM!

THE FAR SIDE FROM OUR BARN FELL DOWN A LITTLE...

MY GOD! WH-WHAT HAPPENED?!

THE WEHRMACHT IS RETREATING AND BLEW UP THE BRIDGE TO SEAL THEIR TRAIL. IT MEANS WE'RE FREE!

LET'S LOOK AROUND. IT'S SAFE NOW!

UH-UH. I'M NOT GOING ANYWHERE!

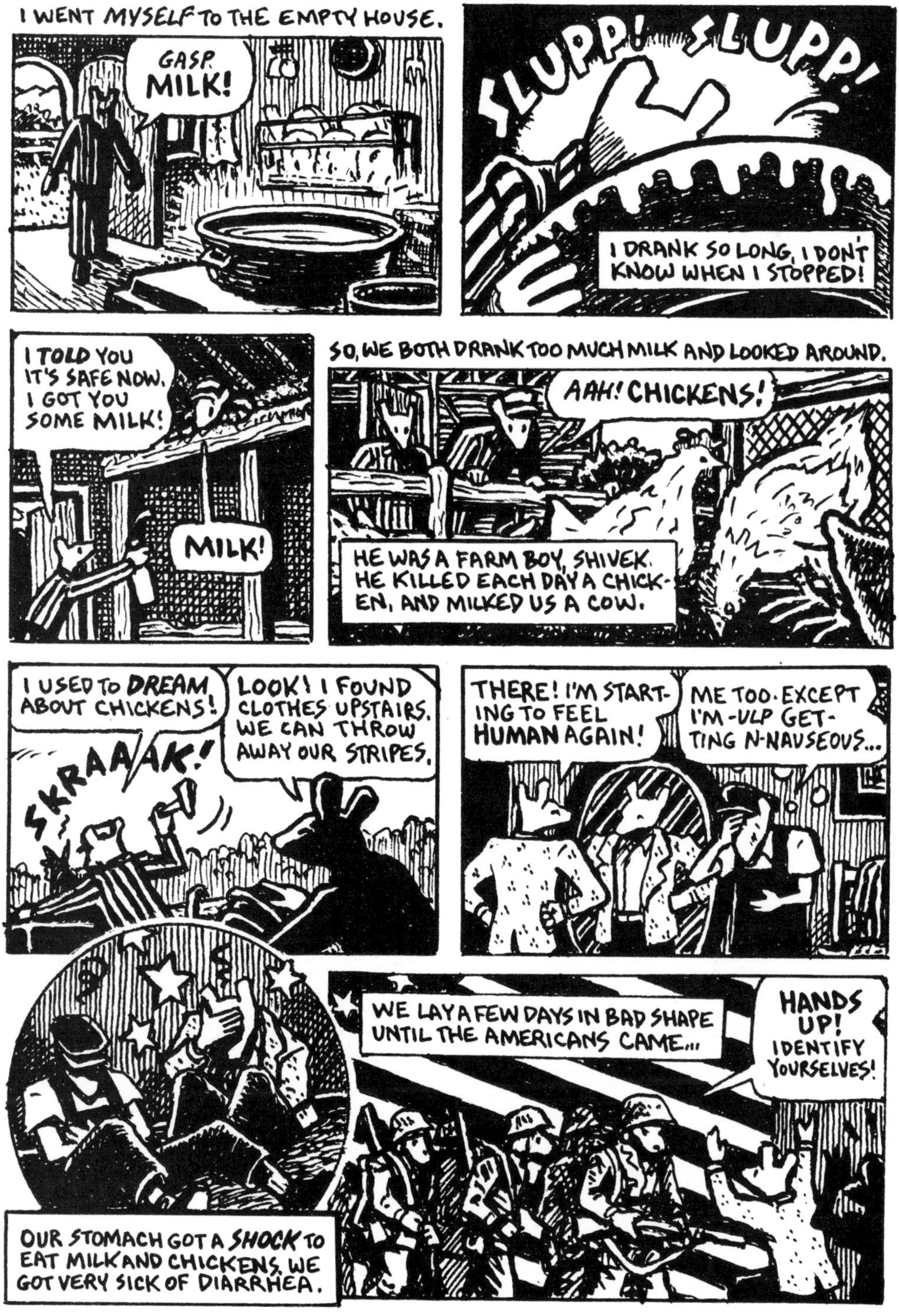
I WENT MYSELF TO THE EMPTY HOUSE.
GASP. MILK!
SLUPP! SLUPP!
I DRANK SO LONG, I DON'T KNOW WHEN I STOPPED!
I TOLD YOU IT'S SAFE NOW. I GOT YOU SOME MILK!
MILK!
SO, WE BOTH DRANK TOO MUCH MILK AND LOOKED AROUND.
AAH! CHICKENS!
HE WAS A FARM BOY, SHIVEK. HE KILLED EACH DAY A CHICKEN, AND MILKED US A COW.
I USED TO DREAM ABOUT CHICKENS!
SKRAAAK!
LOOK! I FOUND CLOTHES UPSTAIRS. WE CAN THROW AWAY OUR STRIPES.
THERE! I'M STARTING TO FEEL HUMAN AGAIN!
ME TOO. EXCEPT I'M-ULP GETTING N-NAUSEOUS...
OUR STOMACH GOT A SHOCK TO EAT MILK AND CHICKENS. WE GOT VERY SICK OF DIARRHEA.
WE LAY A FEW DAYS IN BAD SHAPE UNTIL THE AMERICANS CAME...
HANDS UP! IDENTIFY YOURSELVES!

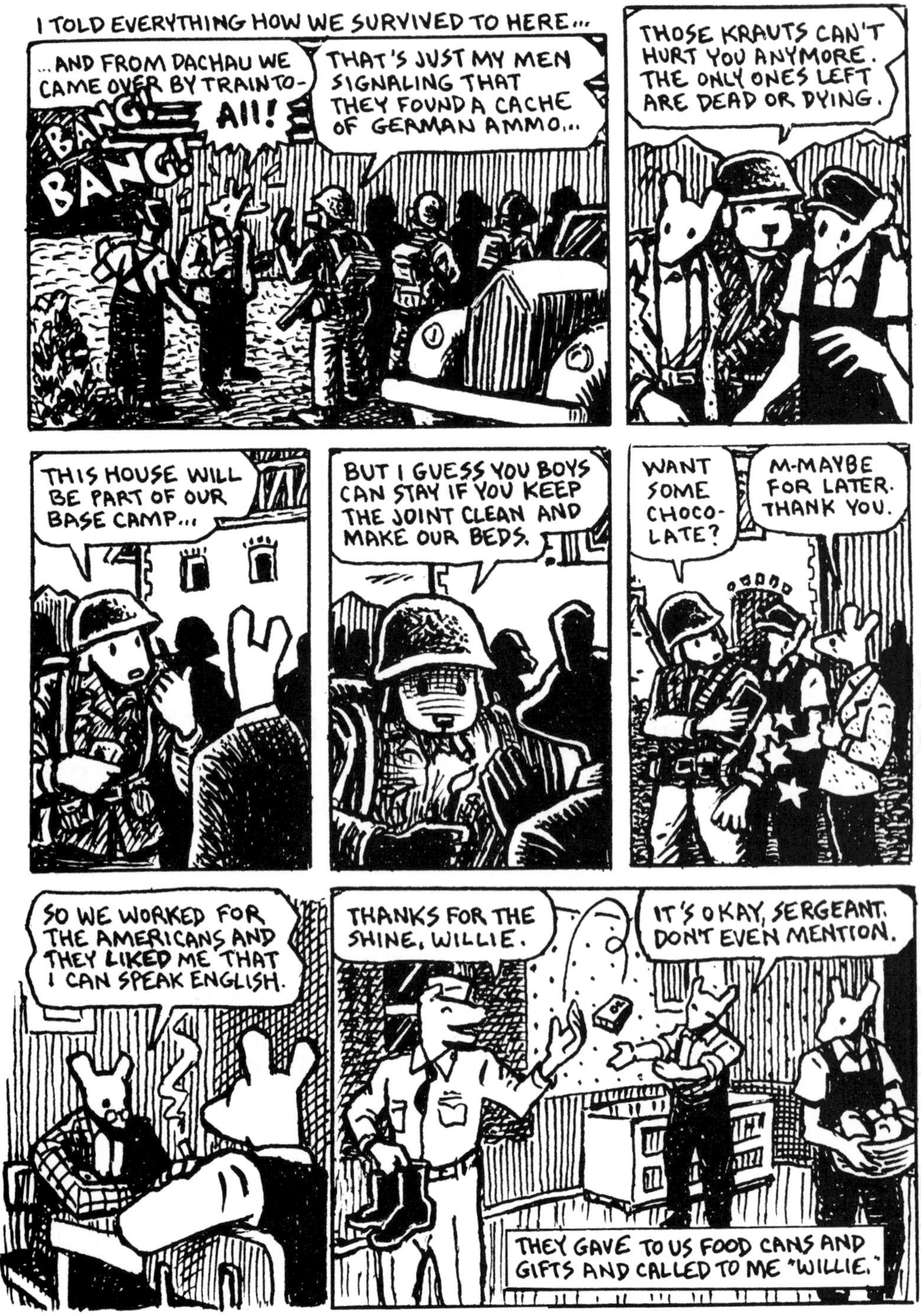
I TOLD EVERYTHING HOW WE SURVIVED TO HERE...
...AND FROM DACHAU WE CAME OVER BY TRAIN TO-
BANG! BANG!
AII!
THAT'S JUST MY MEN SIGNALING THAT THEY FOUND A CACHE OF GERMAN AMMO...
THOSE KRAUTS CAN'T HURT YOU ANYMORE. THE ONLY ONES LEFT ARE DEAD OR DYING.
THIS HOUSE WILL BE PART OF OUR BASE CAMP...
BUT I GUESS YOU BOYS CAN STAY IF YOU KEEP THE JOINT CLEAN AND MAKE OUR BEDS.
WANT SOME CHOCO-LATE?
M-MAYBE FOR LATER. THANK YOU.
SO WE WORKED FOR THE AMERICANS AND THEY LIKED ME THAT I CAN SPEAK ENGLISH.
THANKS FOR THE SHINE, WILLIE.
IT'S OKAY, SERGEANT. DON'T EVEN MENTION.
THEY GAVE TO US FOOD CANS AND GIFTS AND CALLED TO ME "WILLIE."

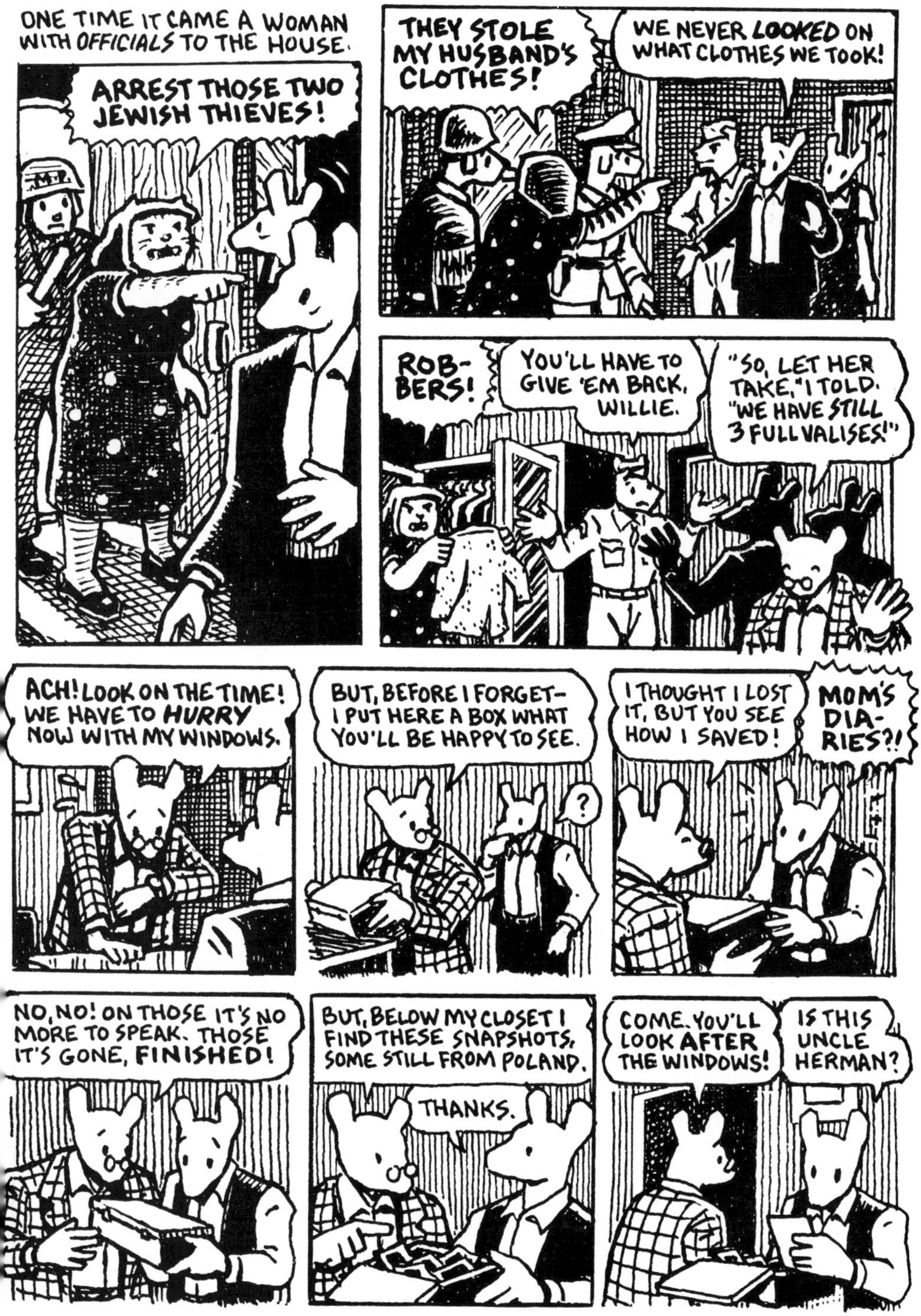
ONE TIME IT CAME A WOMAN WITH OFFICIALS TO THE HOUSE.
ARREST THOSE TWO JEWISH THIEVES!
M.P.
THEY STOLE MY HUSBAND'S CLOTHES!
WE NEVER LOOKED ON WHAT CLOTHES WE TOOK!
ROBBERS!
YOU'LL HAVE TO GIVE 'EM BACK, WILLIE.
"SO, LET HER TAKE," I TOLD. "WE HAVE STILL 3 FULL VALISES!"
ACH! LOOK ON THE TIME! WE HAVE TO HURRY NOW WITH MY WINDOWS.
BUT, BEFORE I FORGET- I PUT HERE A BOX WHAT YOU'LL BE HAPPY TO SEE.
?
I THOUGHT I LOST IT, BUT YOU SEE HOW I SAVED!
MOM'S DIARIES?!
NO, NO! ON THOSE IT'S NO MORE TO SPEAK. THOSE IT'S GONE, FINISHED!
BUT, BELOW MY CLOSET I FIND THESE SNAPSHOTS, SOME STILL FROM POLAND.
THANKS.
COME. YOU'LL LOOK AFTER THE WINDOWS!
IS THIS UNCLE HERMAN?

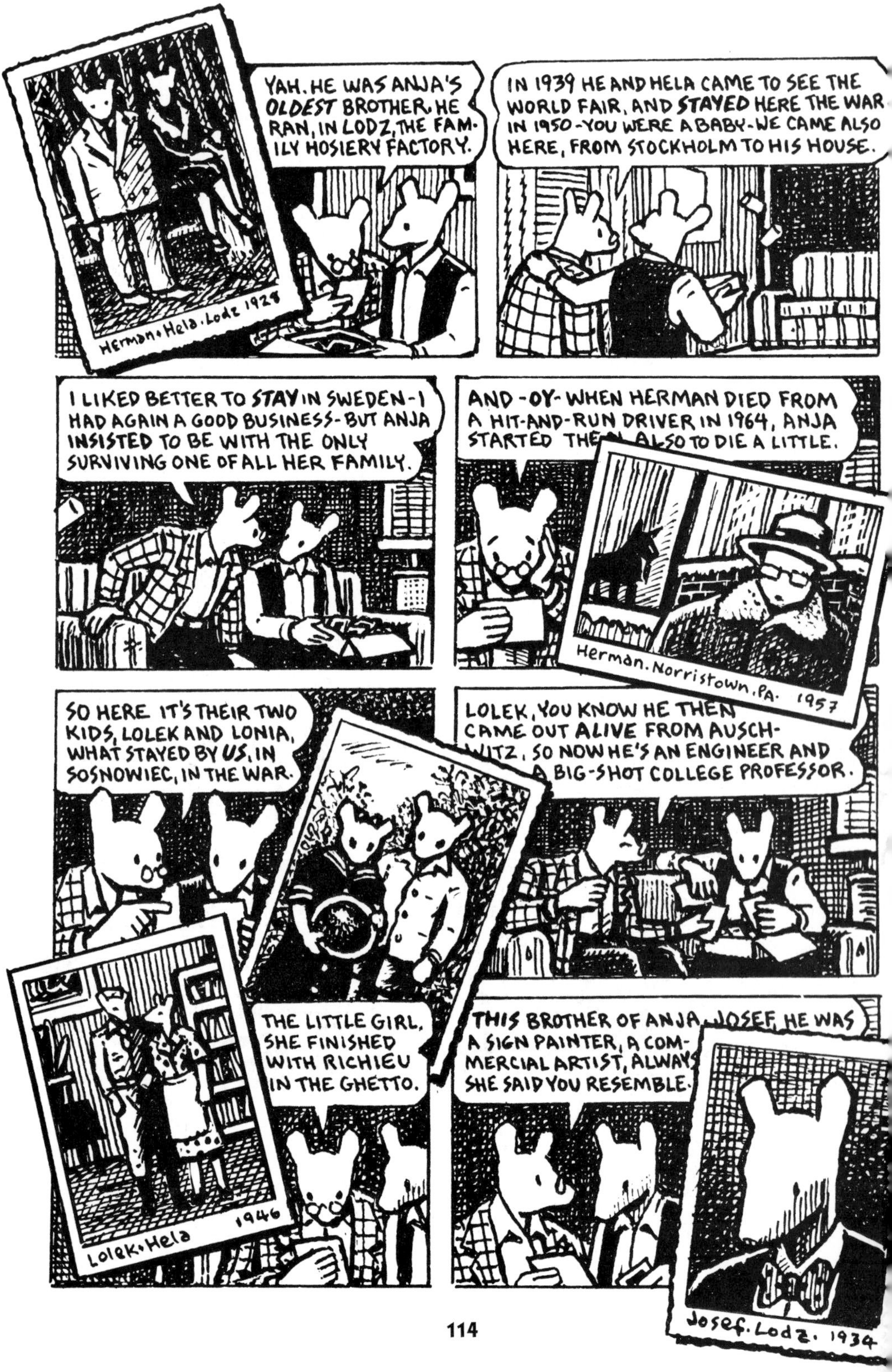
Herman. Hela. Lodz 1928
YAH. HE WAS ANJA'S OLDEST BROTHER. HE RAN, IN LODZ, THE FAMILY HOSIERY FACTORY.
IN 1939 HE AND HELA CAME TO SEE THE WORLD FAIR, AND STAYED HERE THE WAR. IN 1950 - YOU WERE A BABY - WE CAME ALSO HERE, FROM STOCKHOLM TO HIS HOUSE.
I LIKED BETTER TO STAY IN SWEDEN - I HAD AGAIN A GOOD BUSINESS - BUT ANJA INSISTED TO BE WITH THE ONLY SURVIVING ONE OF ALL HER FAMILY.
AND - OY - WHEN HERMAN DIED FROM A HIT-AND-RUN DRIVER IN 1964, ANJA STARTED THE ALSO TO DIE A LITTLE.
Herman. Norristown, PA. 1957
SO HERE IT'S THEIR TWO KIDS, LOLEK AND LONIA, WHAT STAYED BY US, IN SOSNOWIEC, IN THE WAR.
LOLEK, YOU KNOW HE THEN CAME OUT ALIVE FROM AUSCHWITZ, SO NOW HE'S AN ENGINEER AND A BIG-SHOT COLLEGE PROFESSOR.
Lolek. Hela 1946
THE LITTLE GIRL, SHE FINISHED WITH RICHIEU IN THE GHETTO.
THIS BROTHER OF ANJA, JOSEF, HE WAS A SIGN PAINTER, A COMMERCIAL ARTIST, ALWAYS SHE SAID YOU RESEMBLE.
Josef. Lodz. 1934

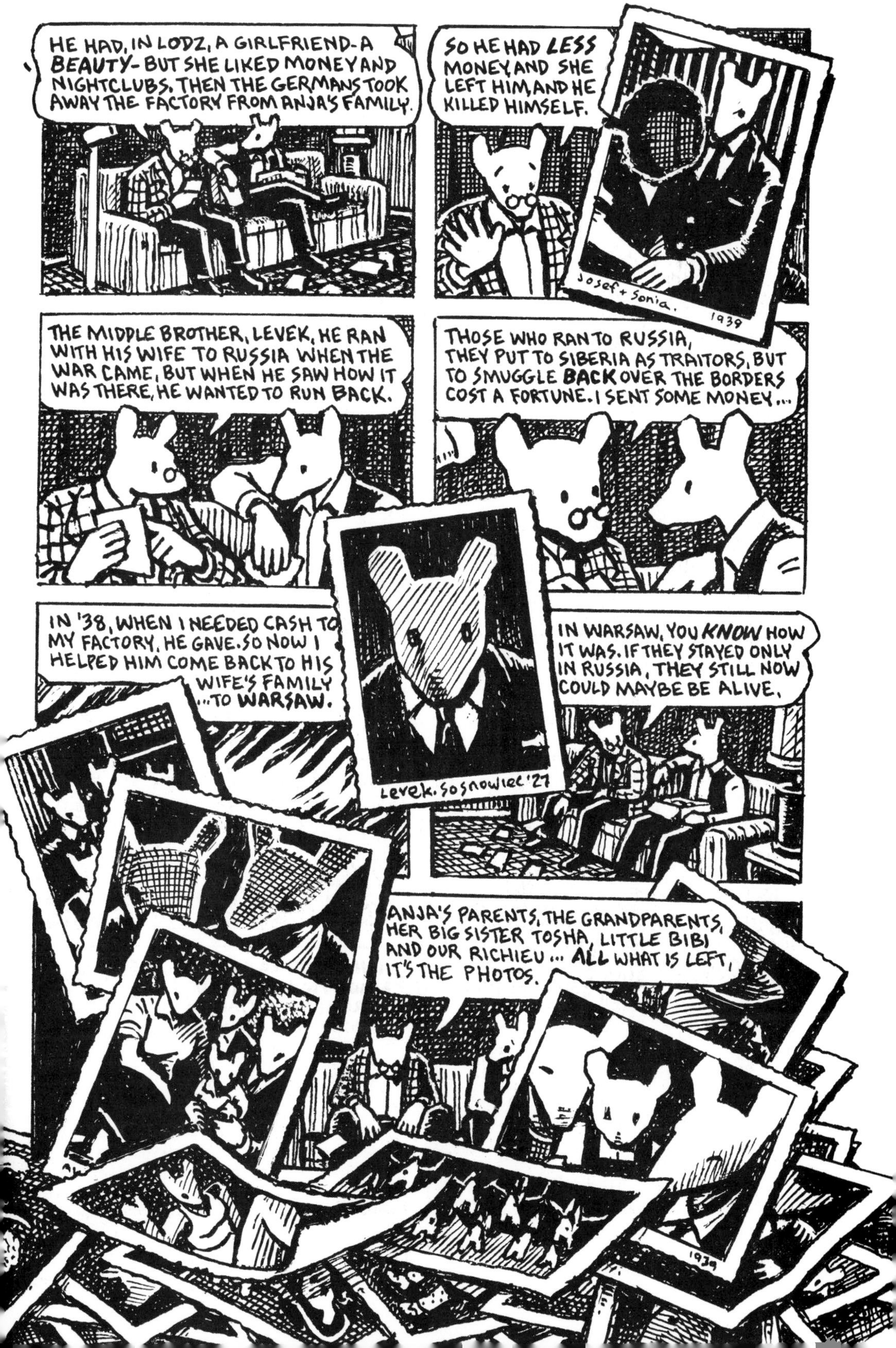
HE HAD, IN LODZ, A GIRLFRIEND- A BEAUTY- BUT SHE LIKED MONEY AND NIGHTCLUBS. THEN THE GERMANS TOOK AWAY THE FACTORY FROM ANJA'S FAMILY.
SO HE HAD LESS MONEY, AND SHE LEFT HIM, AND HE KILLED HIMSELF.
Josef + Sonia. 1939
THE MIDDLE BROTHER, LEVEK, HE RAN WITH HIS WIFE TO RUSSIA WHEN THE WAR CAME, BUT WHEN HE SAW HOW IT WAS THERE, HE WANTED TO RUN BACK.
THOSE WHO RAN TO RUSSIA, THEY PUT TO SIBERIA AS TRAITORS, BUT TO SMUGGLE BACK OVER THE BORDERS COST A FORTUNE. I SENT SOME MONEY...
IN '38, WHEN I NEEDED CASH TO MY FACTORY, HE GAVE. SO NOW I HELPED HIM COME BACK TO HIS WIFE'S FAMILY ...TO WARSAW.
Levek. Sosnowiec '27
IN WARSAW, YOU KNOW HOW IT WAS. IF THEY STAYED ONLY IN RUSSIA, THEY STILL NOW COULD MAYBE BE ALIVE.
ANJA'S PARENTS, THE GRANDPARENTS, HER BIG SISTER TOSHA, LITTLE BIBI AND OUR RICHIEU... ALL WHAT IS LEFT, IT'S THE PHOTOS.
1939

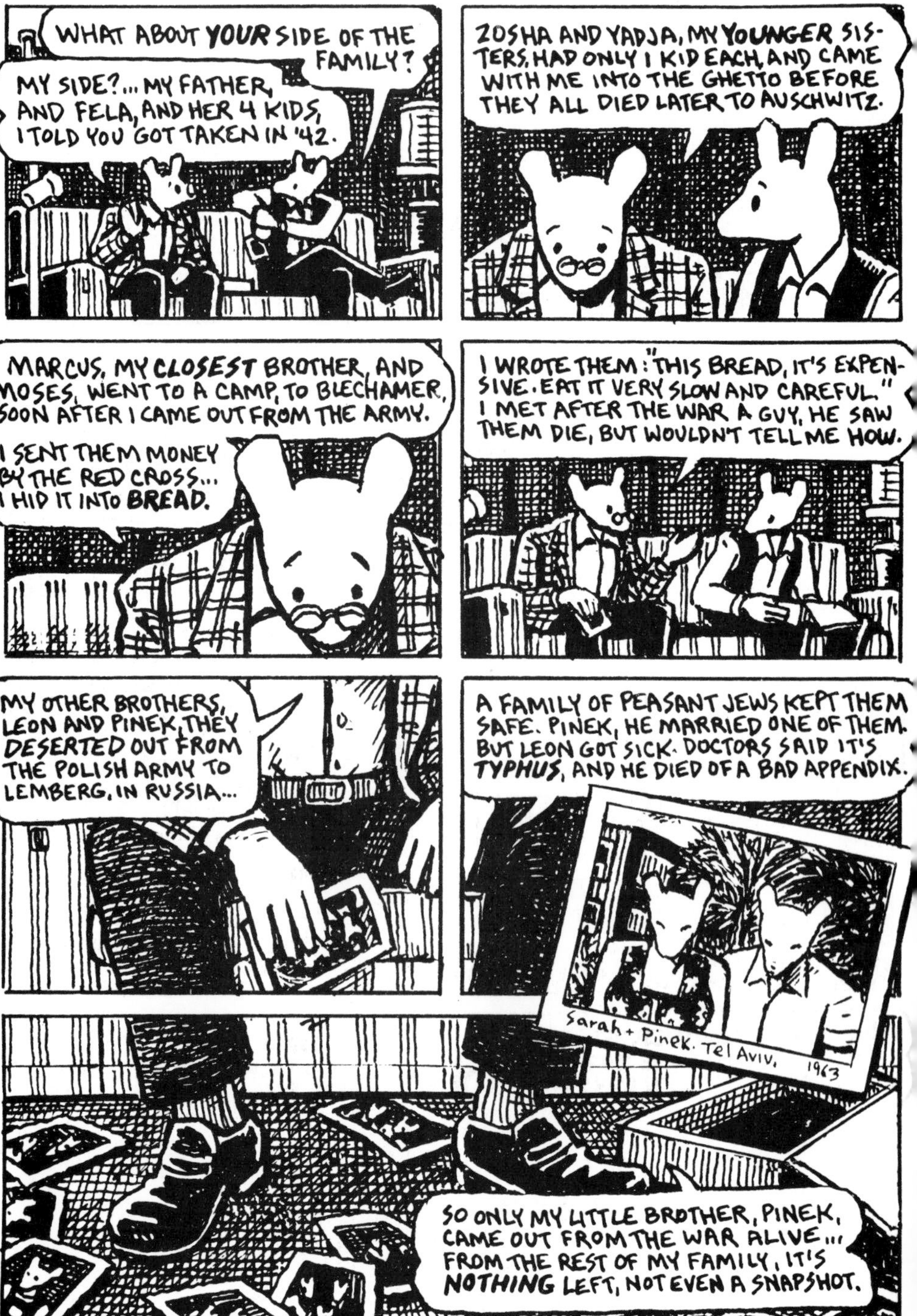
WHAT ABOUT YOUR SIDE OF THE FAMILY?
MY SIDE?... MY FATHER, AND FELA, AND HER 4 KIDS, I TOLD YOU GOT TAKEN IN '42.
ZOSHA AND YADJA, MY YOUNGER SISTERS, HAD ONLY 1 KID EACH, AND CAME WITH ME INTO THE GHETTO BEFORE THEY ALL DIED LATER TO AUSCHWITZ.
MARCUS, MY CLOSEST BROTHER, AND MOSES, WENT TO A CAMP, TO BLECHAMER, SOON AFTER I CAME OUT FROM THE ARMY.
I SENT THEM MONEY BY THE RED CROSS... I HID IT INTO BREAD.
I WROTE THEM: "THIS BREAD, IT'S EXPENSIVE. EAT IT VERY SLOW AND CAREFUL." I MET AFTER THE WAR A GUY, HE SAW THEM DIE, BUT WOULDN'T TELL ME HOW.
MY OTHER BROTHERS, LEON AND PINEK, THEY DESERTED OUT FROM THE POLISH ARMY TO LEMBERG, IN RUSSIA...
A FAMILY OF PEASANT JEWS KEPT THEM SAFE. PINEK, HE MARRIED ONE OF THEM. BUT LEON GOT SICK. DOCTORS SAID IT'S TYPHUS, AND HE DIED OF A BAD APPENDIX.
Sarah + Pinek. Tel Aviv. 1963
SO ONLY MY LITTLE BROTHER, PINEK, CAME OUT FROM THE WAR ALIVE... FROM THE REST OF MY FAMILY, IT'S NOTHING LEFT, NOT EVEN A SNAPSHOT.

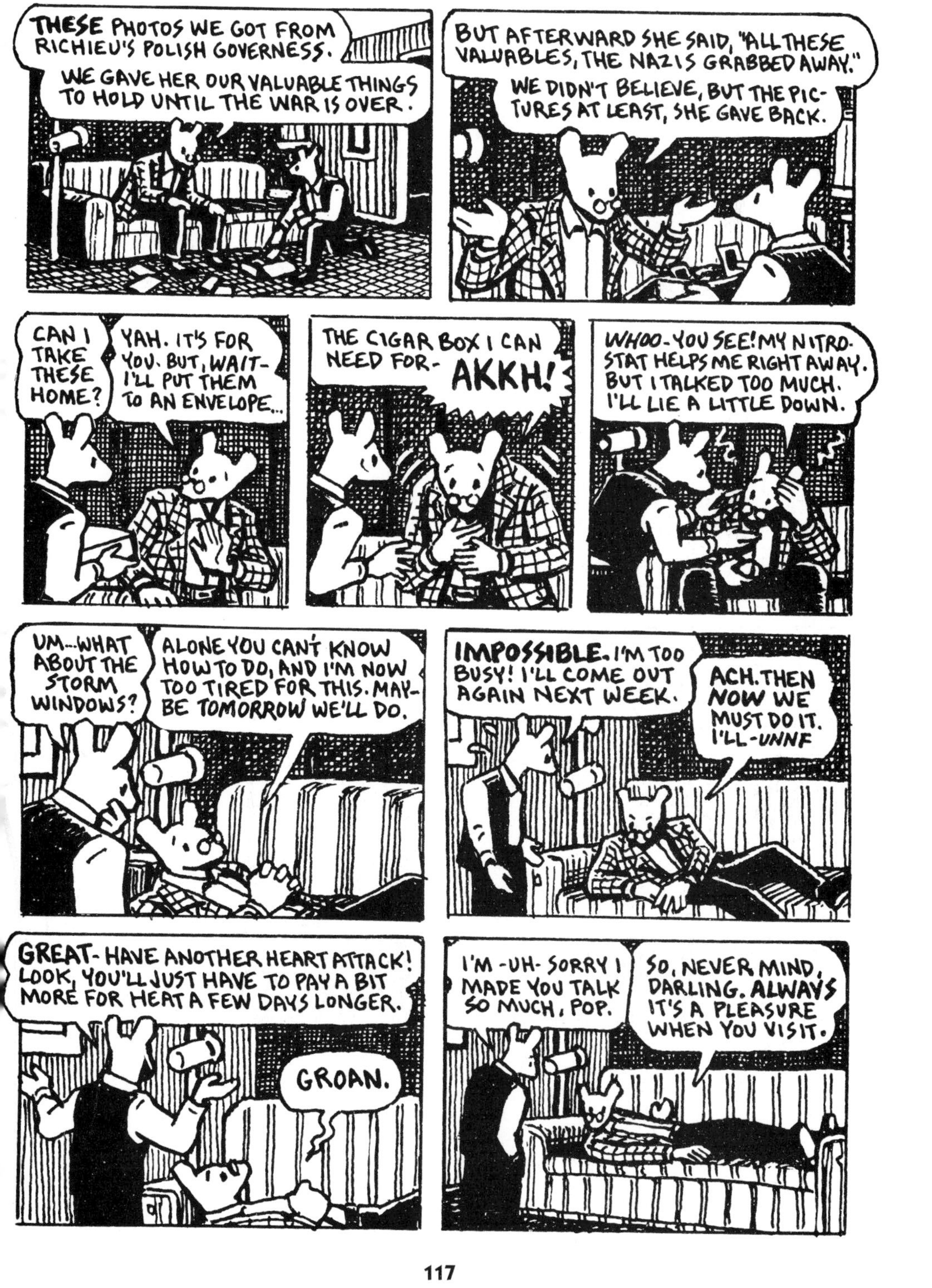
THESE PHOTOS WE GOT FROM RICHIEU'S POLISH GOVERNESS.
WE GAVE HER OUR VALUABLE THINGS TO HOLD UNTIL THE WAR IS OVER.
BUT AFTERWARD SHE SAID, "ALL THESE VALUABLES, THE NAZIS GRABBED AWAY."
WE DIDN'T BELIEVE, BUT THE PICTURES AT LEAST, SHE GAVE BACK.
CAN I TAKE THESE HOME?
YAH. IT'S FOR YOU. BUT, WAIT- I'LL PUT THEM TO AN ENVELOPE...
THE CIGAR BOX I CAN NEED FOR-
AKKH!
WHOO- YOU SEE! MY NITROSTAT HELPS ME RIGHT AWAY. BUT I TALKED TOO MUCH. I'LL LIE A LITTLE DOWN.
UM...WHAT ABOUT THE STORM WINDOWS?
ALONE YOU CAN'T KNOW HOW TO DO, AND I'M NOW TOO TIRED FOR THIS. MAYBE TOMORROW WE'LL DO.
IMPOSSIBLE. I'M TOO BUSY! I'LL COME OUT AGAIN NEXT WEEK.
ACH. THEN NOW WE MUST DO IT. I'LL-UNNF
GREAT- HAVE ANOTHER HEART ATTACK! LOOK, YOU'LL JUST HAVE TO PAY A BIT MORE FOR HEAT A FEW DAYS LONGER.
GROAN.
I'M -UH- SORRY I MADE YOU TALK SO MUCH, POP.
SO, NEVER MIND, DARLING. ALWAYS IT'S A PLEASURE WHEN YOU VISIT.

CHAPTER FIVE

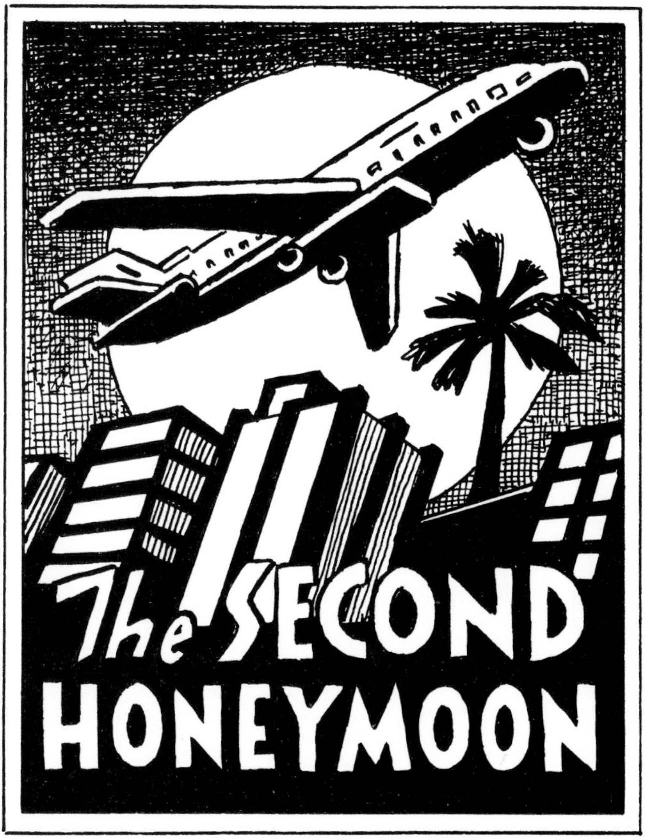
The SECOND
HONEYMOON

Winter...

WANT SOME COFFEE?

AND SHE SAID: "NO! I WILL NOT GO IN THE GAS CHAMBERS. AND MY *CHILDREN* WILL NOT—CLIK

YOU BET!

Y'KNOW, I'VE GOT OVER 20 HOURS OF VLADEK'S STORY ON TAPE NOW. WE WERE JUST ABOUT *FINISHED* WHEN HE RAN OFF TO FLORIDA.

HE HASN'T CALLED US ONCE. I HOPE HE'S OKAY...

MALA IS DOWN THERE. MAYBE THEY MET AND KILLED EACH OTHER.

ACTUALLY, I THINK THEIR BATTLE KEEPS HIM GOING. HE'S BEEN A BIZARRE COMBINATION OF HELPLESSNESS AND MANIACAL ENERGY EVER SINCE SHE LEFT.

WHAT ARE WE GONNA DO WITH VLADEK? WE SURE AS HELL CAN'T MOVE OUT TO REGO PARK!

MAYBE HE COULD MOVE IN HERE WITH US.

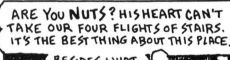

ARE YOU **NUTS**? HIS HEART CAN'T TAKE OUR FOUR FLIGHTS OF STAIRS. IT'S THE BEST THING ABOUT THIS PLACE.

BESIDES, WHAT IF HE SAYS YES!

WELL...IT'S UP TO YOU... HE'S YOUR FATHER.

STOP! I FEEL GUILTY ENOUGH ALREADY!

GREAT. THAT SOLVES EV-ERYTHING!

I WISH HE AND MALA COULD PATCH THINGS UP AND MAKE EACH OTHER MISERABLE AGAIN.

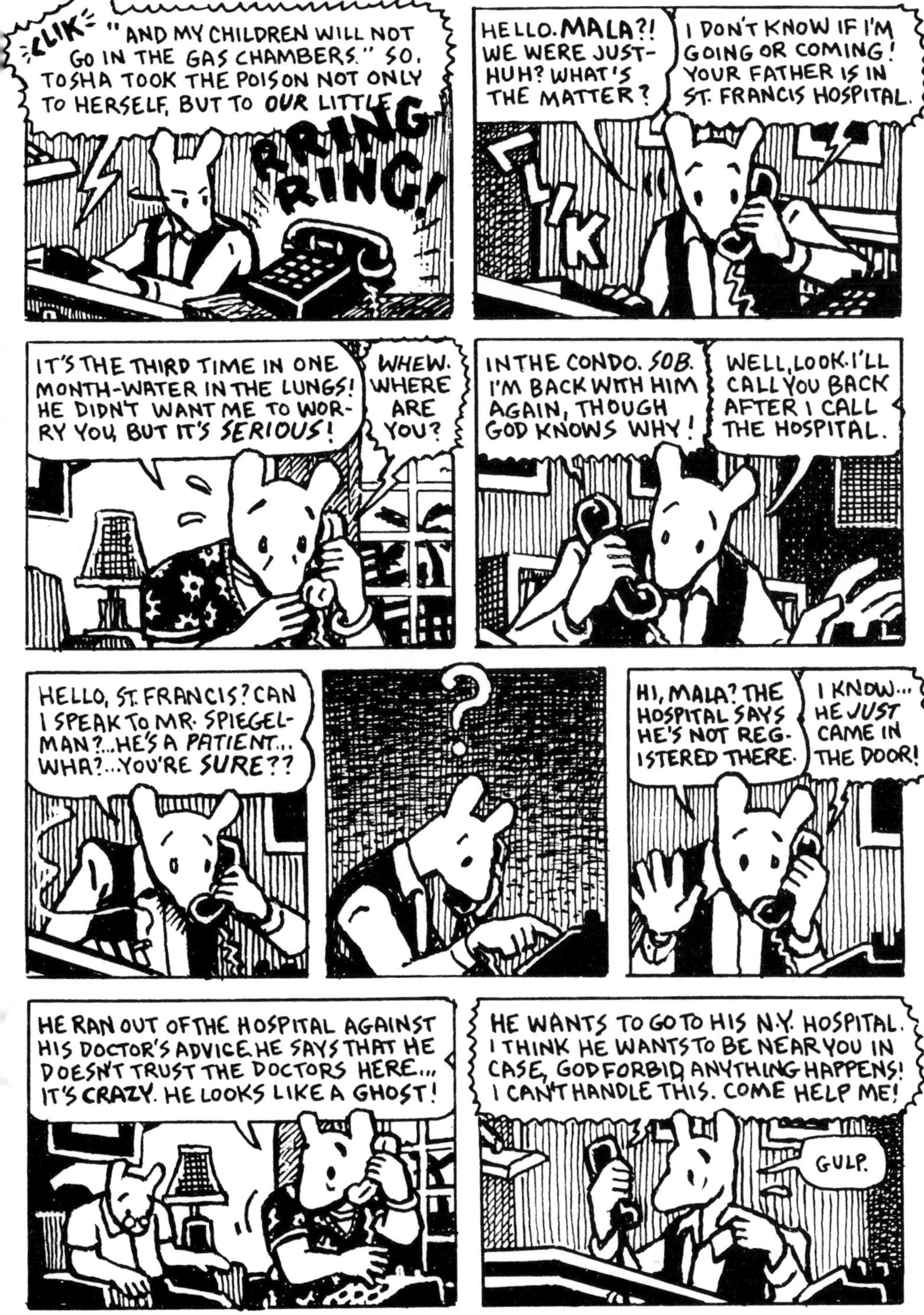
CLIK
"AND MY CHILDREN WILL NOT GO IN THE GAS CHAMBERS." SO, TOSHA TOOK THE POISON NOT ONLY TO HERSELF, BUT TO OUR LITTLE
RRING RING!
HELLO. MALA?! WE WERE JUST- HUH? WHAT'S THE MATTER?
I DON'T KNOW IF I'M GOING OR COMING! YOUR FATHER IS IN ST. FRANCIS HOSPITAL.
CLIK
IT'S THE THIRD TIME IN ONE MONTH-WATER IN THE LUNGS! HE DIDN'T WANT ME TO WORRY YOU, BUT IT'S SERIOUS!
WHEW. WHERE ARE YOU?
IN THE CONDO. SOB. I'M BACK WITH HIM AGAIN, THOUGH GOD KNOWS WHY!
WELL, LOOK. I'LL CALL YOU BACK AFTER I CALL THE HOSPITAL.
HELLO, ST. FRANCIS? CAN I SPEAK TO MR. SPIEGELMAN?...HE'S A PATIENT... WHA?...YOU'RE SURE??
?
HI, MALA? THE HOSPITAL SAYS HE'S NOT REGISTERED THERE.
I KNOW... HE JUST CAME IN THE DOOR!
HE RAN OUT OF THE HOSPITAL AGAINST HIS DOCTOR'S ADVICE. HE SAYS THAT HE DOESN'T TRUST THE DOCTORS HERE... IT'S CRAZY. HE LOOKS LIKE A GHOST!
HE WANTS TO GO TO HIS N.Y. HOSPITAL. I THINK HE WANTS TO BE NEAR YOU IN CASE, GOD FORBID, ANYTHING HAPPENS! I CAN'T HANDLE THIS. COME HELP ME!
GULP.

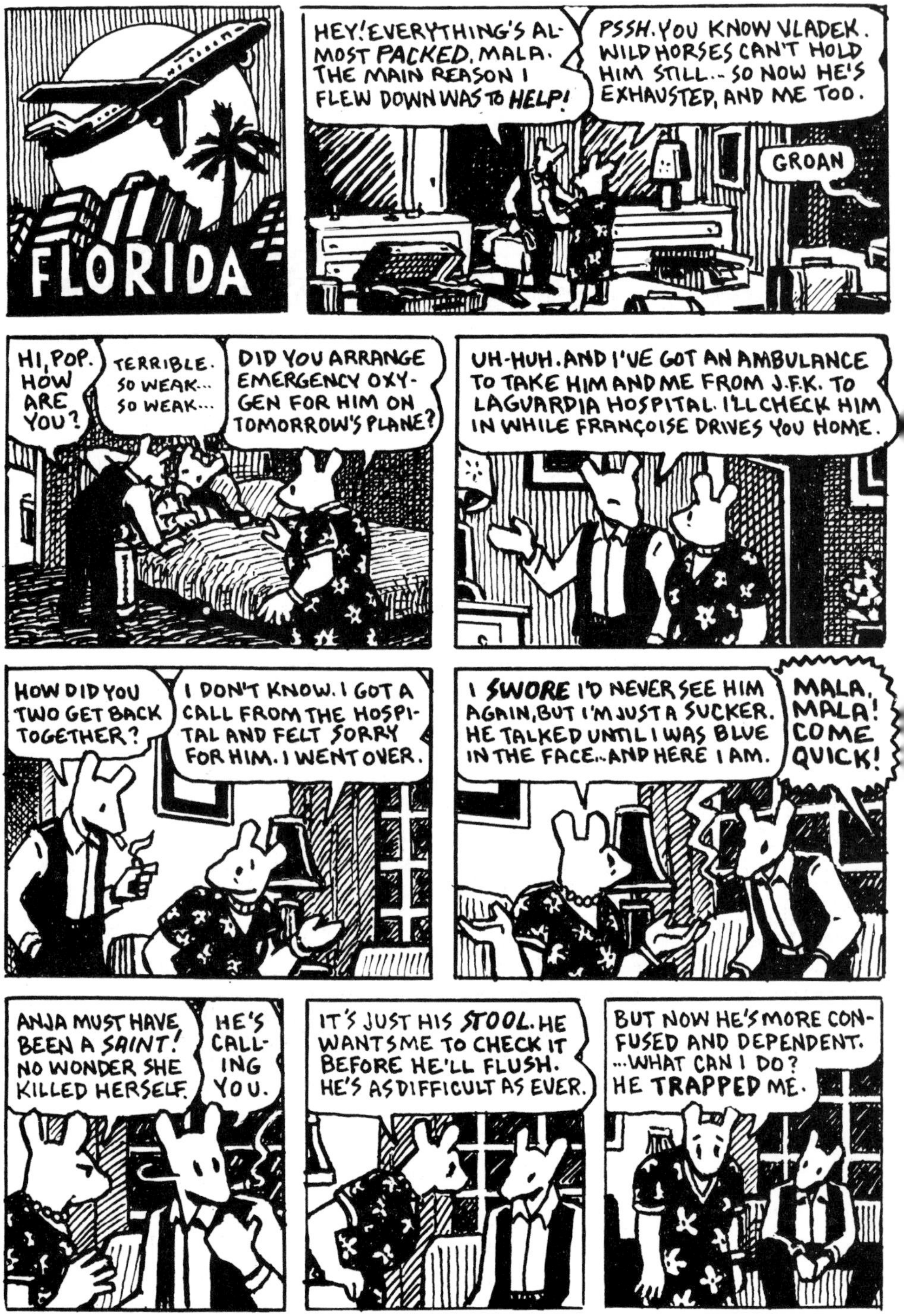
FLORIDA
HEY! EVERYTHING'S ALMOST PACKED, MALA. THE MAIN REASON I FLEW DOWN WAS TO HELP!
PSSH. YOU KNOW VLADEK. WILD HORSES CAN'T HOLD HIM STILL.. SO NOW HE'S EXHAUSTED, AND ME TOO.
GROAN
HI, POP. HOW ARE YOU?
TERRIBLE. SO WEAK... SO WEAK...
DID YOU ARRANGE EMERGENCY OXYGEN FOR HIM ON TOMORROW'S PLANE?
UH-HUH. AND I'VE GOT AN AMBULANCE TO TAKE HIM AND ME FROM J.F.K. TO LAGUARDIA HOSPITAL. I'LL CHECK HIM IN WHILE FRANÇOISE DRIVES YOU HOME.
HOW DID YOU TWO GET BACK TOGETHER?
I DON'T KNOW. I GOT A CALL FROM THE HOSPITAL AND FELT SORRY FOR HIM. I WENT OVER.
I SWORE I'D NEVER SEE HIM AGAIN, BUT I'M JUST A SUCKER. HE TALKED UNTIL I WAS BLUE IN THE FACE.. AND HERE I AM.
MALA, MALA! COME QUICK!
ANJA MUST HAVE BEEN A SAINT! NO WONDER SHE KILLED HERSELF.
HE'S CALLING YOU.
IT'S JUST HIS STOOL. HE WANTS ME TO CHECK IT BEFORE HE'LL FLUSH. HE'S AS DIFFICULT AS EVER.
BUT NOW HE'S MORE CONFUSED AND DEPENDENT. ...WHAT CAN I DO? HE TRAPPED ME.

Next morning...

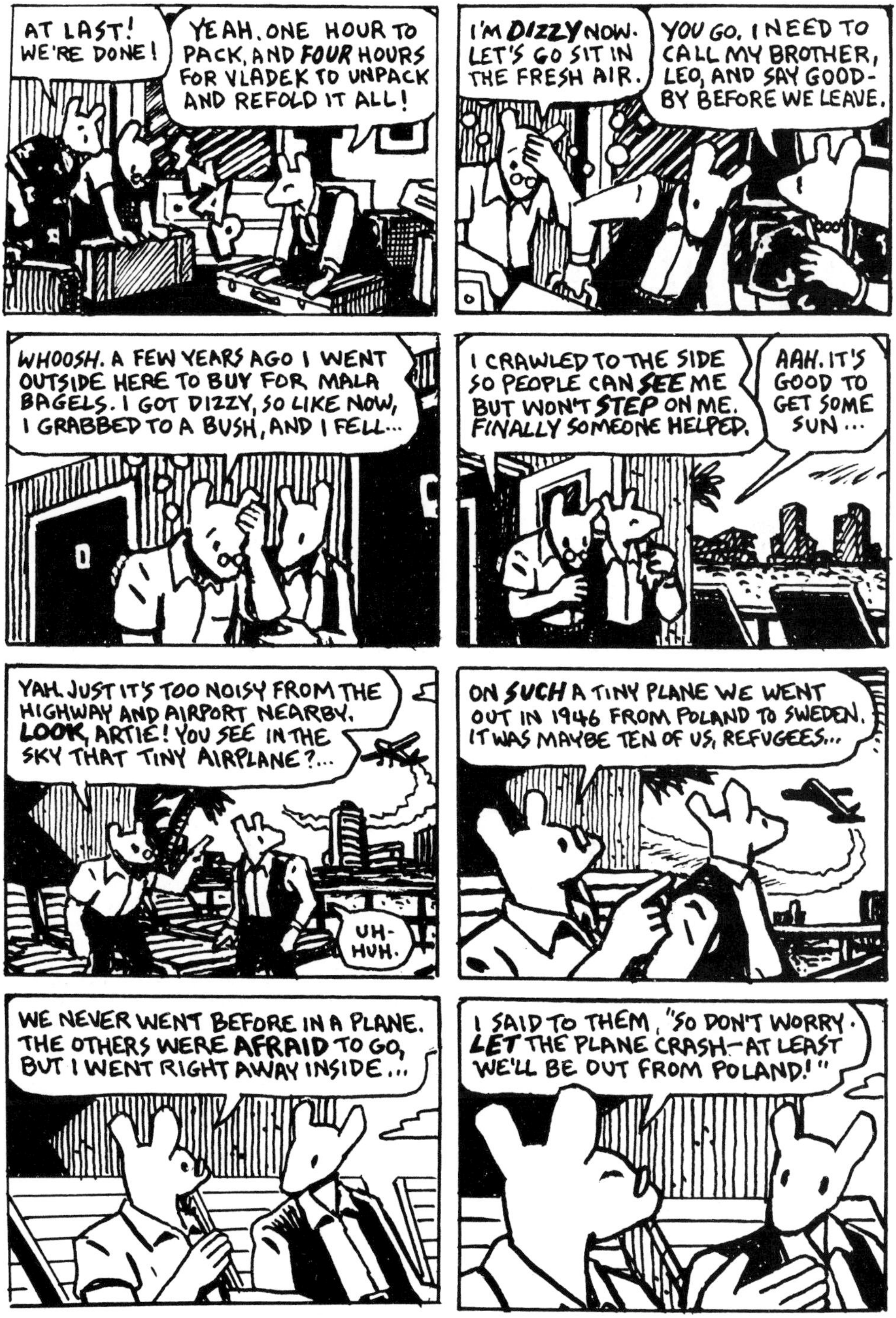
AT LAST! WE'RE DONE!
YEAH. ONE HOUR TO PACK, AND FOUR HOURS FOR VLADEK TO UNPACK AND REFOLD IT ALL!
I'M DIZZY NOW. LET'S GO SIT IN THE FRESH AIR.
YOU GO. I NEED TO CALL MY BROTHER, LEO, AND SAY GOOD-BY BEFORE WE LEAVE.
WHOOSH. A FEW YEARS AGO I WENT OUTSIDE HERE TO BUY FOR MALA BAGELS. I GOT DIZZY, SO LIKE NOW, I GRABBED TO A BUSH, AND I FELL...
I CRAWLED TO THE SIDE SO PEOPLE CAN SEE ME BUT WON'T STEP ON ME. FINALLY SOMEONE HELPED.
AAH. IT'S GOOD TO GET SOME SUN...
YAH. JUST IT'S TOO NOISY FROM THE HIGHWAY AND AIRPORT NEARBY. LOOK, ARTIE! YOU SEE IN THE SKY THAT TINY AIRPLANE?...
UH-HUH.
ON SUCH A TINY PLANE WE WENT OUT IN 1946 FROM POLAND TO SWEDEN. IT WAS MAYBE TEN OF US, REFUGEES...
WE NEVER WENT BEFORE IN A PLANE. THE OTHERS WERE AFRAID TO GO, BUT I WENT RIGHT AWAY INSIDE...
I SAID TO THEM, "SO DON'T WORRY. LET THE PLANE CRASH—AT LEAST WE'LL BE OUT FROM POLAND!"

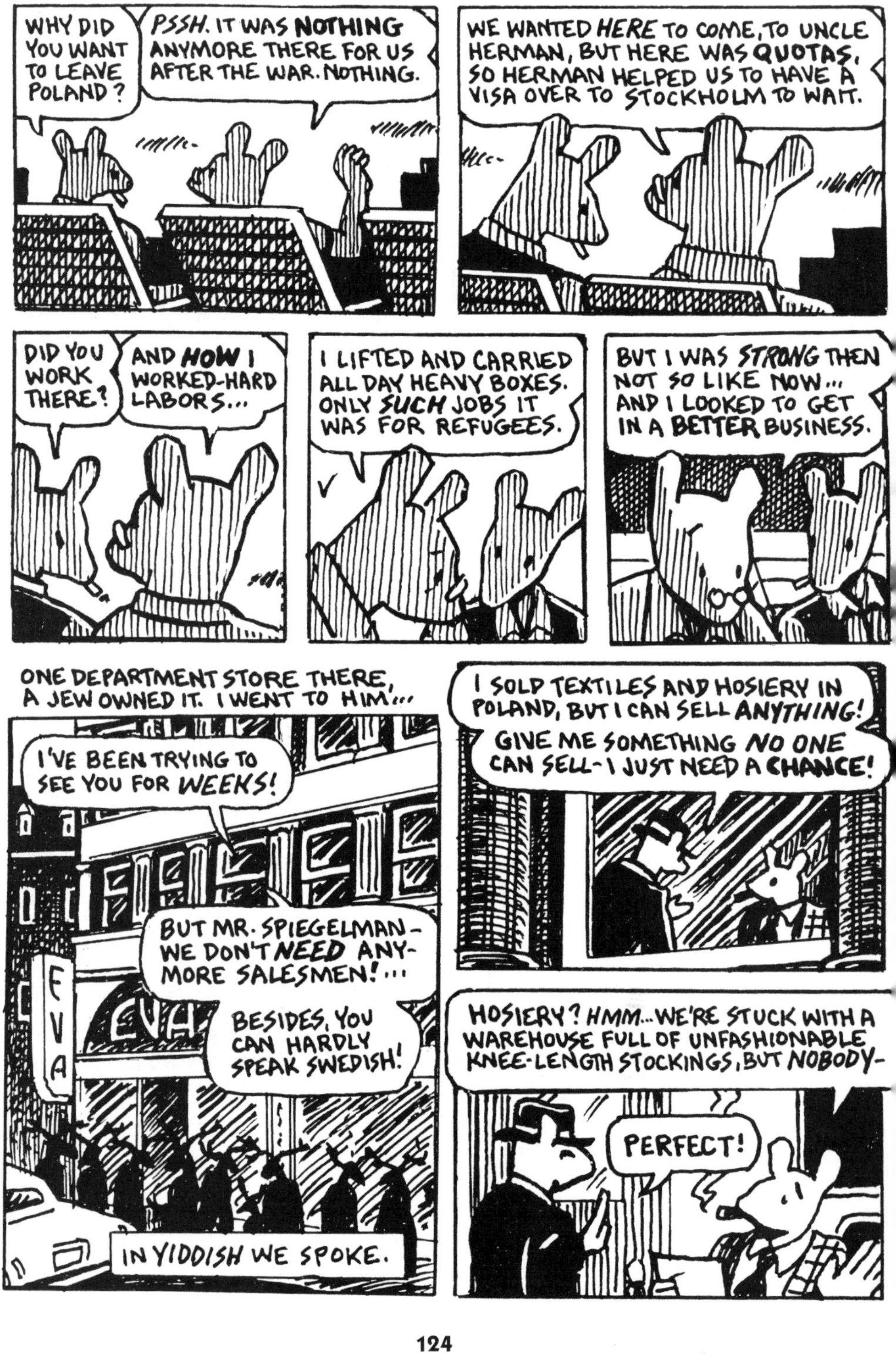
WHY DID YOU WANT TO LEAVE POLAND?
PSSH. IT WAS NOTHING ANYMORE THERE FOR US AFTER THE WAR. NOTHING.
WE WANTED HERE TO COME, TO UNCLE HERMAN, BUT HERE WAS QUOTAS, SO HERMAN HELPED US TO HAVE A VISA OVER TO STOCKHOLM TO WAIT.
DID YOU WORK THERE?
AND HOW I WORKED-HARD LABORS...
I LIFTED AND CARRIED ALL DAY HEAVY BOXES. ONLY SUCH JOBS IT WAS FOR REFUGEES.
BUT I WAS STRONG THEN NOT SO LIKE NOW... AND I LOOKED TO GET IN A BETTER BUSINESS.
ONE DEPARTMENT STORE THERE, A JEW OWNED IT. I WENT TO HIM...
I'VE BEEN TRYING TO SEE YOU FOR WEEKS!
BUT MR. SPIEGELMAN - WE DON'T NEED ANY-MORE SALESMEN!...
BESIDES, YOU CAN HARDLY SPEAK SWEDISH!
EVA
IN YIDDISH WE SPOKE.
I SOLD TEXTILES AND HOSIERY IN POLAND, BUT I CAN SELL ANYTHING!
GIVE ME SOMETHING NO ONE CAN SELL - I JUST NEED A CHANCE!
HOSIERY? HMM... WE'RE STUCK WITH A WAREHOUSE FULL OF UNFASHIONABLE KNEE-LENGTH STOCKINGS, BUT NOBODY-
PERFECT!

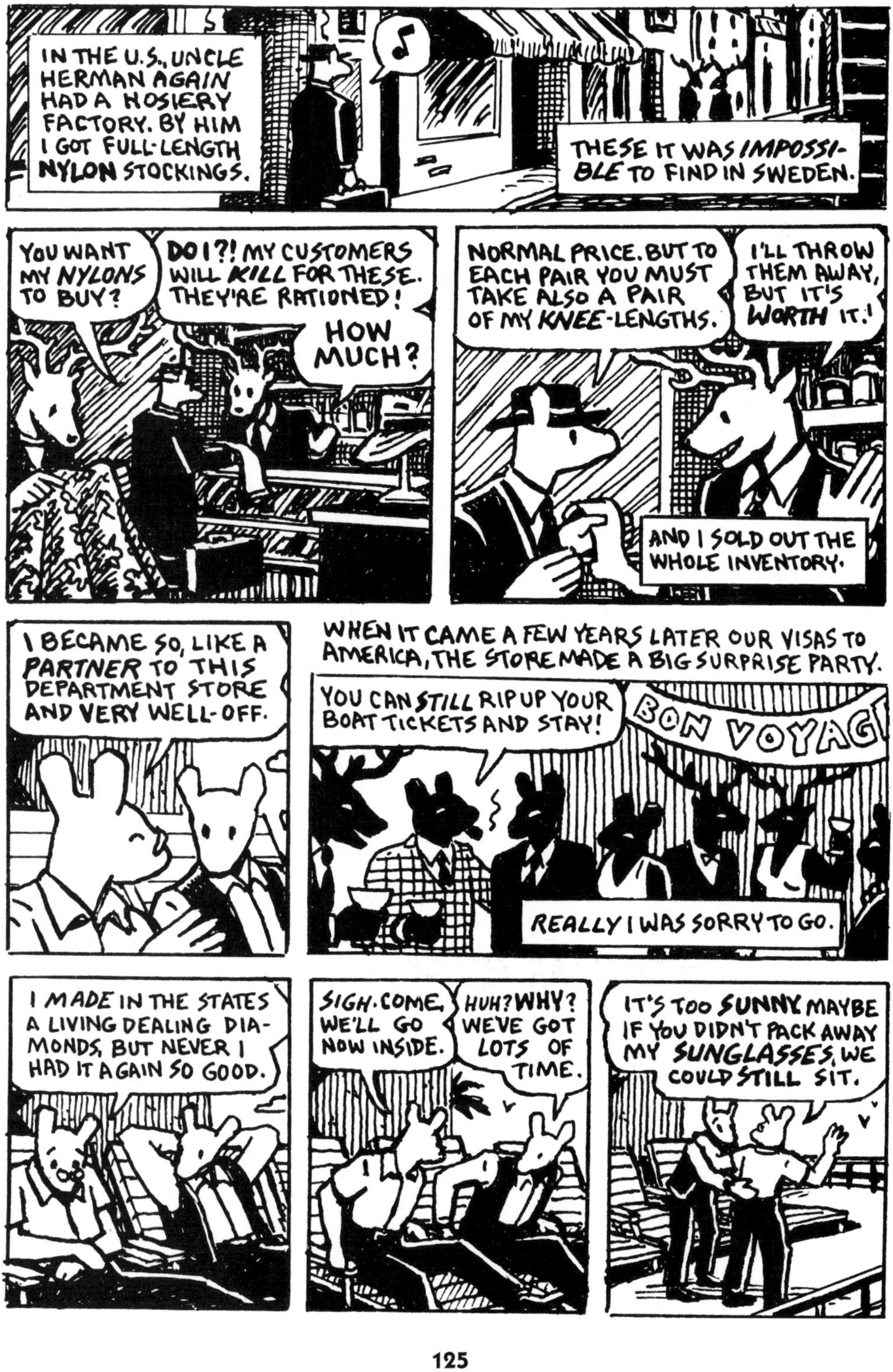
IN THE U.S., UNCLE HERMAN AGAIN HAD A HOSIERY FACTORY. BY HIM I GOT FULL-LENGTH NYLON STOCKINGS.
THESE IT WAS IMPOSSIBLE TO FIND IN SWEDEN.
YOU WANT MY NYLONS TO BUY?
DO I?! MY CUSTOMERS WILL KILL FOR THESE. THEY'RE RATIONED!
HOW MUCH?
NORMAL PRICE. BUT TO EACH PAIR YOU MUST TAKE ALSO A PAIR OF MY KNEE-LENGTHS.
I'LL THROW THEM AWAY, BUT IT'S WORTH IT.!
AND I SOLD OUT THE WHOLE INVENTORY.
I BECAME SO, LIKE A PARTNER TO THIS DEPARTMENT STORE AND VERY WELL-OFF.
WHEN IT CAME A FEW YEARS LATER OUR VISAS TO AMERICA, THE STORE MADE A BIG SURPRISE PARTY.
YOU CAN STILL RIP UP YOUR BOAT TICKETS AND STAY!
BON VOYAG
REALLY I WAS SORRY TO GO.
I MADE IN THE STATES A LIVING DEALING DIAMONDS, BUT NEVER I HAD IT AGAIN SO GOOD.
SIGH. COME, WE'LL GO NOW INSIDE.
HUH? WHY? WE'VE GOT LOTS OF TIME.
IT'S TOO SUNNY. MAYBE IF YOU DIDN'T PACK AWAY MY SUNGLASSES, WE COULD STILL SIT.

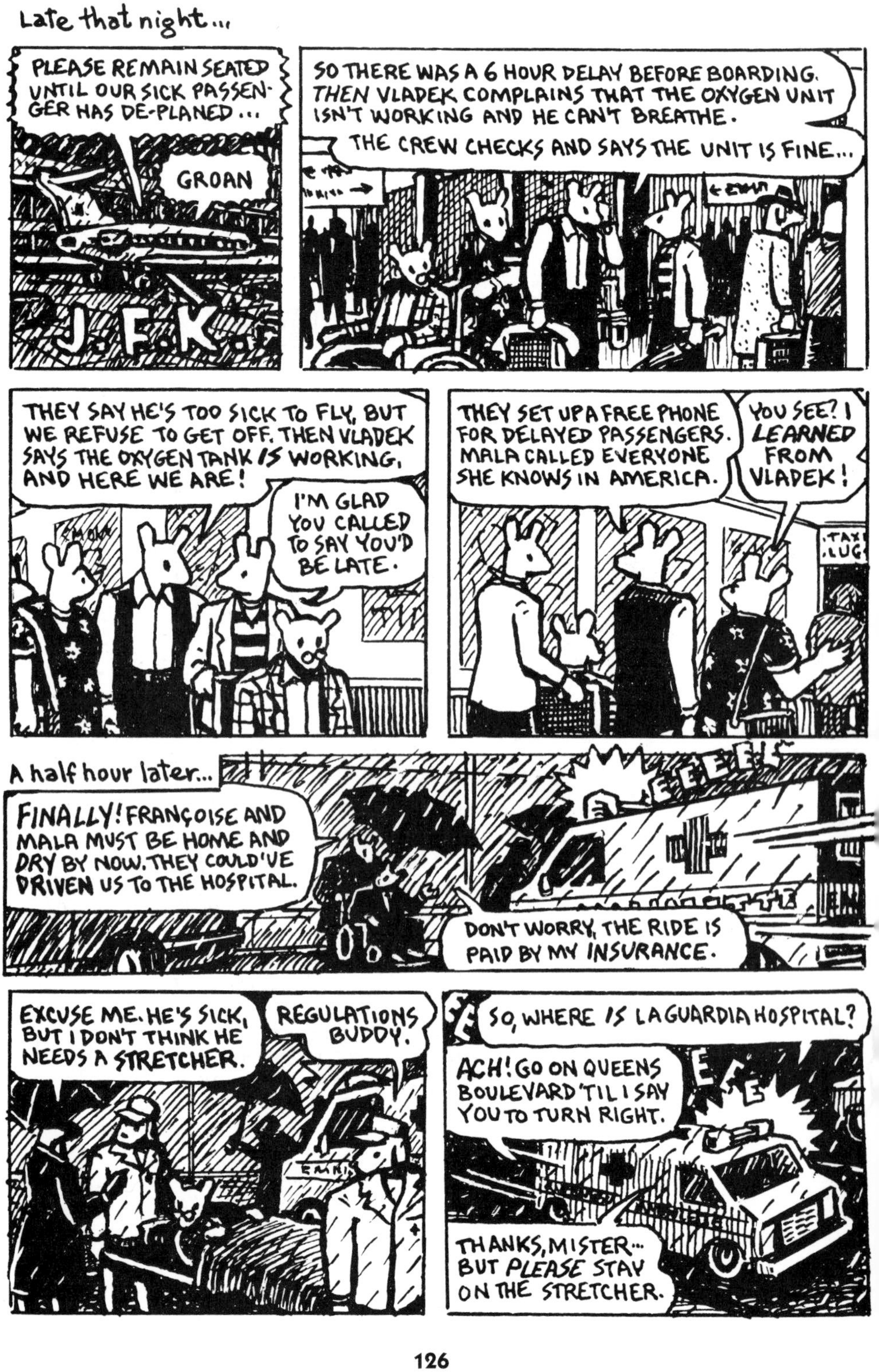

Late that night...
PLEASE REMAIN SEATED UNTIL OUR SICK PASSENGER HAS DE-PLANED...
GROAN
J.F.K.
SO THERE WAS A 6 HOUR DELAY BEFORE BOARDING. THEN VLADEK COMPLAINS THAT THE OXYGEN UNIT ISN'T WORKING AND HE CAN'T BREATHE.
THE CREW CHECKS AND SAYS THE UNIT IS FINE...
THEY SAY HE'S TOO SICK TO FLY, BUT WE REFUSE TO GET OFF. THEN VLADEK SAYS THE OXYGEN TANK IS WORKING, AND HERE WE ARE!
I'M GLAD YOU CALLED TO SAY YOU'D BE LATE.
THEY SET UP A FREE PHONE FOR DELAYED PASSENGERS. MALA CALLED EVERYONE SHE KNOWS IN AMERICA.
YOU SEE? I LEARNED FROM VLADEK!
A half hour later...
FINALLY! FRANÇOISE AND MALA MUST BE HOME AND DRY BY NOW. THEY COULD'VE DRIVEN US TO THE HOSPITAL.
DON'T WORRY, THE RIDE IS PAID BY MY INSURANCE.
EXCUSE ME. HE'S SICK, BUT I DON'T THINK HE NEEDS A STRETCHER.
REGULATIONS BUDDY.
SO, WHERE IS LA GUARDIA HOSPITAL?
ACH! GO ON QUEENS BOULEVARD 'TIL I SAY YOU TO TURN RIGHT.
THANKS, MISTER... BUT PLEASE STAY ON THE STRETCHER.

LaGuardia Hospital...

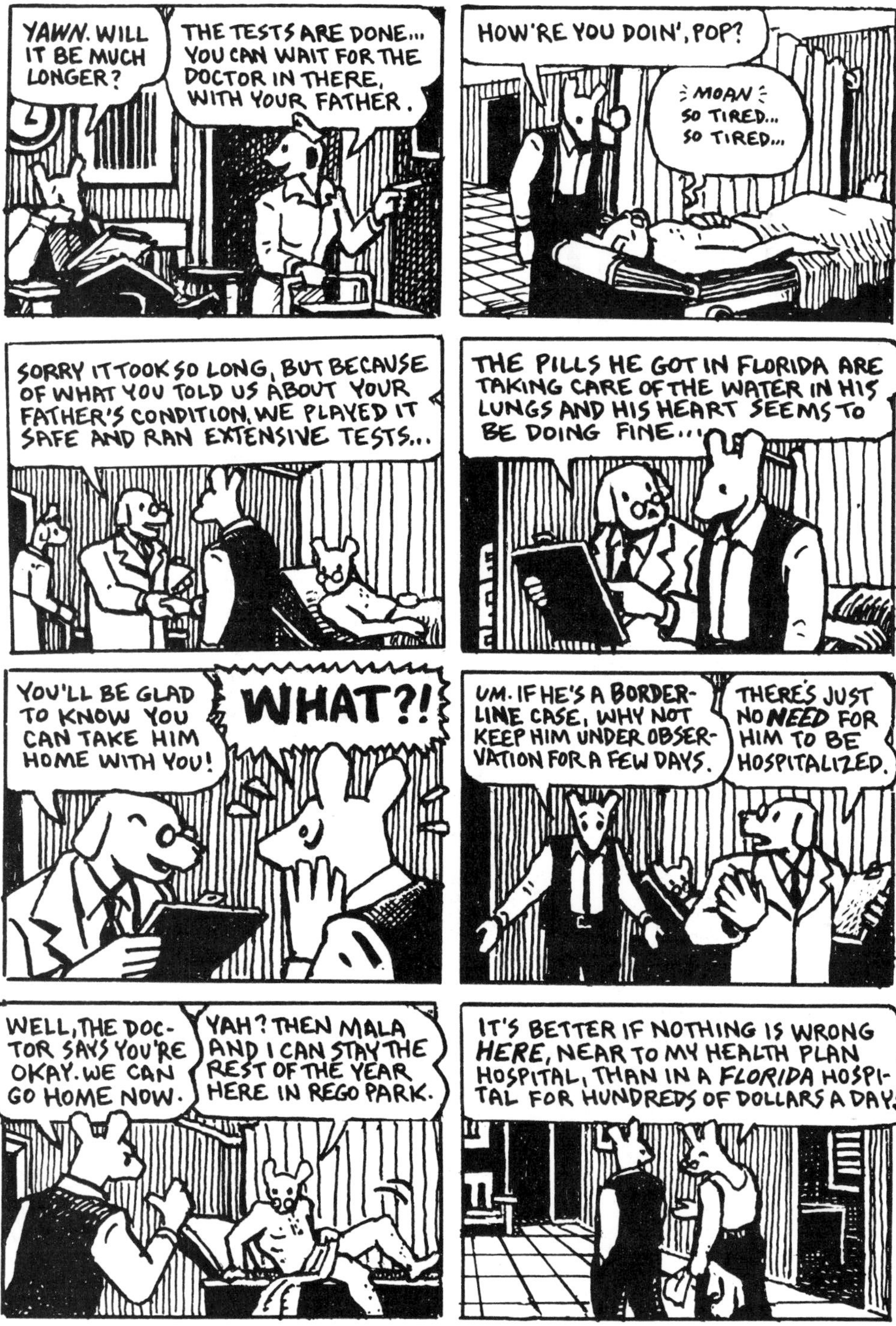
YAWN. WILL IT BE MUCH LONGER?
THE TESTS ARE DONE... YOU CAN WAIT FOR THE DOCTOR IN THERE, WITH YOUR FATHER.
HOW'RE YOU DOIN', POP?
MOAN SO TIRED... SO TIRED...
SORRY IT TOOK SO LONG, BUT BECAUSE OF WHAT YOU TOLD US ABOUT YOUR FATHER'S CONDITION, WE PLAYED IT SAFE AND RAN EXTENSIVE TESTS...
THE PILLS HE GOT IN FLORIDA ARE TAKING CARE OF THE WATER IN HIS LUNGS AND HIS HEART SEEMS TO BE DOING FINE...
YOU'LL BE GLAD TO KNOW YOU CAN TAKE HIM HOME WITH YOU!
WHAT?!
UM. IF HE'S A BORDER-LINE CASE, WHY NOT KEEP HIM UNDER OBSERVATION FOR A FEW DAYS.
THERE'S JUST NO NEED FOR HIM TO BE HOSPITALIZED.
WELL, THE DOCTOR SAYS YOU'RE OKAY. WE CAN GO HOME NOW.
YAH? THEN MALA AND I CAN STAY THE REST OF THE YEAR HERE IN REGO PARK.
IT'S BETTER IF NOTHING IS WRONG HERE, NEAR TO MY HEALTH PLAN HOSPITAL, THAN IN A FLORIDA HOSPITAL FOR HUNDREDS OF DOLLARS A DAY!

A month or so later...

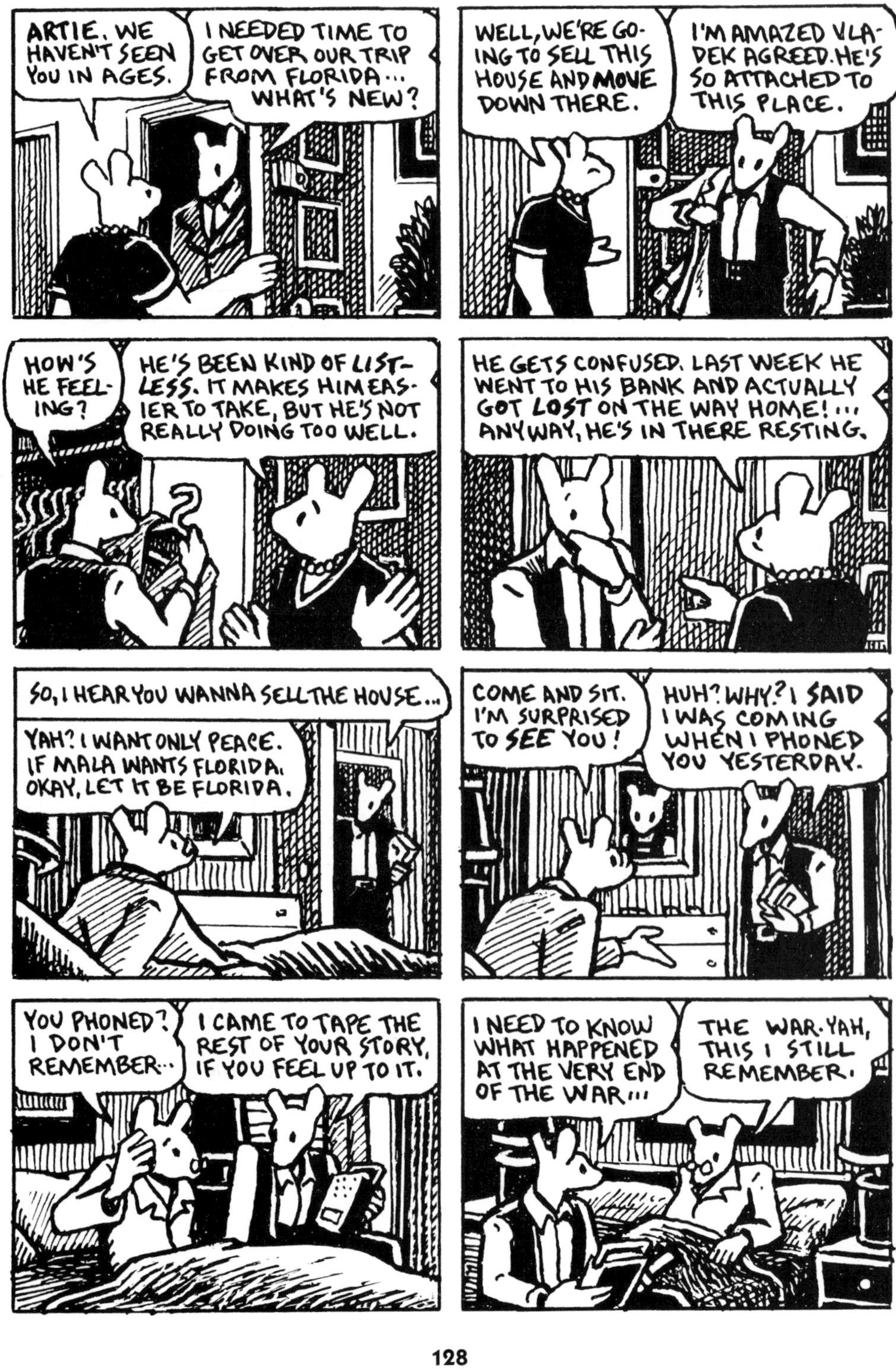
ARTIE. WE HAVEN'T SEEN YOU IN AGES.
I NEEDED TIME TO GET OVER OUR TRIP FROM FLORIDA... WHAT'S NEW?
WELL, WE'RE GOING TO SELL THIS HOUSE AND MOVE DOWN THERE.
I'M AMAZED VLADEK AGREED. HE'S SO ATTACHED TO THIS PLACE.
HOW'S HE FEELING?
HE'S BEEN KIND OF LISTLESS. IT MAKES HIM EASIER TO TAKE, BUT HE'S NOT REALLY DOING TOO WELL.
HE GETS CONFUSED. LAST WEEK HE WENT TO HIS BANK AND ACTUALLY GOT LOST ON THE WAY HOME!... ANYWAY, HE'S IN THERE RESTING.
SO, I HEAR YOU WANNA SELL THE HOUSE...
YAH? I WANT ONLY PEACE. IF MALA WANTS FLORIDA, OKAY, LET IT BE FLORIDA.
COME AND SIT. I'M SURPRISED TO SEE YOU!
HUH? WHY? I SAID I WAS COMING WHEN I PHONED YOU YESTERDAY.
YOU PHONED? I DON'T REMEMBER...
I CAME TO TAPE THE REST OF YOUR STORY, IF YOU FEEL UP TO IT.
I NEED TO KNOW WHAT HAPPENED AT THE VERY END OF THE WAR...
THE WAR. YAH, THIS I STILL REMEMBER.

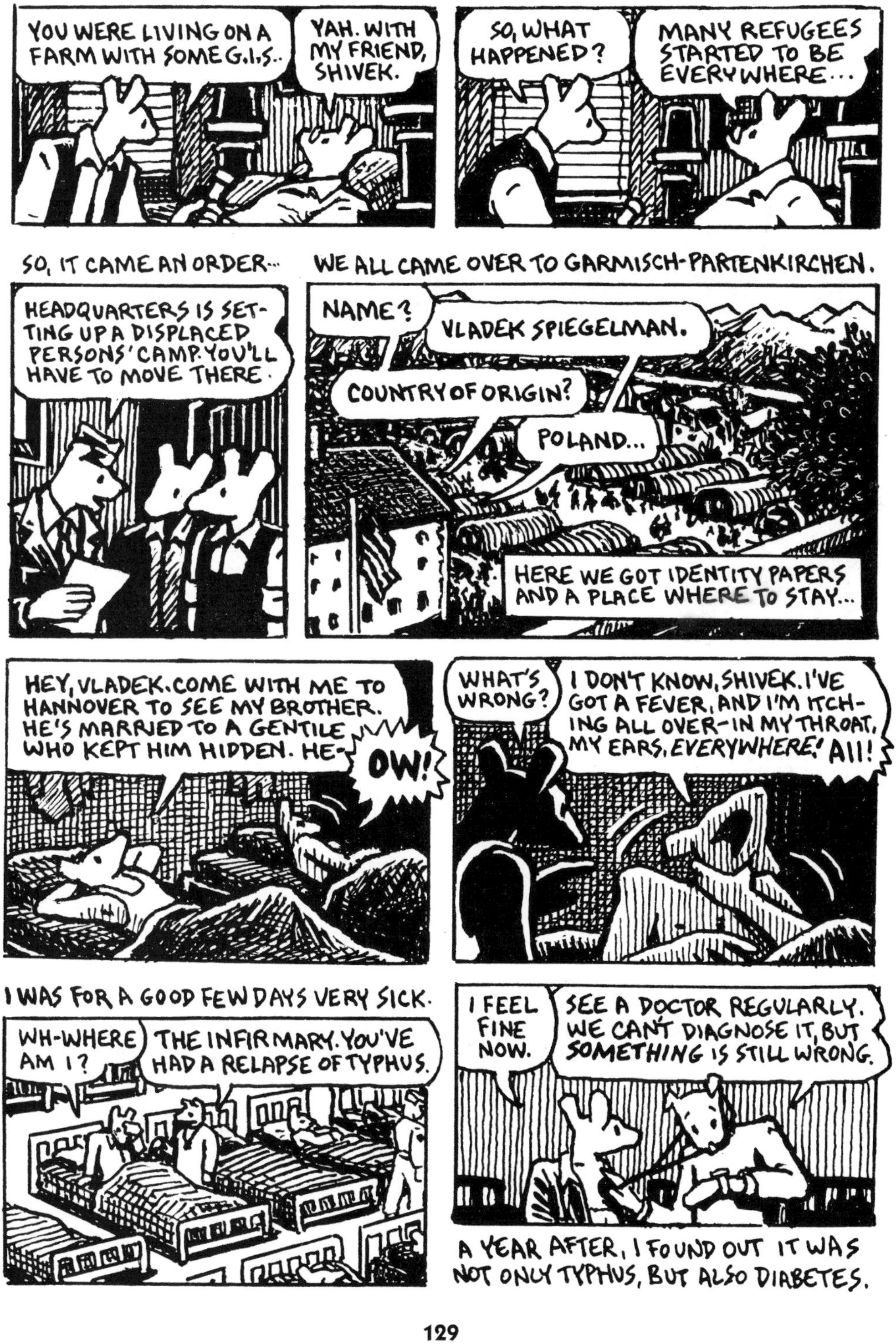
YOU WERE LIVING ON A FARM WITH SOME G.I.S..
YAH. WITH MY FRIEND, SHIVEK.
SO, WHAT HAPPENED?
MANY REFUGEES STARTED TO BE EVERYWHERE...
SO, IT CAME AN ORDER...
HEADQUARTERS IS SETTING UP A DISPLACED PERSONS' CAMP. YOU'LL HAVE TO MOVE THERE.
WE ALL CAME OVER TO GARMISCH-PARTENKIRCHEN.
NAME?
VLADEK SPIEGELMAN.
COUNTRY OF ORIGIN?
POLAND...
HERE WE GOT IDENTITY PAPERS AND A PLACE WHERE TO STAY...
HEY, VLADEK. COME WITH ME TO HANNOVER TO SEE MY BROTHER. HE'S MARRIED TO A GENTILE WHO KEPT HIM HIDDEN. HE-
OW!
WHAT'S WRONG?
I DON'T KNOW, SHIVEK. I'VE GOT A FEVER, AND I'M ITCHING ALL OVER- IN MY THROAT, MY EARS, EVERYWHERE! AII!
I WAS FOR A GOOD FEW DAYS VERY SICK.
WH-WHERE AM I?
THE INFIRMARY. YOU'VE HAD A RELAPSE OF TYPHUS.
I FEEL FINE NOW.
SEE A DOCTOR REGULARLY. WE CAN'T DIAGNOSE IT, BUT SOMETHING IS STILL WRONG.
A YEAR AFTER, I FOUND OUT IT WAS NOT ONLY TYPHUS, BUT ALSO DIABETES.

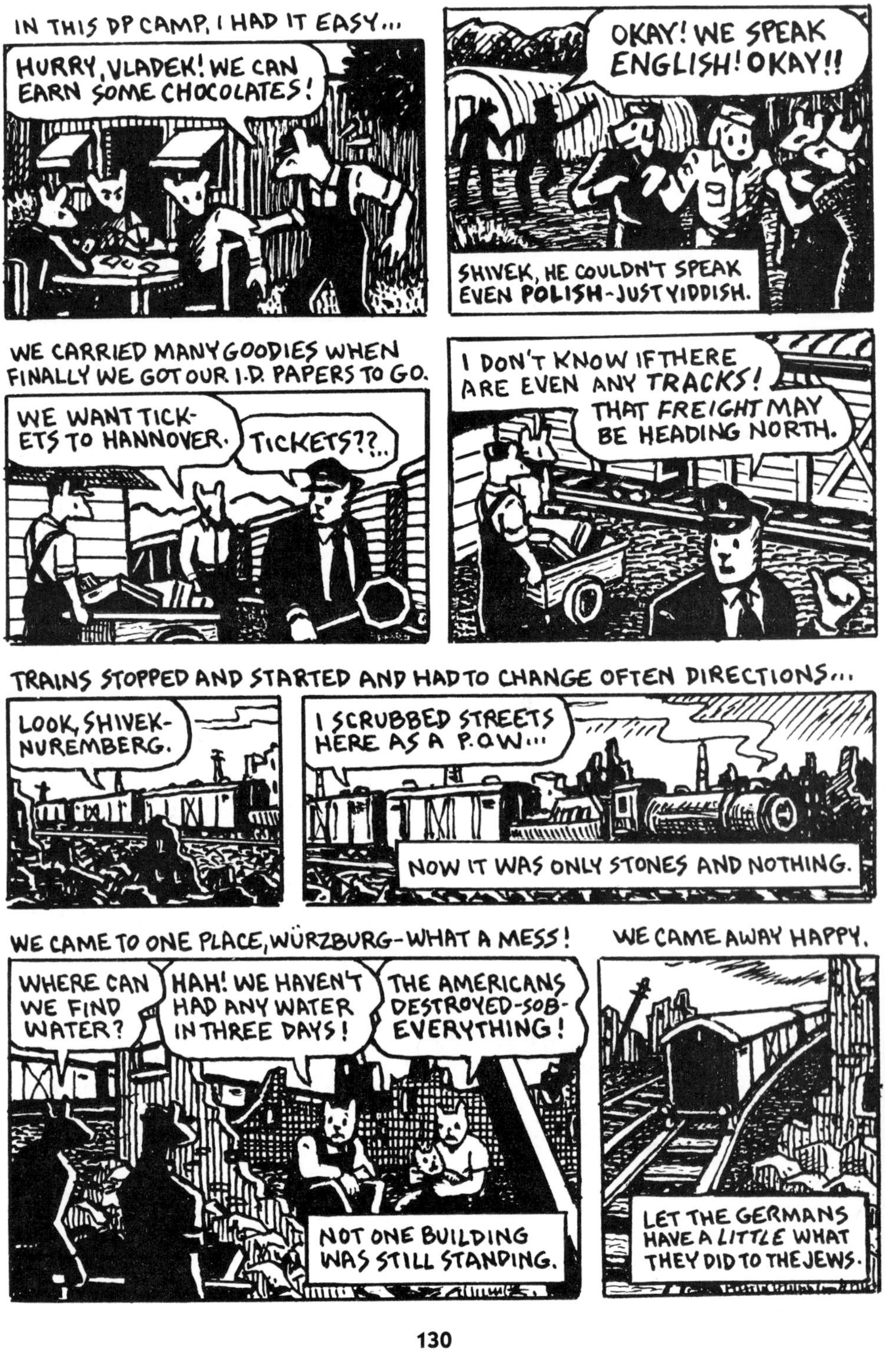
IN THIS DP CAMP, I HAD IT EASY...
HURRY, VLADEK! WE CAN EARN SOME CHOCOLATES!
OKAY! WE SPEAK ENGLISH! OKAY!!
SHIVEK, HE COULDN'T SPEAK EVEN POLISH - JUST YIDDISH.
WE CARRIED MANY GOODIES WHEN FINALLY WE GOT OUR I.D. PAPERS TO GO.
WE WANT TICK-ETS TO HANNOVER.
TICKETS??...
I DON'T KNOW IF THERE ARE EVEN ANY TRACKS!
THAT FREIGHT MAY BE HEADING NORTH.
TRAINS STOPPED AND STARTED AND HAD TO CHANGE OFTEN DIRECTIONS...
LOOK, SHIVEK - NUREMBERG.
I SCRUBBED STREETS HERE AS A P.O.W...
NOW IT WAS ONLY STONES AND NOTHING.
WE CAME TO ONE PLACE, WÜRZBURG - WHAT A MESS!
WHERE CAN WE FIND WATER?
HAH! WE HAVEN'T HAD ANY WATER IN THREE DAYS!
THE AMERICANS DESTROYED - SOB - EVERYTHING!
NOT ONE BUILDING WAS STILL STANDING.
WE CAME AWAY HAPPY.
LET THE GERMANS HAVE A LITTLE WHAT THEY DID TO THE JEWS.

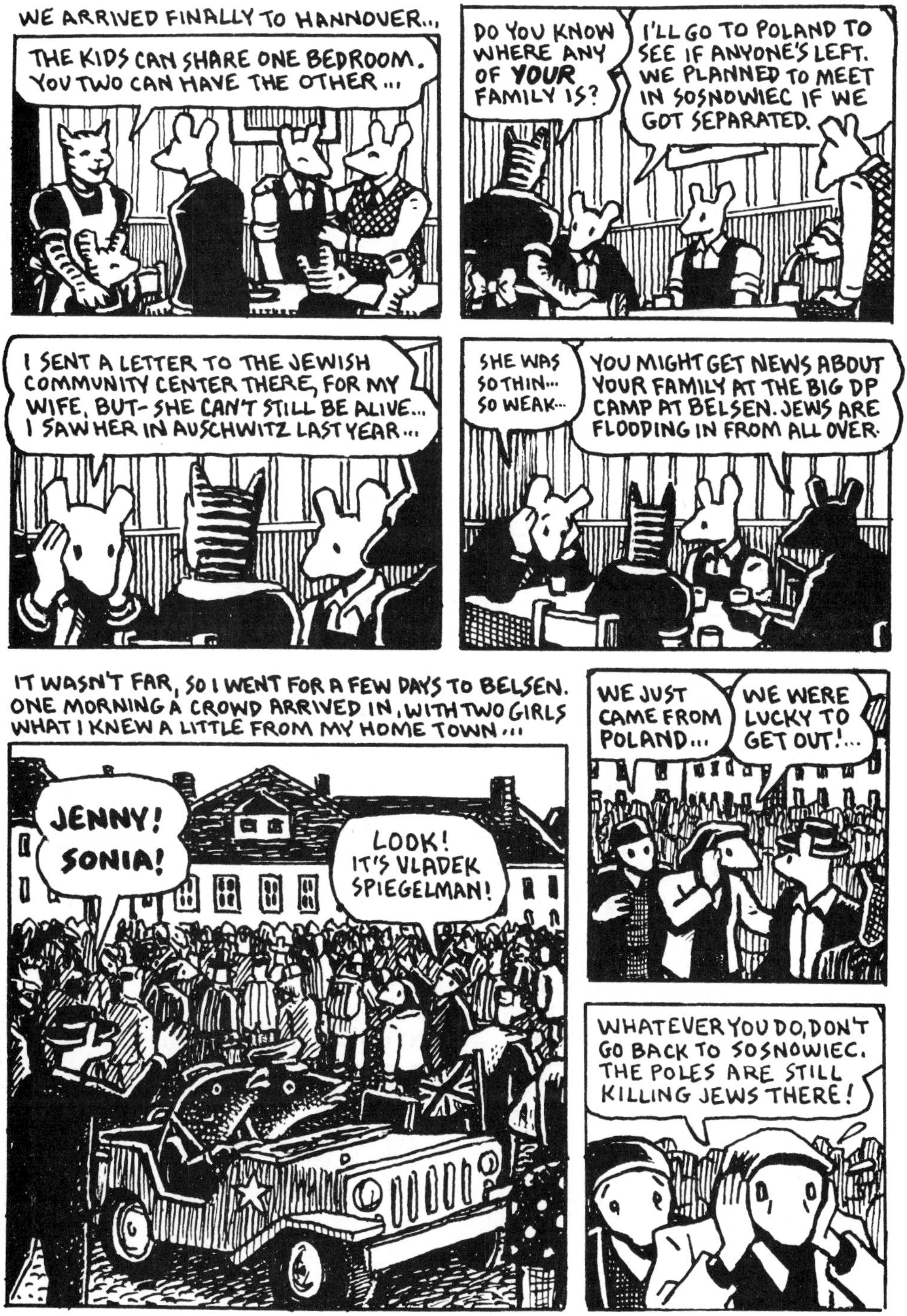
WE ARRIVED FINALLY TO HANNOVER...
THE KIDS CAN SHARE ONE BEDROOM. YOU TWO CAN HAVE THE OTHER...
DO YOU KNOW WHERE ANY OF YOUR FAMILY IS?
I'LL GO TO POLAND TO SEE IF ANYONE'S LEFT. WE PLANNED TO MEET IN SOSNOWIEC IF WE GOT SEPARATED.
I SENT A LETTER TO THE JEWISH COMMUNITY CENTER THERE, FOR MY WIFE, BUT- SHE CAN'T STILL BE ALIVE... I SAW HER IN AUSCHWITZ LAST YEAR...
SHE WAS SO THIN... SO WEAK...
YOU MIGHT GET NEWS ABOUT YOUR FAMILY AT THE BIG DP CAMP AT BELSEN. JEWS ARE FLOODING IN FROM ALL OVER.
IT WASN'T FAR, SO I WENT FOR A FEW DAYS TO BELSEN. ONE MORNING A CROWD ARRIVED IN, WITH TWO GIRLS WHAT I KNEW A LITTLE FROM MY HOME TOWN...
JENNY! SONIA!
LOOK! IT'S VLADEK SPIEGELMAN!
WE JUST CAME FROM POLAND...
WE WERE LUCKY TO GET OUT!...
WHATEVER YOU DO, DON'T GO BACK TO SOSNOWIEC. THE POLES ARE STILL KILLING JEWS THERE!

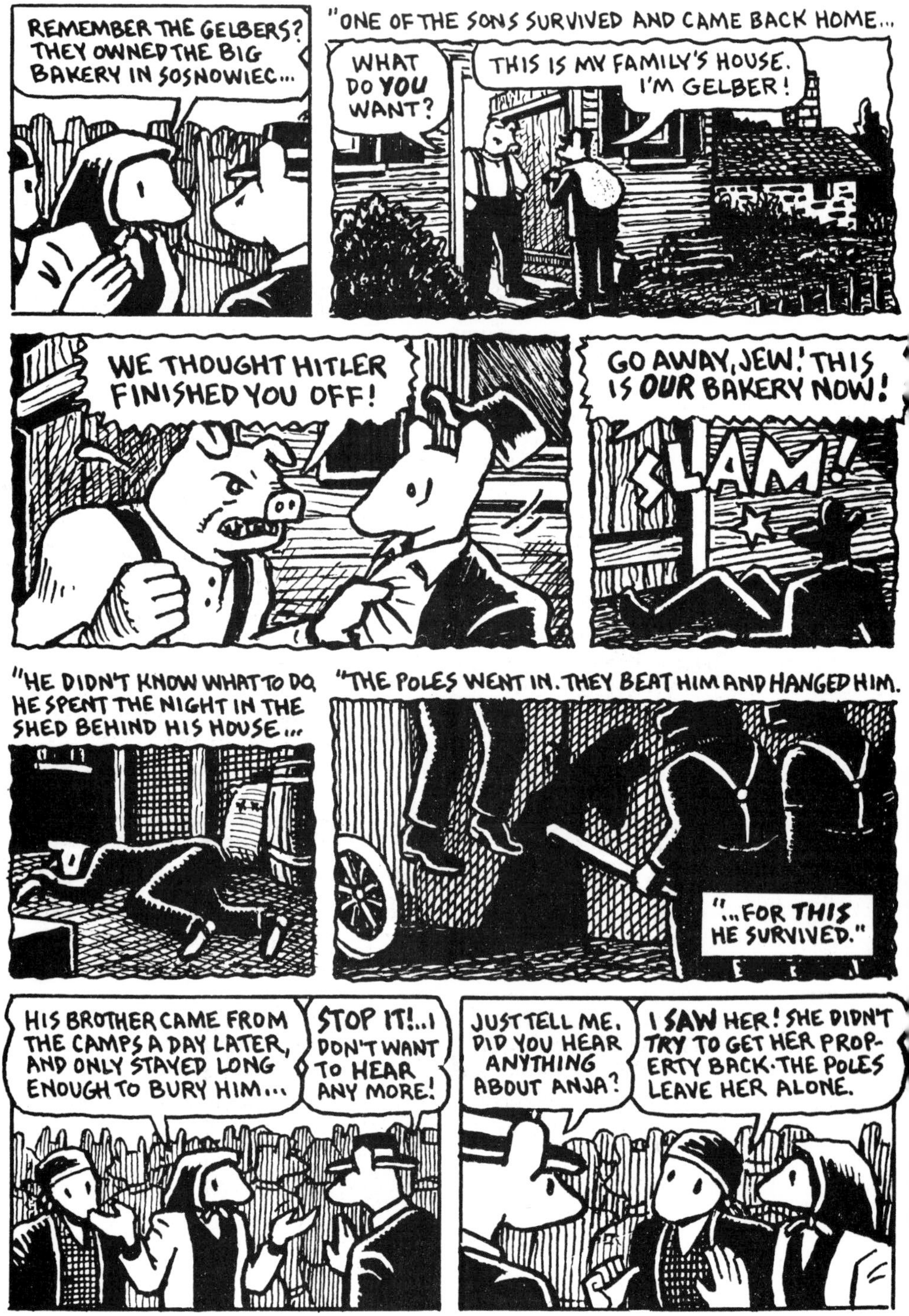
REMEMBER THE GELBERS? THEY OWNED THE BIG BAKERY IN SOSNOWIEC...
"ONE OF THE SONS SURVIVED AND CAME BACK HOME...
WHAT DO YOU WANT?
THIS IS MY FAMILY'S HOUSE. I'M GELBER!
WE THOUGHT HITLER FINISHED YOU OFF!
GO AWAY, JEW! THIS IS OUR BAKERY NOW!
SLAM!
"HE DIDN'T KNOW WHAT TO DO. HE SPENT THE NIGHT IN THE SHED BEHIND HIS HOUSE...
"THE POLES WENT IN. THEY BEAT HIM AND HANGED HIM.
"...FOR THIS HE SURVIVED."
HIS BROTHER CAME FROM THE CAMPS A DAY LATER, AND ONLY STAYED LONG ENOUGH TO BURY HIM...
STOP IT!..I DON'T WANT TO HEAR ANY MORE!
JUST TELL ME. DID YOU HEAR ANYTHING ABOUT ANJA?
I SAW HER! SHE DIDN'T TRY TO GET HER PROPERTY BACK. THE POLES LEAVE HER ALONE.

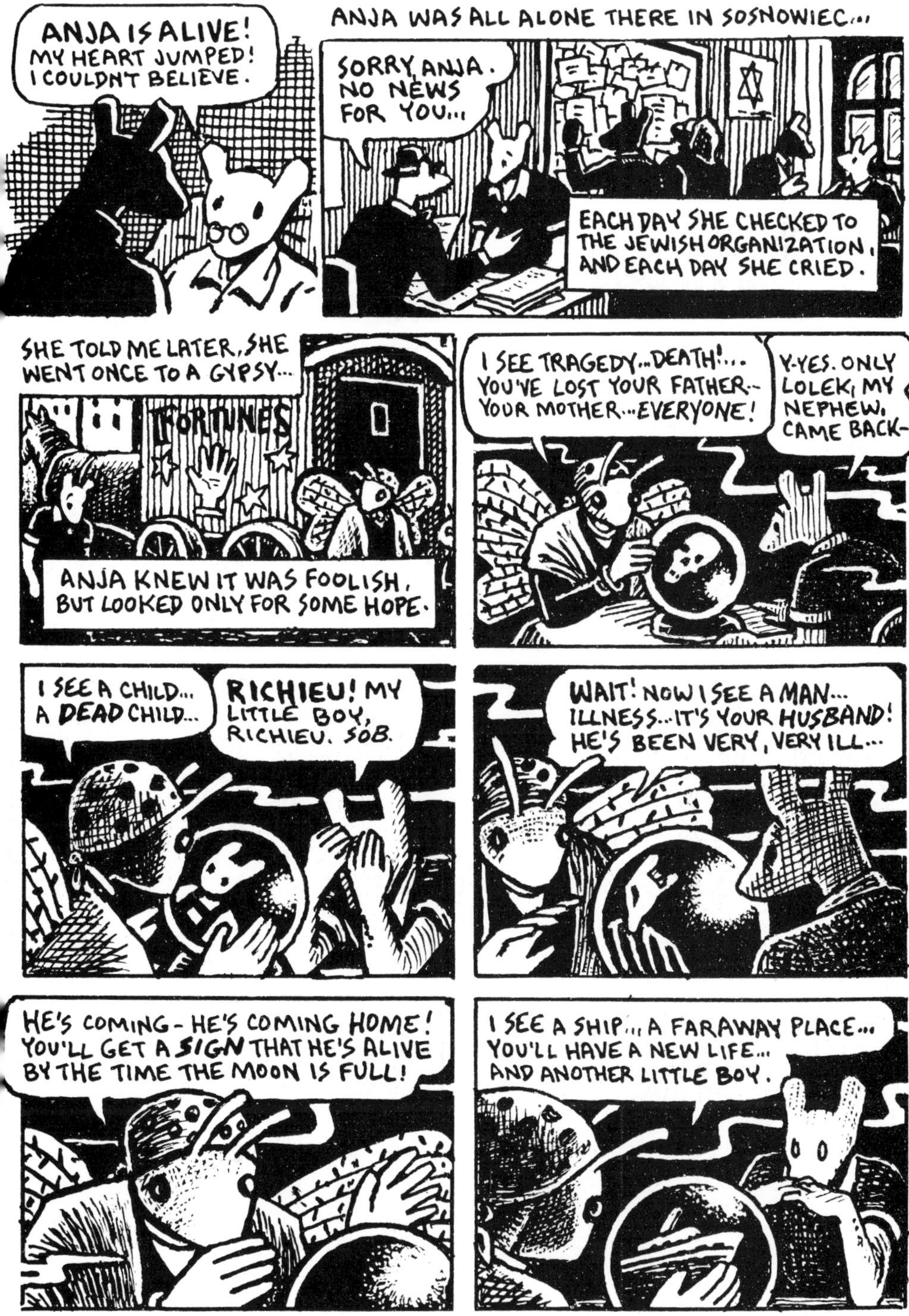
ANJA IS ALIVE! MY HEART JUMPED! I COULDN'T BELIEVE.
ANJA WAS ALL ALONE THERE IN SOSNOWIEC...
SORRY, ANJA. NO NEWS FOR YOU...
EACH DAY SHE CHECKED TO THE JEWISH ORGANIZATION, AND EACH DAY SHE CRIED.
SHE TOLD ME LATER, SHE WENT ONCE TO A GYPSY...
FORTUNES
ANJA KNEW IT WAS FOOLISH, BUT LOOKED ONLY FOR SOME HOPE.
I SEE TRAGEDY...DEATH!... YOU'VE LOST YOUR FATHER-- YOUR MOTHER...EVERYONE!
Y-YES. ONLY LOLEK, MY NEPHEW, CAME BACK-
I SEE A CHILD... A DEAD CHILD...
RICHIEU! MY LITTLE BOY, RICHIEU. SOB.
WAIT! NOW I SEE A MAN... ILLNESS...IT'S YOUR HUSBAND! HE'S BEEN VERY, VERY ILL...
HE'S COMING - HE'S COMING HOME! YOU'LL GET A SIGN THAT HE'S ALIVE BY THE TIME THE MOON IS FULL!
I SEE A SHIP... A FARAWAY PLACE... YOU'LL HAVE A NEW LIFE... AND ANOTHER LITTLE BOY.

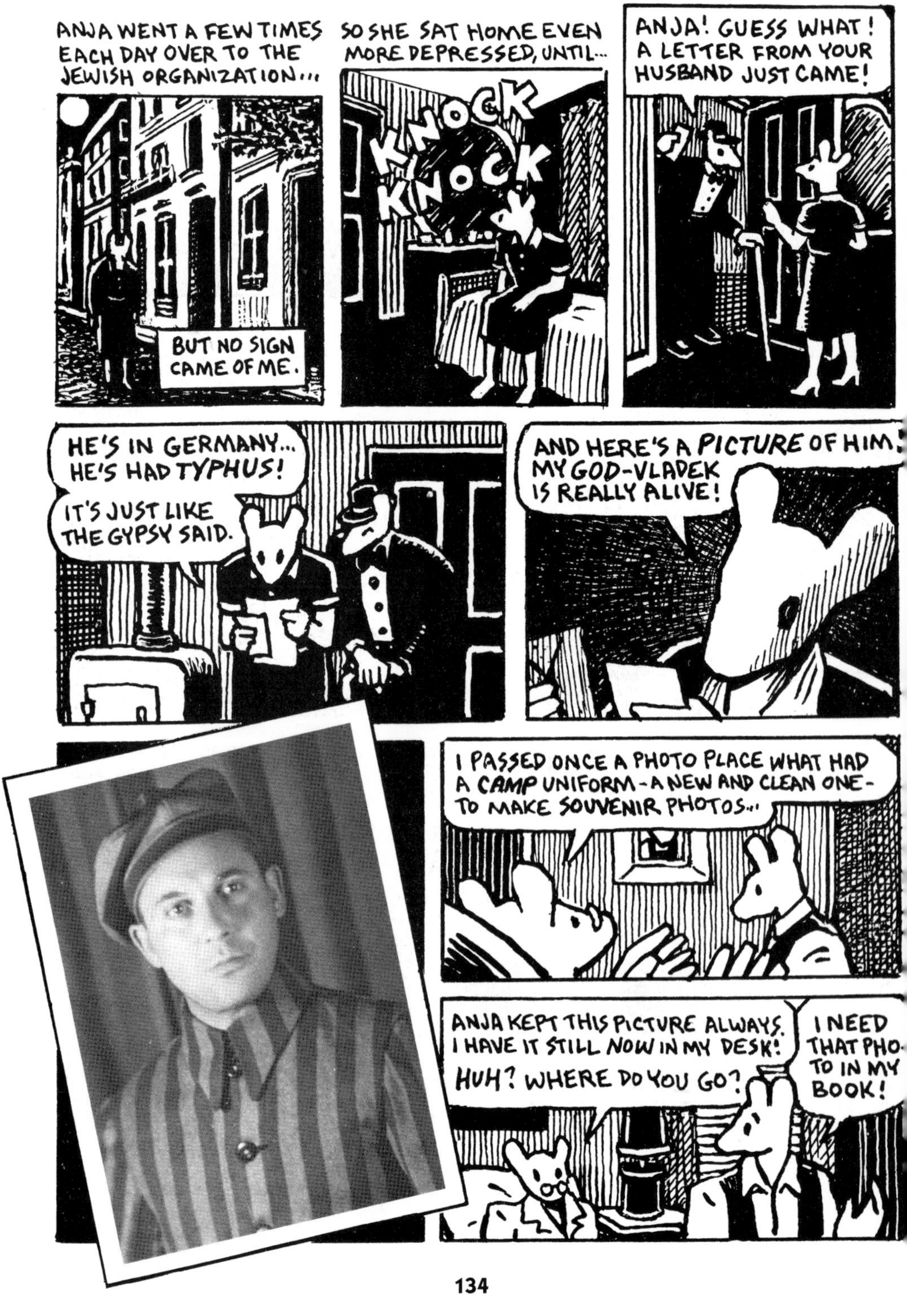
ANJA WENT A FEW TIMES EACH DAY OVER TO THE JEWISH ORGANIZATION...
BUT NO SIGN CAME OF ME.
SO SHE SAT HOME EVEN MORE DEPRESSED, UNTIL...
KNOCK KNOCK KNOCK
ANJA! GUESS WHAT! A LETTER FROM YOUR HUSBAND JUST CAME!
HE'S IN GERMANY... HE'S HAD TYPHUS!
IT'S JUST LIKE THE GYPSY SAID.
AND HERE'S A PICTURE OF HIM!
MY GOD-VLADEK IS REALLY ALIVE!
I PASSED ONCE A PHOTO PLACE WHAT HAD A CAMP UNIFORM - A NEW AND CLEAN ONE - TO MAKE SOUVENIR PHOTOS...
ANJA KEPT THIS PICTURE ALWAYS. I HAVE IT STILL NOW IN MY DESK!
HUH? WHERE DO YOU GO?
I NEED THAT PHOTO IN MY BOOK!

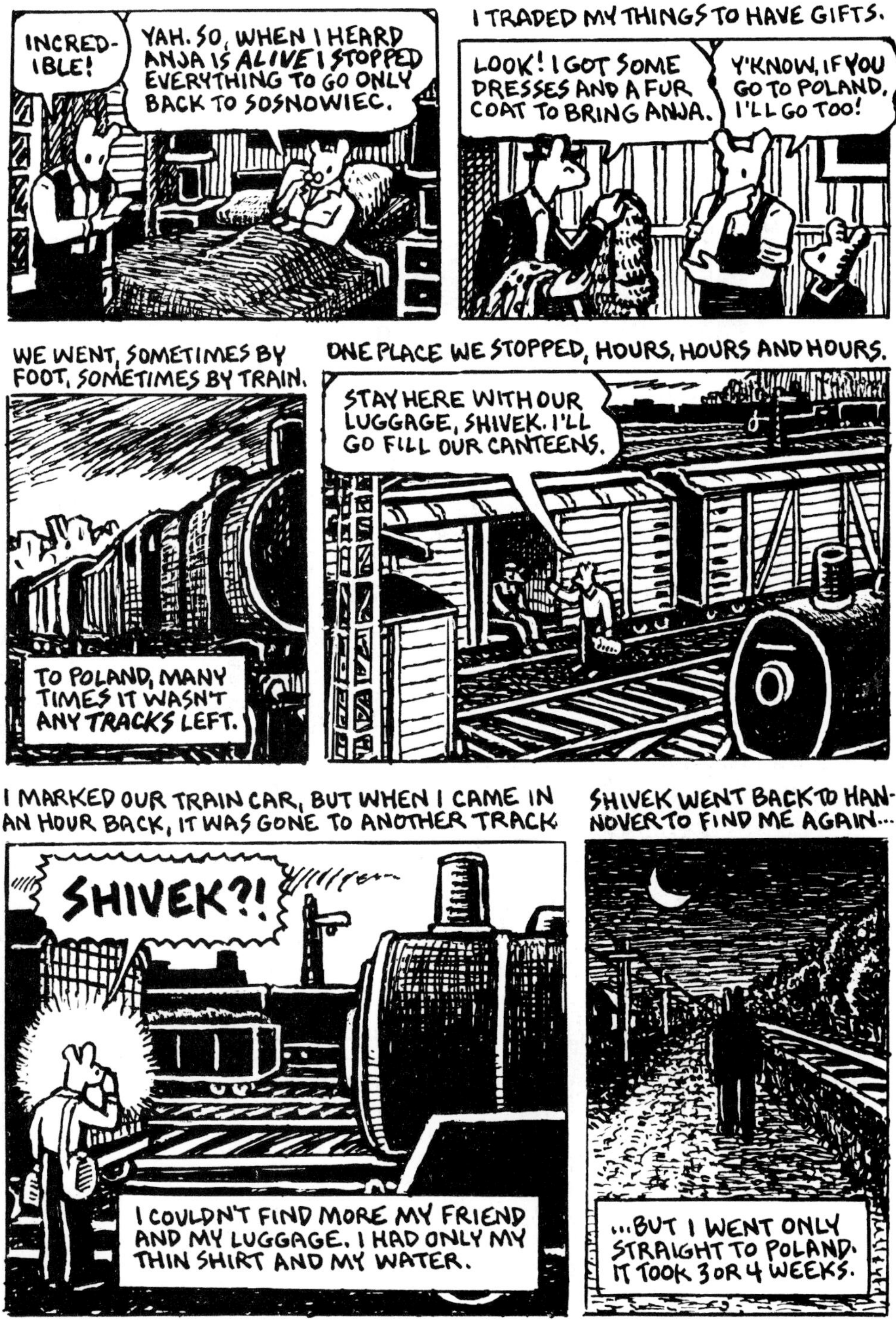
INCREDIBLE!
YAH. SO, WHEN I HEARD ANJA IS ALIVE I STOPPED EVERYTHING TO GO ONLY BACK TO SOSNOWIEC.
I TRADED MY THINGS TO HAVE GIFTS.
LOOK! I GOT SOME DRESSES AND A FUR COAT TO BRING ANJA.
Y'KNOW, IF YOU GO TO POLAND, I'LL GO TOO!
WE WENT, SOMETIMES BY FOOT, SOMETIMES BY TRAIN.
TO POLAND, MANY TIMES IT WASN'T ANY TRACKS LEFT.
ONE PLACE WE STOPPED, HOURS, HOURS AND HOURS.
STAY HERE WITH OUR LUGGAGE, SHIVEK. I'LL GO FILL OUR CANTEENS.
I MARKED OUR TRAIN CAR, BUT WHEN I CAME IN AN HOUR BACK, IT WAS GONE TO ANOTHER TRACK.
SHIVEK?!
I COULDN'T FIND MORE MY FRIEND AND MY LUGGAGE. I HAD ONLY MY THIN SHIRT AND MY WATER.
SHIVEK WENT BACK TO HANNOVER TO FIND ME AGAIN...
...BUT I WENT ONLY STRAIGHT TO POLAND. IT TOOK 3 OR 4 WEEKS.

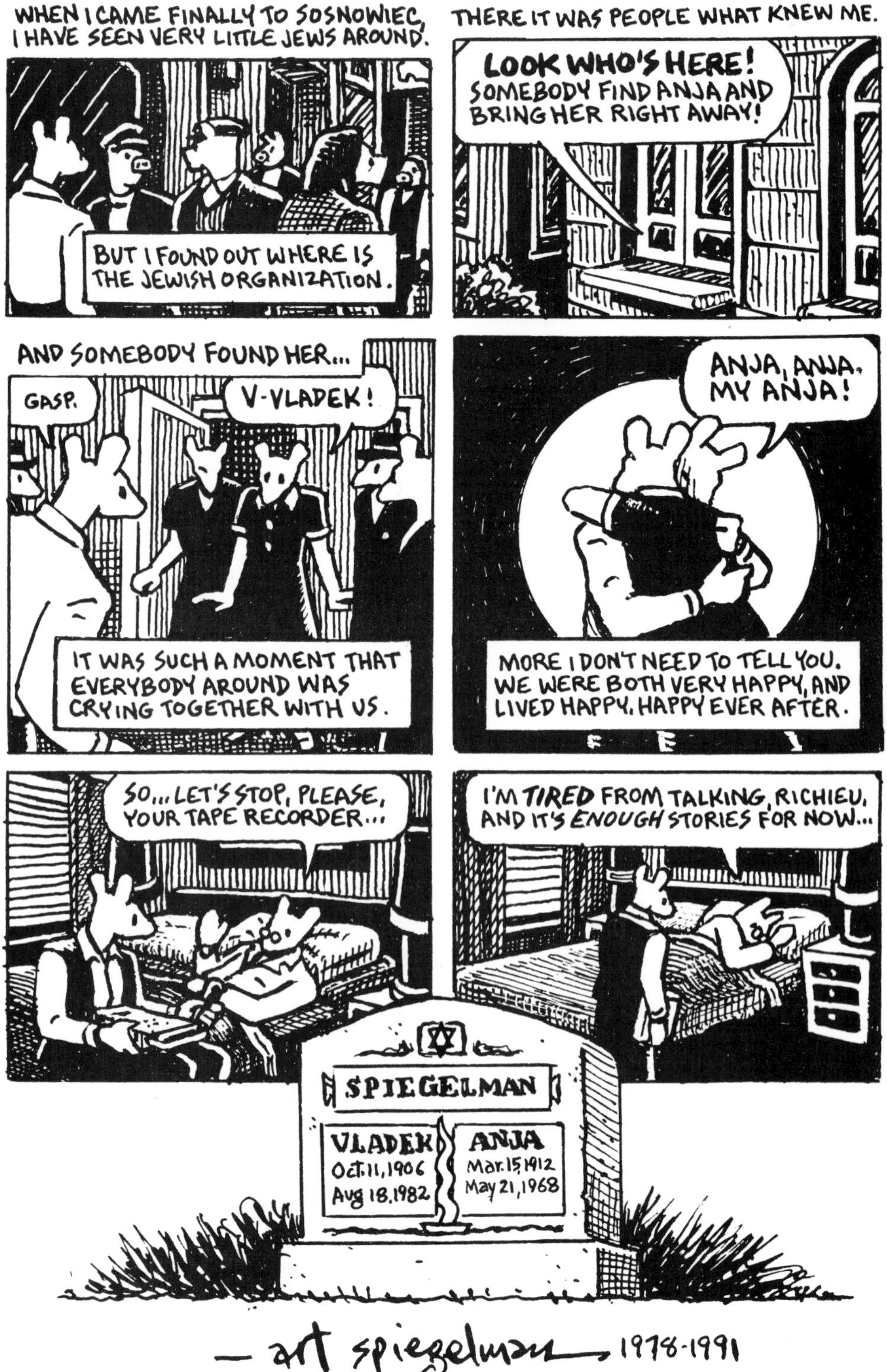
WHEN I CAME FINALLY TO SOSNOWIEC, I HAVE SEEN VERY LITTLE JEWS AROUND.
BUT I FOUND OUT WHERE IS THE JEWISH ORGANIZATION.
THERE IT WAS PEOPLE WHAT KNEW ME.
LOOK WHO'S HERE! SOMEBODY FIND ANJA AND BRING HER RIGHT AWAY!
AND SOMEBODY FOUND HER...
GASP.
V-VLADEK!
IT WAS SUCH A MOMENT THAT EVERYBODY AROUND WAS CRYING TOGETHER WITH US.
ANJA, ANJA, MY ANJA!
MORE I DON'T NEED TO TELL YOU. WE WERE BOTH VERY HAPPY, AND LIVED HAPPY, HAPPY EVER AFTER.
SO... LET'S STOP, PLEASE, YOUR TAPE RECORDER...
I'M *TIRED* FROM TALKING, RICHIEU, AND IT'S *ENOUGH* STORIES FOR NOW...
SPIEGELMAN
VLADEK
Oct. 11, 1906
Aug 18, 1982
ANJA
Mar. 15, 1912
May 21, 1968

— art spiegelman 1978-1991

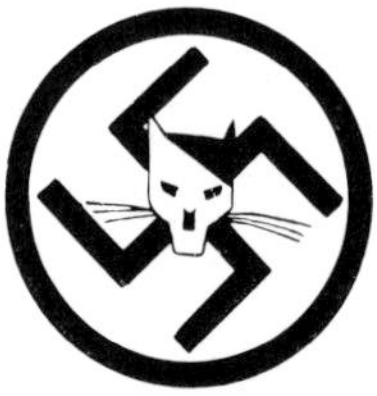

ALSO AVAILABLE:

Maus: A Survivor's Tale

Part I: My Father Bleeds History

(Mid-1930s to Winter 1944)

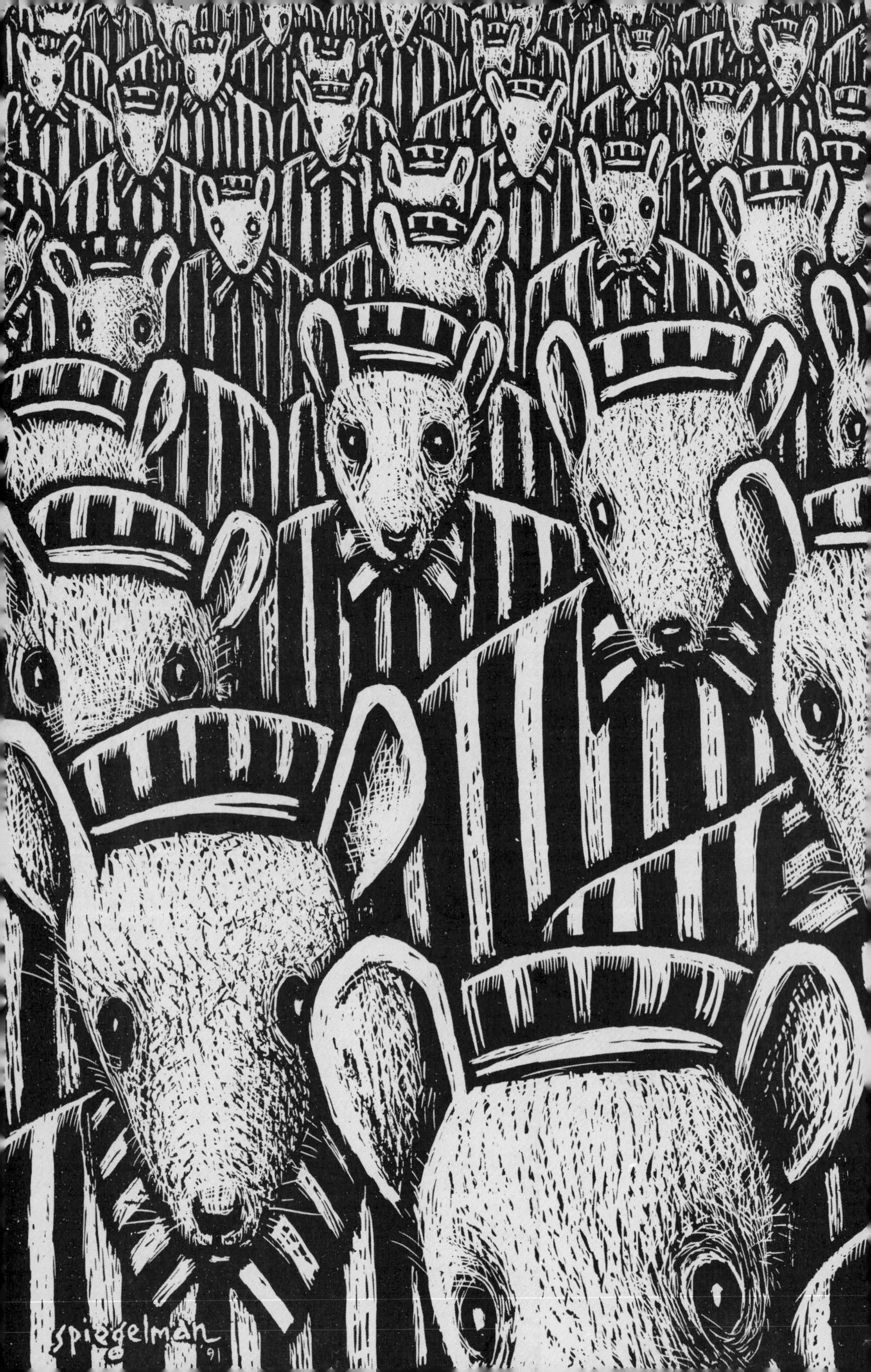
spiegelman
'91